Where Are
the Workers?

THE WORKING CLASS
IN AMERICAN HISTORY

Editorial Advisors
James R. Barrett, Julie Greene,
William P. Jones, Thavolia Glymph,
and Nelson Lichtenstein

*A list of books in the series appears
at the end of this book.*

Where Are the Workers?

Labor's Stories at Museums and Historic Sites

Edited by
ROBERT FORRANT AND
MARY ANNE TRASCIATTI

UNIVERSITY OF
ILLINOIS PRESS
Urbana, Chicago, and Springfield

Library of Congress Cataloging-in-Publication Data
Names: Forrant, Robert, 1947– editor. | Trasciatti, Mary
    Anne, editor.
Title: Where are the workers?: labor's stories at museums
    and historic sites / edited by Robert Forrant and Mary
    Anne Trasciatti.
Description: Urbana: University of Illinois Press, [2022]
    | Series: The working class in American history |
    Includes bibliographical references and index.
Identifiers: LCCN 2021057671 (print) | LCCN
    2021057672 (ebook) | ISBN 9780252044397 (hardback
    ; alk. paper) | ISBN 9780252086465 (paperback; alk.
    paper) | ISBN 9780252053382 (ebook)
Subjects: LCSH: Labor—United States—History. | Labor
    movement—United States—History. | Labor—United
    States—History—Sources. | Labor movement—
    United States—History—Sources. | Labor—History—
    Museums—United States. | BISAC: HISTORY /
    United States / General | SOCIAL SCIENCE / Social
    Classes & Economic Disparity Classification: LCC
    HD8066 .W485 2022 (print) | LCC HD8066 (ebook) |
    DDC 331.0973—dc23/eng/20211209
LC record available at https://lccn.loc.gov/2021057671
LC ebook record available at https://lccn.loc.gov/2021057672

We dedicate this book to the 146 workers who lost their lives in the 1911 Triangle Shirtwaist Factory fire, to the 1912 Bread & Roses strikers, and to the countless frontline workers who stepped forward to take care of us in the 2020–2021 COVID-19 pandemic. May their stories be collected, preserved, and told in the coming years.

Contents

Acknowledgments

We are grateful to Philip Levy and Fraser Ottanelli for offering insights and suggestions that helped us to strengthen and focus the book's introduction. A special thanks to James Engelhardt, who, while acquisitions editor at the University of Illinois Press, supported this project. Also, thanks to Alison Syring Bassford, acquisitions editor, and everyone at the University of Illinois Press for their efforts to bring the project to fruition.

Uncovering
Labor's History

ROBERT FORRANT AND
MARY ANNE TRASCIATTI

> Those genuinely interested in a history from the
> bottom up, those who feel the limits of the historical
> reality defined by the powerful, must understand that
> presuming to "allow" the "inarticulate" to speak is
> not enough. We must listen, and we must share the
> responsibility for historical explication and judgment.
> . . . Only in this way can the arrogance of the powerful
> be confronted by the truth of another reality, by those
> history-makers whose consciousness provides the record
> of that reality and the measure of its challenging power.
> —Michael Frisch

Michael Frisch presents an outline of how to present the truth of history.[1]
Class is central to everyday life, and labor issues are woven throughout U.S.
history and culture. Yet the stories of how working-class people have fought
for fair wages; humane hours of work and leisure time; the right to join a
union; safe, sanitary, and democratic workplaces; and a host of other things
that make life worth living remain unfamiliar to large numbers of Americans.
Mainstream academic and popular culture narratives, even those that claim
an "intersectional" approach, typically minimize the importance of class as
a category of social analysis and class struggle as a pervasive element of U.S.
history. As a result, stories of working-class activism and, with a few notable
exceptions such as the 1911 Triangle Shirtwaist Factory fire, of the violence
visited upon working people under capitalism are typically relegated to the
margins of public memory. Even a "murderous assault" on workers like the
April 20, 1914, Ludlow Massacre—in which police and armed guards killed
21 people, including young children, during a coal-miners' strike—was not

widely commemorated until 2003, and then only after purposeful physical damage had been done to a granite monument placed in 1918 at the massacre site by the United Mine Workers of America.[2]

In 1980, historian David Montgomery advocated that historians needed to study the people, and by the people, he meant the working class.[3] In the ensuing decades, public historians have taken up Montgomery's challenge. As Thomas Klubock and Paulo Fontes observe, there are "countless versions" today of what they term "public-labor history alliances" around the world.[4] In the U.S., many of those projects place labor history squarely in front of an audience not often exposed to it by connecting the history to the sites where it happened. Examples include labor history walking tours in Chicago and other cities; books like *A Peoples Guide to Greater Boston* and "history tourism" in places like Homestead, Pennsylvania, site of the epic 1892 steel strike, and Calumet, Michigan, site of the 1913 Italian Hall Massacre, in which more than six dozen striking workers and family members were killed while attending a holiday party.[5]

In the second decade of the twenty-first century, public historians have called for more public histories of labor.[6] They ground their arguments in the specificity of the moment—renewed union activism, anti-union campaigns, a declining standard of living, and rising social unrest—and the importance of the labor movement to the maintenance of democratic institutions and the struggle for social and economic equality. With *Interpreting Labor and Working-Class History at Museums and Historic Sites*, we join that call. We see in the present moment an urgent need to tell the stories of working people and working-class organizations and movements, but we also know that class struggle is a defining feature of capitalist societies and the time for active engagement with labor history in the U.S. is always *now*.

As the title suggests, place is a central concern of our project. With their material and aesthetic components, physical structures and natural landscapes can appeal to us in deep and embodied ways. When we attach a story to a place, we join the symbolic with the material to enable a feeling of connection that can resonate long after the physical encounter is over. The chapters in this book, written by academics, historical preservationists, archivists, and museum curators, offer models and inspiration for labor and working-class public history projects that vivify places and other material objects through the power of narrative.

We recognize that the field of labor history has traditionally defined itself as the study of industrial workers, unions, and strikes. Thus, this history "from the bottom up" excludes workers whose stories lie "beneath the bottom." Unfree and unwaged workers (prisoners, the enslaved, housewives) and participants in the informal economy (sex workers and numbers runners) are not to be found. We do not want to reify this exclusion; we share the belief that for labor history to be inclusive, it must consider all forms of labor.[7] We acknowledge that slaves, prison workers, many homemakers, sex workers, numbers runners, and a host of others who labor outside the traditional paradigm of labor studies are members of the working class. However, ours is not a reclamation project. Instead, our purpose is to show how the practices, methods, and tools of historical interpretation in situ can help address the decline in unionization and worker militancy in the U.S. since the 1980s by providing context for contemporary working-class struggles and inspiring future generations of activists and organizers.

Who We Are

We come to this project as labor academics deeply interested in how historical narratives can inform and inspire contemporary activism and how we can interest our students in engaged scholarship. We believe that who and what is remembered and retold and how historical narratives and their public manifestations get shaped by power are critical concerns.[8] Robert Forrant has taught labor, working-class, and immigration history at the University of Massachusetts Lowell for 25 years and is an advisor to the university's Labor Studies program. A principal historian on numerous public history projects focused on working-class and immigrant communities, Forrant has worked as a consultant to the International Labor Organization, the International Metalworkers' Federation, and the United Nations International Development Program. Mary Anne Trasciatti teaches rhetoric and directs the Labor Studies program at Hofstra University. She regularly offers classes and workshops on public speaking and women's history for union activists on Long Island and serves on the Advisory Board of Long Island Jobs with Justice. In 2019, she codirected the United Association for Labor Education's Northeast Summer School for Women in Unions and Worker Organizations.

The work that we both do is deeply rooted in place. In 2012, Forrant worked extensively with students; residents of Lawrence, Massachusetts; and the Lawrence History Center to produce a full-scale exhibit in English and Spanish and coordinate a year-long commemoration of the 1912 Bread & Roses Strike. Some 25,000 people visited the exhibit and attended commemoration-related events. A Lawrence History Center board member since 2012, with Susan Grabski, Director of the Lawrence History Center, he produced a history of the strike found on the Digital Public Library of America's website and with Jurg Siegenthaler, *The Great Lawrence Textile Strike of 1912: New Scholarship on the Bread and Roses Strike.*[9] Trasciatti is President of the Remember the Triangle Fire Coalition, a nonprofit public history/memory/arts activist organization that connects individuals and groups in the U.S. and worldwide to the 1911 fire in New York City. Since 2010, the Coalition has worked with unions and community groups to organize the annual official commemoration of the fire in front of the Brown (formerly Asch) Building where it happened. Trasciatti is spearheading the Coalition's project to build a permanent memorial of the fire. Scheduled for dedication in 2022, it will be New York City's first labor memorial.[10] Our shared vision of teaching and scholarship as resources for activism and our respective commitments to place-based public history and commemoration have inspired and shaped this collaboration.

Background: Why Such a Volume?

In *Organizing the Curriculum*, a collection of essays on labor history in the schools, teacher-educator Leigh Benin asks: "Why does our culture obscure the true significance of labor?" Benin contends that the obscuring of labor's significance is purposeful and an effort to "render the very existence of labor invisible, even to those who labor." A survey of the U.S. landscape supports Benin's contention. At National Parks and at numerous other sites where significant labor and working-class history occurred, much of that history is unmarked. Visitors can spend time at the overwhelming majority of U.S. National Parks, museums, and historical sites and not even casually bump into treatments focused on work, workers, and labor history. Places that do make an effort to present labor history sometimes offer simplified or sanitized accounts that minimize or even erase aspects to promote a particular point of view or avoid controversy. Museums, galleries, and archives also further the impression—sometimes unwittingly—that labor history is not a part of U.S. history. Labor and working-class history can be placed on a proverbial milk carton and labeled "missing." The authors herein discuss the implications of working-class history gone missing and how to rectify such omissions.[11]

The time is ripe for an expansion of place-based public labor history. An enormous wealth gap, exacerbated by the global COVID-19 pandemic, divides U.S. society.[12] That a small group of people possesses extraordinary resources while large numbers struggle daily to make ends meet is no accident. On the contrary, the wealth gap is a product of a concerted effort to destroy labor unions. Research shows that both stagnating wages and rising inequality are a direct result of declining union membership. Although the situation is dire, there is hope. The U.S. labor movement is in a moment of transition marked by historic levels of popular support and increased militancy, on the one hand, and a stream of antilabor initiatives from the Supreme Court, federal agencies, and various state governments, on the other. This combination of growing support and increased threats makes labor history more relevant than ever. The labor movement's future may depend to a degree on our understanding of its past.[13]

The potential for a resurgent labor movement is palpable. Interest in and support for labor unions is on the rise in the United States, especially among millennials. Many younger Americans view unions as one of the few organizations offering a voice for workers in an increasingly precarious economic environment. Support for unions is growing among other segments of the population, as well. A 2019 Gallup poll released in time for Labor Day reported that 64 percent of Americans overall approve of labor unions, the highest rating in half a century.[14]

This renewed support comes after the labor movement spent more than three decades in the doldrums. Although unions suffered a significant setback in the post–World War II era with the Taft-Hartley Act's passage, membership remained stable until the 1970s. The election of Ronald Reagan marked a decisive turning point. Until then, except for the AFL-CIO's neutrality in the 1972 contest between Republican Richard Nixon and Democrat George McGovern, organized labor had primarily supported Democrats at the ballot box since AFL president Samuel Gompers exhorted members to vote to "reward friends and punish enemies" in 1906. In 1980, the Professional Air Traffic Controllers Organization (PATCO) endorsed Reagan against incumbent Democrat Jimmy Carter. The next year Reagan repaid the favor by firing and blacklisting nearly 11,000 air traffic controllers for striking illegally.[15] His move against PATCO strengthened large employers' hand and dealt a crushing blow to labor through a significant loss of membership and influence.

Democrats have not engaged in the same type of blatant union-busting, but the lip service they pay to labor has done little to help the movement regain its momentum. In recent years, efforts to secure the Employee Free Choice Act and other pro-labor legislation under Democratic administrations have largely floundered at both state and federal levels. The 2016 election of Republican Donald Trump entailed an all-out assault on workers' ability to engage in collective action. A conservative majority on the Supreme Court has dealt some hard blows, arguably the most serious being the 2018 ruling in *Janus v. AFSCME*. The court found that public-sector workers represented by unions could not be required to pay for collective bargaining, even though unions must continue to bargain collectively for those workers. This decision effectively imposed a "right to work" rule on public-sector unions across the U.S.

In the wake of the *Janus* decision, Alaska, Montana, Kansas, and Pennsylvania proposed laws to impose additional restrictions on union enrollments.[16] Decisions by the NLRB have also sought to restrain collective action by workers. In June 2019, the NLRB decided that Uber drivers and, by extension, other app-based workers, are independent contractors rather than employees. As such, they do not receive government protections during unionization drives. The board may succeed in curtailing labor's right to free speech as well. In July 2019, NLRB counsel filed a brief against "Scabby the Rat," a large, inflatable rodent used by building trades and other unions to draw attention to contractors who employ non-union labor, arguing that "Scabby" is a form of unlawful picketing.[17] The 2020 election of Democrat Joe Biden appears to have saved "Scabby," but unless Democrats succeed in overturning the Supreme Court's 2010 *Citizens United* decision, which defined political spending as a form of protected speech under the First Amendment, corporations with deep pockets will continue to exercise undue influence on U.S. elections. Damage inflicted by the Citizens United and Janus decisions and by the corporate assault on unions could be mitigated by the Protecting the Right to Organize Act (PRO Act). If passed, the bill would offer necessary protections to workers trying to organize and limit what corporations can do to disrupt union organizing drives. The House of Representatives passed the PRO Act in March 2021 but it has stalled in the Senate. It remains to be seen whether the bill, which has the support of President Biden, will become law.

An uptick in militant labor activism is meeting the assault on unions. In 2018, nearly 500,000 workers were involved in strikes, up from 25,000 the year before.[18] Strike fever showed no sign of abating in 2019. Teachers, nurses, autoworkers, copper miners, hotel workers, grocery store workers, and janitors walked off the job in numbers unseen since the 1980s. Workers are organizing or have organized in the tech, digital media, and cannabis industries. Even yoga teachers formed a union, the first-ever in their profession.[19] In 2019 flight attendants at Delta Airlines, the most profitable carrier in the U.S. began organizing themselves into the Association of Flight Attendants/ Communications Workers of America. The union, which represents approximately 50,000 flight attendants at 20 airlines, is under the leadership of one of labor's most charismatic and formidable figures, Sara Nelson. President of the AFA since 2014, Nelson catapulted into national prominence when she forced President Trump to back down and end the federal government shutdown by threatening a general strike in early 2019.[20]

The COVID-19 pandemic focused national attention on healthcare, warehouse, transportation, meat processing, janitorial, and retail food workers in frontline industries. These essential workers provided necessary goods and services to Americans under stay-at-home orders, often at high personal cost to themselves and their families. Not surprisingly, many employers met their requests for a modicum of necessary safety precautions, including personal protective equipment (PPE), workplace ventilation, and social distancing requirements, as well as hazard pay and paid sick leave, with indifference or hostility. Amazon's firing of Chris Smalls, an organizer in the company's Staten Island warehouse, exemplifies this kind of employer hostility.[21] Workers at Amazon and elsewhere fought back, staging strikes and walkouts that highlighted the discrepancy between the rhetoric of appreciation for essential workers and the reality of their working conditions. At DHL Express in South Boston, workers resisted continually 60-hour workweeks during the Pandemic and Sunday overtime. An arbitrator ruled in November 2020 that such Sunday shifts could be mandated and DHL fired 25 drivers. Perhaps ironically, possibly not, the union fighting to get the terminated workers back on the job is Teamsters Local 25.[22]

Workers also struck in support of the Black Lives Matter movement, which gained momentum during the pandemic when a video of Minneapolis police officer Derek Chauvin killing George Floyd by pressing his knee on Floyd's neck for almost nine minutes went viral. On Juneteenth, the day commemorating the end of slavery in the U.S., the International Longshore and Warehouse Union (ILWU) shut down California ports in solidarity with Black Lives Matter. A month later, the Service Employees International Union (SEIU), Fight for $15 and a Union, and Poor People's Campaign joined forces in the Strike for Black Lives to press business to confront systemic racism.[23]

As the Black Lives Matter strikes indicate, increasing numbers are only a part of the story. The nature of labor activism has also changed as the struggle over *bread and butter* issues (wages, hours, and benefits) has given way to *social justice unionism*—classwide campaigns for racial, gender, environmental, and other forms of justice. In its 2012 strike, the Chicago Teachers' Union (CTU) pioneered *bargaining for the common good*. Bargaining in this way involves coalition-building between labor, community, and social justice groups to demand concessions from governments, corporations, and the wealthy that benefit the community as a whole, not just the bargaining unit. In 2019, when the CTU struck again, its demands included affordable housing for students and teachers, dual-language classes, and sanctuary for undocumented immigrants on school grounds.[24]

History (Mis)Remembered and Untaught

The turn to social justice initiatives is also evident in historical interpretation. In introducing a volume on interpreting difficult history at museums and historic sites, Julia Rose notes, "Museums and historical sites, since the last quarter of the past century, have increasingly recognized their social responsibilities as educational institutions and, more recently, are placing stronger emphasis on museums' relevance to social issues. These museums serve as advocates for social justice and responsible citizenship."[25] That most Americans lack even basic historical context to understand and evaluate the significance of strikes, organizing drives, and antilabor decisions by the Supreme Court and the National Labor Relations Board poses a challenge for museum-based social justice advocates who present labor-themed exhibits.

Despite organized labor's significant contributions to U.S. culture and values and its role in improving the material conditions of everyday life for working people, the state of labor education in most public-school systems in the U.S. is abysmal. Few states require or encourage labor history in their standards. Not surprisingly, states that include labor history have a strong labor activism tradition and high union density. They include California, Connecticut, Illinois, Massachusetts, New York, West Virginia, and Wisconsin. In contrast, Texas mandates teaching economics "with Emphasis on the Free Enterprise System and its Benefits."[26] In 2009, Wisconsin became the first state to incorporate labor history into its state standards for social studies. In New York, labor activism and progressive reform are mandated middle-school teaching topics. The West Virginia Legislature passed a resolution in 2010 designating the week following Labor Day as Labor History Week in West Virginia and encouraging schools to provide instruction during that week on labor history events. With an initiative signed into law in 2012, California has designated May as Labor History Month, replacing Labor History Week, established in 2002. California's Labor History Month encourages schools "to commemorate this month with appropriate educational exercises that make pupils aware of the role the labor movement has played in shaping California and the United States."[27]

Connecticut's standards call for teaching about labor movements and how they affected working conditions, influenced the political process, and shaped the concept of the U.S. as a land of opportunity. The causes and effects of labor conflict in various industries and geographic regions are also covered. The rise and decline of organized labor from the late-nineteenth century to today are included, along with material focused on New Deal reforms like Social Security, the Fair Labor Standards Act, the National Labor Relations Act and labor's role in the passage of the Civil Rights Acts of 1964 and 1968.[28]

By contrast, the Massachusetts curriculum standards make no mention of labor history covering the 1800 to 1860 time period. For the post-Civil War era—Rebuilding the United States: industry and immigration—there is a focus on the role of business leaders, entrepreneurs, and inventors such as Alexander Graham Bell, Andrew Carnegie, Thomas Edison, J. P. Morgan, John D. Rockefeller, and Cornelius Vanderbilt in the Industrial Revolution. Teachers are encouraged to "make connections among the critical consequences of the Industrial Revolution"; for example, economic growth and the rise of big business; environmental impact of industries; the expansion of cities; the emergence of labor unions such as the Knights of Labor and the American Federation of Labor under Samuel Gompers; workers' distrust of monopolies; the rise of either the Populist Party under the leadership of William Jennings Bryan or the Socialist Party under Eugene Debs. The frameworks also call for coverage of the 1912 Bread & Roses Strike in Lawrence, the 1919 Boston police strike, and the Massachusetts trials, appeals, and execution of Nicola Sacco and Bartolomeo Vanzetti in the 1920s. However, there is a paucity of materials to deliver this content and almost no opportunity within the Massachusetts school day to explore this history through field trips to important historical sites.[29]

Consider four of the premier historic sites in New England that pride themselves on telling the country's industrialization story: the Lowell National Historical Park, the Museum of Springfield History, and the Springfield Armory National Historic Site, all in Massachusetts, and the American Precision Museum in Windsor, Vermont. A significant focus in all four sites is the art of invention, advanced technology, and precision machinery. *Forging Arms for the Nation* notes that the U.S. Armed Forces and American industry looked to the Springfield Armory "for innovative engineering." It "commemorates the critical role of the nation's first armory by preserving and interpreting the world's largest historic U.S. military small arms collection, along with historic archives, buildings, and landscapes." Showcased are the Armory's leading engineers, and there is a brief reference on the website that 40 percent of the staff during the Second World War were women. However, there is very little interpretation done on what work was like, who the workers were, where they lived, and the like, and a word search of the site reveals little online information. The Armory website, *The Forge of Innovation*, probes further into some of these questions. With the University of Massachusetts Amherst history faculty's assistance, more is being done to tell women and immigrant workers' stories.

The dominant exhibits in the physical spaces at the Armory Museum and the Museum of Springfield History fail to dig deeply into and interpret Springfield's and the region's working-class history through artifacts or detailed museum signage. Both sites are in the city's historic African American neighborhood, yet this story is mostly missing. Mason Square, named for philanthropist Primus P. Mason and formerly known as Winchester Square after Mayor Charles A. Winchester, was the commercial heart of the McKnight District, Springfield's African American neighborhood. Adjacent to the neighborhood sat the Springfield Armory and nearby were many of the city's premier metalworking industries. Mason (1817–1892) was an African American entrepreneur and real estate investor in Springfield. His parents were free people of color. Upon his death, a newspaper headline acknowledged that he left most of his property and wealth to a charity organization he envisioned would be a home for aged men, in Springfield, Massachusetts.

The small numbers of Black workers hired at the Armory and other industrial sites "were disproportionately relegated to less skilled labor." During World War I, the Armory's monthly newspaper, *The Armorer*, regularly printed derogatory humor solicited from fellow employees in columns called "Squinty's Column" and "Jest Fer Fun" that maligned African Americans.[30]

During the Second World War, more hiring of African Americans took place due to President Franklin D. Roosevelt's Executive Order 8802, barring discrimination in the government-funded defense sector. By 1943, "almost half of the facility's 13,500 employees were women, and 7.9 percent were African American. In wartime Springfield, as across America, significantly more women and blacks were in skilled defense jobs. This did not last once the war concluded. In 1971, the Justice Department entered a consent decree against AMBAC Industries, owners of the American Bosch plant in Springfield, prohibiting them from discriminating against African American and Puerto Rican workers in hiring. The decree ordered back pay damages for 29 workers discriminated against in filling internal job vacancies and also ordered significant changes in how it went about publicly announcing new hiring.[31]

In Lowell, the story is much the same, with the significant focus on workers largely focused on the period from 1830–1860. Overall, mill managers, investors, waterpower, canals, and intricate textile machinery receive their due—workers not so much. Lowell's labor history remains unexplored in any substantial ways in the National Park exhibit cases, displays, and narratives, while the myth of "fortunate mill girls" is perpetuated despite archival research to the contrary.

The American Precision Museum in Windsor, Vermont, closes out our New England tour. There, you will find a terrific display of the machinery designed and built in the Connecticut River Valley. Much of the machinery in Henry Ford's River Rouge complex got built in factories in and around Windsor and in nearby Springfield, Vermont. These sites discuss invention, creation, and development, but this is almost entirely individualized, with the hands-on workforce's role thoroughly minimized. Finally, these sites do not consider the effects technologies have on skilled workers, nor do they take up the lasting impact of deindustrialization on workers and their communities. In many ways, it is as though history stopped in 1960.[32]

What to Do?

As was pointed out in a recent issue of the Labor and Working-Class History Association's (LAWCHA) journal, "One of the ultimate joys and biggest challenges facing labor historians is connecting their work with the people about whom they write and teach." The Iowa Labor History Oral Project (ILHOP), established during the mid-1970s and dedicated to recording Iowa workers' oral histories, is one vehicle for doing such work. Attempts to get the material adopted in Iowa's schools, however, have met with limited success.[33] LAWCHA is committed to teaching labor history in the classroom, from K-12 to colleges and universities. Its website has a *Resources in Teaching Labor's Story* repository with materials contributed by members designed for incorporation into the school curriculum. Links there include a labor history chronology and access to primary source materials. Organizations such as Teaching for Change, the Zinn Education Project, and the Gilder Lehrman Institute of American History also provide classroom teachers with similar materials. The Kheel Center at Cornell University curates the preeminent online resource for teaching and learning about the Triangle fire. It houses a wealth of primary materials, including oral history recordings, as well as secondary sources. The Lawrence History Center has curated materials designed to help classroom teachers deliver content on the 1912 Bread and Roses Strike. In California, labor history lesson plans exist thanks to the California Federation of Teachers.[34]

In higher education, several state universities have labor studies programs, and many have a labor extension effort designed to offer education to union members, including labor history and stewards' training. However, many of these programs are marginalized within the larger university community and subject to frequent funding cut-off threats. The financial strains caused by COVID-19 have handed university administrators a way to eliminate these programs and rid themselves of one of the very few places on campuses where conversations regarding working conditions, discrimination, and wages occur.

A handful of universities offer Master's Degrees in Labor Studies, but these degree-granting programs are routinely threatened with closure by their administrations. City University of New York (CUNY) offers a full-time semester-long program combining academic study with firsthand experiences within the labor movement. Students in the program are paired with unions and worker-rights organizations to gain practical skills and learn first-hand the strategies these organizations use to fight for workers' rights. During class time, students study the history of—and current debates within—the U.S. labor movement. The University of Massachusetts Lowell offers a Labor Studies minor. Students in the program's required course have an internship very similar to CUNY.[35]

Given that most people are not learning labor history in high school or college, aside from the examples mentioned earlier, exposure to that history in alternative settings is essential for building and supporting a viable and formidable labor movement. Labor unions and worker organizations offer classes, workshops, and even summer schools that teach, among other things, the history of their movement and the relevance of past struggles to present and future ones. Such programs have a rich history of their own, and they are an essential way to share knowledge and build solidarity among workers. Both editors of this volume have participated and taught in them. However, they reach a relatively small audience composed primarily of people already involved in labor activism. For everyone else, the more likely places to encounter labor history—even if sometimes unwittingly—are the places where it happened. The factory, the mill, the quarry, the farm, the home, the meeting hall, the bakery, the streets—contributors to *Where Are the Workers* explore the resonance of working-class stories in all these places. This itinerary, we know, is incomplete. The plantation, the prison, the brothel are also labor sites. The stories they tell make many people uncomfortable. White visitors to plantations, for example, recoil at the idea that these stately homes and the elegant lifestyle of those who inhabited them were secondary to the significance of the plantation as a center of production based on slave labor.[36] We applaud the extraordinary dynamism transforming interpretation at these places and hope that this book inspires projects at sites of working-class and union organizing that are not traditionally viewed as within the purview of labor history.

This volume is focused on why we should and how we can bring the complexities of labor and working-class history to life. In so doing, we offer a reason for the communities depicted in this history to engage with it in vibrant public spaces. In the essay "Art for Whose Sake? Working-Class Life in Visual Art," Sara Hattfield focuses on who attends museums and gallery space and why. She describes growing up in a working-class household and being supremely interested in career possibilities in art. "Working-class people may visit galleries on school visits at an early age," she writes, "but could the lack of working-class self-representation in the displays make them feel that art is not for them? But there was also something missing. Very rarely did I come across a work that represented me, or the people I knew." Much the same can be said for the overwhelming majority of K-12 fieldtrips to museums and historic sites taken by students from working-class households. Something fundamental is missing when stories of working-class people are missing or not curated and interpreted in interesting and accessible ways.[37]

Conclusion

Authors of a 2018 article in *The Public Historian* recall Howard Zinn exhorting archivists in 1970 to reject a false neutrality enacted through professionalism and to refuse to serve as "instruments of social control in an essentially undemocratic society." Instead, he pushed them to "play some small part in the creation of a real democracy." Zinn sought an "archival rebellion" to develop new critical and creative approaches to archival practice.[38] A similar appeal can be made as materials get collected and archived, to democratize access to oral history and artifacts collecting and to create public legacies in public spaces that accurately reflect the complex histories told by the authors in this book.

The story of the fiery airplane crash of a Douglas DC-3 aircraft, owned by Airline Transport Carriers of Burbank, California, on January 28, 1948, indicates why the purposeful approach to recover and present to the public labor and working-class history discussed in this volume is essential. Thirty-two people lost their lives, including 28 Mexican farmworkers, most of whom remained unidentified. Some of the people on the flight were in the U.S. as part of a guest-worker program. Others had crossed the border without documents. Chartered by the Immigration and Naturalization Service to fly the farmworkers to the INS Deportation Center in El Centro, California, the airplane was seven hours overdue for a required safety inspection. Placed in a mass grave at Holy Cross Cemetery in Fresno, California were the twenty-seven men and one woman. Just twelve were identified.

Angered by the fact that radio and newspaper coverage of the crash did not give the Mexican victims' names but referred to them as 'deportees,' Woody Guthrie composed *Deportee: Plane Wreck at Los Gatos*. In 2010, Tim Z. Hernandez, the son and grandson of Mexican farmworkers, discovered newspaper articles about the crash while researching a novel in the Fresno library. He identified and memorialized the twenty-eight. "When I saw the newspaper stories, Woody Guthrie's lyrics became real to me. I thought, someone somewhere must have those names." Many descendants attended the unveiling of a memorial, which listed all of the names, at Holy Cross Cemetery. At the ceremony, while Guthrie's song played, musicians read each victim's name and the crowd chanted "descansa en Paz," rest in peace.[39]

Andrew Flinn and Mary Stevens describe the sort of purposeful collection and commemoration that this example and the chapters herein discuss:

> Endeavors by individuals and social groups to document their history, particularly if that history is subordinated or marginalized, is political and subversive. "Recast" histories and their making undermine the distortions and omissions of orthodox historical narratives and the archive and heritage collections sustaining them.[40]

Zinn's exhortation against false neutrality disguised as professionalism applies to anyone engaged in the public history field. The wealth gap dividing the U.S. shows no signs of closing on its own. COVID 19 exacerbated these inequalities and placed a growing number of immigrants, African Americans, and workers of color on the frontlines feeding and caring for the nation. Their stories need to be captured so that the arrogance of the powerful is challenged by the reality of a fierce, vibrant people who know their past and are forging their future.

This book makes a case for placing labor history in relevant museums, historic sites, and landscapes to create meaningful opportunities for working people to learn about their struggles and triumphs (elusive though they may sometimes seem). We have divided the book into two parts. Part I contains essays by historians, preservationists, curators, and archivists engaged in interpreting labor history at various sites around the U.S. Part II's essays offer critical insights into the possibilities and limitations of place-based public labor history initiatives. A brief introduction precedes each section. The place-based labor history initiatives presented are not meant to exhaust all possibilities but to inspire and model practices that others may follow to promote understanding of past struggles, create awareness of present challenges, and support ongoing efforts to build power, expand democracy, and achieve justice for working people.

Notes

1. Michael Frisch, *A Shared Authority: Essays on the Craft and Meaning of Oral and Public History* (Albany: State University of New York Press, 1990), 71.

2. James Green and Elizabeth Jameson, "Marking Labor History on the National

Landscape: The Restored Ludlow Memorial and Its Significance," *International Labor and Working-Class History*, Fall 2009, No. 76, 6–25. See "Restore Ludlow Monument," *Denver Post*, May 31, 2003.

3. David Montgomery, "To Study the People: The American Working Class," *Labor History*, No. 21, 1980, 485–512.

4. Thomas Miller Klubock and Paulo Fontes, "Labor History and Public History: Introduction," *International Labor and Working-Class History*, Fall 2009, No. 76, 2–5, 2.

5. Joseph Nevins, Suren Moodliar, and Eleni Macrakis, *A Peoples Guide to Greater Boston*, University of California Press, 2020. For an overview of this history, see Erik Loomis, *A History of America in Ten Strikes*, The New Press, 2020. For how labor history scholarship has evolved, see the collection of essays by Jeffrey Sklansky, Talitha LeFlouria, and Jefferson Cowie in *Labor: Studies in Working-Class History*, Vol. 16, No. 4, December 2019, 11–48. Chicago's labor trail gets explored in Jeffrey Helgeson, "Chicago's Labor Trail: Labor History as Collaborative Public History," *International Labor and Working-Class History*, Fall 2009, No. 76, 60–64. On remembering the Italian Hall tragedy, see the Keweenaw National Historical Park's site; for Homestead, one site presenting the strike's history to the general public is curated by the Senator John Heinz History Center. Robert Weyeneth, "What I've Learned Along the Way: A Public Historian's Intellectual Odyssey," *The Public Historian*, Vol. 36, No. 2, May 2014, 9–25.

6. See, for example, Richard Anderson, "We Need Public Histories of Organized Labor," *History@Work*, January 25, 2013; https://ncph.org/history-at-work/we-need -public-histories-of-organized-labor/; Tracy Neumann, "Incorporating Labor History in a Public History Curriculum," *Labor@Work*, August 11, 2020, https://ncph .org/history-at-work/incorporating-labor-history-in-a-public-history-curriculum/.

7. Talitha LeFlouria, "Writing Working-Class History from the Bottom Up and Beyond," *Labor: Studies in Working-Class History* Vol. 16 No 4. 2016 (30–34).

8. See Dennis Deslippe, Eric Fure-Slocum, and John W. McKerley, *Civic Labors: Scholar Activism and Working-Class Studies*, University of Illinois Press, 2016; Michel-Rolph Trouillot, *Silencing the Past: Power and the Production of History*, Beacon Press, 1995.

9. Robert Forrant and Jurg Siegenthaler, *The Great Lawrence Textile Strike of 1912: New Scholarship on the Bread and Roses Strike*, Baywood Publishing, 2014; The Digital Public Library's "Bread and Roses Strike of 1912: Two Months that Changed Labor History," For information on the Lawrence History Center and its work documenting that city's history, https://dp.la/exhibitions/breadandroses www.lawrencehistory.org.

10. www.RememberetheTriangleFire.org.

11. Rob Linné, Leigh Benin, Adrienne Sosin, eds. *Organizing the Curriculum: Perspectives on Teaching the U.S. Labor Movement* (Rotterdam: Sense Publishing, 2009) xi, 4; Michelle Caswell, "Seeing Yourself in History: Community Archives and the Fight Against Symbolic Annihilation," *The Public Historian*, Vol. 36, No. 4, 2014, 26–37; Andrew Flinn, Mary Stevens, and Elizabeth Shepherd, "Whose Memories,

Whose Archives? Independent Community Archives, Autonomy and the Mainstream," *Archival Science*, Vol. 9, Nos. 1–2, 2009, 71–86; Michelle Caswell and Samip Mallick, "Collecting the Easily Missed Stories: Digital Participatory Microhistory and the South Asian American Digital Archive," *Archives and Manuscripts*, Vol. 42, No. 1, 2014, 73–86; Jay Winston Driskell Jr., A Review of "The Sweat of Their Face: Portraying American Workers." Smithsonian's National Portrait Gallery, Washington, D.C., November 3, 2017-September 3, 2018; Dorothy Moss, Curator, and David C. Ward, Historian Emeritus. Review in *The Public Historian*, Vol. 41, No. 1, February 2019, 140–147.

12. *New York Times*, "Measuring the Impact of the Pandemic on the Economy," December 18, 2020, B.5; Michael Batty, Jesse Bricker, Joseph Briggs, Elizabeth Holmquist, Susan McIntosh, Kevin Moore, Eric Nielsen, Sarah Reber, Molly Shatto, Kamila Sommer, Tom Sweeney, and Alice Henriques Volz (2019), "Introducing the Distributional Financial Accounts of the United States," Finance and Economics Discussion Series 2019–017. Washington: Board of Governors of the Federal Reserve System, https://doi.org/10.17016/FEDS.2019.017; Pedro Nicolaci da Costa, "America's Humungous Wealth Gap Is Widening Further," Forbes, May 29, 2019.

13. Malcolm Gay, "MFA Workers Unionize in Landslide Vote," *Boston Globe*, November 21, 2020, B1; Estelle Sommeiller and Mark Price, "The new gilded age: Income inequality in the U.S. by state, metropolitan area, and county," Economic Policy Institute, July 19, 2018, https://www.epi.org/publication/the-new-gilded-age-income-inequality-in-the-u-s-by-state-metropolitan-area-and-county/; Ryan Nunn, Jimmy O'Donnell, and Jay Shambaugh, "The Shift in Private Sector Union Participation: Explanation and Effects," The Hamilton Project at Brookings, August 2019.

14. Michelle Chen, 2018. Millennials Are Keeping Labor Unions Alive. *The Nation*. February 5. https://www.thenation.com/article/millennials-are-keeping-unions-alive/; Jeffrey M. Jones, "As Labor Day Turns 125, Union Approval Nears 50-Year High," Gallup, August 28, 2019. https://news.gallup.com/poll/265916/labor-day-turns-125-union-approval-near-year-high.aspx.

15. On the PATCO strike, see Joseph A. McCartin, *Collision Course: Ronald Reagan, the Air Traffic Controllers, and the Strike that Changed America* (New York: Oxford University Press, 2011).

16. Mike Baker, "Already under Siege, Labor Unions Face a New Threat from Alaska," *New York Times*, October 9, 2019.

17. Noam Scheiber, "Uber Drivers Are Contractors, Not Employees, Labor Board Says," *New York Times*, May 14, 2019; Michael Gold, "Scabby, the Giant Inflatable Union Protest Rat, Faces Extermination," *New York Times*, July 31, 2019.

18. U.S. Bureau of Labor Statistics, "Work Stoppages Summary," February 8, 2019, https://www.bls.gov/news.release/wkstp.nr0.htm.

19. Eric Blanc, "A Strike for Racial Justice and Democracy in Little Rock Schools," *Jacobin Magazine*, November 14, 2019; Linda Jacobson, "Tracker: Indiana teachers hold 'Red for Ed' rally," *Education Dive*, November 18, 2019; Tonya Riley, "She Injured

Herself Working at Amazon: Then the Real Nightmare Began," *Mother Jones*, March 2019; Samantha Winslow, "Marriott Hotel Strikers Set a New Industry Standard," Labor Notes, December 20, 2018; Drew Philip, "'One Job Should Be Enough': Marriott Hotel Workers' Strike Hits Eight U.S. Cities," *The Guardian*, October 26, 2018.

20. Lane Windham, "Sara Nelson on Next-Gen Leadership and Helping People Find Their Own Power," *Labor: Studies in Working-Class History of the Americas*, Vol. 17, No. 2, May 2020, 73–80; Natalie Kitroeff, "Sara Nelson Is America's Most Powerful Flight Attendant," *New York Times*, February 24, 2019, B.U. 1.

21. Gina Bellafante, "'We Didn't Sign Up for This': Amazon Workers on the Front Lines," *New York Times*, April 3, 2020, MB 3.

22. Katie Johnston, "No Rest on the Seventh Day," *Boston Globe*, December 17, 2020, D1.

23. Peter Cole, "The Most Radical Union in the U.S. Is Shutting Down the Ports on Juneteenth," In *These Times*, June 16, 2020; Jacob Bogage, "Thousands of U.S. Workers Walk Out in 'Strike for Black Lives,'" *Washington Post*, July 20, 2020.

24. Mitch Smith and Monica Davey, "Chicago Teachers' Strike, Longest in Decades, Ends," *New York Times*, October 31, 2019; Jackson Potter, "What Other Unions Can Learn from the Historic Gains We Won in the Chicago Teachers Strike," In *These Times*, November 26, 2019.

25. Julia Rose, *Interpreting Difficult History at Museums and Historic Sites* (Lanham, MD, Rowan and Littlefield, 2016), 7. Rose adds, "Museums and historical sites are emerging as social agents that can take on social responsibilities that go beyond collecting and preserving materials. They have the ability to positively influence and affect society," 8.

26. Texas Adminstrative Code, https://texreg.sos.state.tx.us/public/readtac$ext .TacPage?sl=R&app=9&p_dir=&p_rloc=&p_tloc=&p_ploc=&pg=1&p_tac=&ti= 19&pt=2&ch=113&rl=31.

27. "Labor History Week Resolution," February 16, Wisconsin Department of Public Instruction, "Labor History," Wisc. Stat. sec. 115.28(55), https://dpi.wi.gov/ social-studies/laws/labor-history; State Education Department, University of the State of New York, "New York State K-8 Social Studies Framework," February 2017, http://www.nysed.gov/common/nysed/files/programs/curriculum-instruction/ss -framework-k-8a2.pdf; West Virginia Archives and History, "Labor History Week Resolution," February 16, 2010, http://www.wvculture.org/history/labor/laborhistory weekresolution.html; California Federation of Teachers, "Labor History Month," https://www.cft.org/labor-history-month.

28. Connecticut State Department of Education, "Connecticut Elementary and Secondary Standards," February 2015, https://portal.ct.gov/-/media/SDE/Social -Studies/ssframeworks.pdf.

29. Massachusetts Department of Elementary and Secondary Education. Massachusetts Curriculum Framework 2018: History and Social Science, Grades Pre-Kindergarten to 12. http://www.doe.mass.edu/frameworks/hss/2018–12.pdf.

30. Richard Colton, "African-American workers played role in Springfield Armory history," *The Republican*, February 16, 2014; Rob Wilson, "Crossing Gender and Color Lines at the Springfield Armory: Women and African Americans Changing the WWII Industrial Workplace," past@present, UMass Amherst Department of History, March 24, 2016.

31. "Justice Department Obtains Consent Decrees," Daily Labor Report, December 22, 1971, 1072.

32. Lyman and Merrie Wood Museum of Springfield History, springfieldmuseums. org; Springfield Armory Museum, www.nps.gov/spar/index.htm; Lowell National Historical Park, www.nps.gov/lowe/index.htm; American Precision Museum, www .americanprecision.org. On disinvestment and deindustrialization, Robert Forrant, "The Rise and Demise of the Connecticut River Valley's Industrial Economy: A Photo Essay," *Historical Journal of Massachusetts*, Vol. 46 (1), Winter 2018, 2–21; Forrant, "Springfield, Massachusetts After the Finance Control Board: Is the Way Clear to A Sustainable Recovery? *New England Journal of Public Policy*, 24 (1), 2013, 67–92; Forrant, "Too Many Bends in the River: The Post-World War II Decline of the Connecticut River Valley Machine Tool Industry," *Journal of Industrial History*, 5 (2), 2002, 71–91.

33. John W. McKerley and Jennifer Sherer, "The Iowa Labor History Oral Project," *Labor: Studies in Working-Class History of the Americas*, Vol. 13, Issue 1, 2016, 7–10.

34. Rosemary Feuer, "LAWCHA and the Lesson Plan," *Labor: Studies in Working-Class History of the Americas*, Vol. 10, Issue 3, 7–9; *Labor History for the Classroom and the Public*, www.lawcha.org/labor-history-for-the-classroom-and-public/; Teaching for Change, www.teachingforchange.org; Gilder Lehrman Institute of American History, www.gilderlehrman.org; Remembering the 1911 Triangle Factory Fire, https:// trianglefire.ilr.cornell.edu/; Lawrence History Curriculum, www.lawrencehistory .org/education/unitplans; California Federation of Teachers, "Golden Lands, Working Hands," www.cft.org/california-labor-history.html. Youngstown State University's Center for Working-Class Studies Maintains a Working-Class and Labor Museums. Annotated List: https://ysu.edu/center-working-class-studies/working-class-and -labor-museums.

35. City University of New York School of Labor and Urban Studies, https://slu.cuny .edu/labor-studies/union-semester/. As part of the program, students receive a $7,000 financial allowance to cover tuition and living expenses while working four days a week at their field placement. During the evenings and all day on Fridays, students take classes with the Labor Studies faculty at the School of Labor and Urban Studies.

36. Jorge L. Giovannetti, "Subverting the Master's Narrative: Public Histories of Slavery in Plantation America," *International Labor and Working-Class History* 76, Fall 2009, p. 105–126; see also Randolph Bergstrom, "Still Provoking: The Public History of Race and Slavery," *The Public Historian* 36, 2014, 7–8.

37. Sara Hattfield, "Art for Whose Sake? Working-Class Life in Visual Art," The author is on the faculty of the University of Technology Sydney.

38. Marika Cifor, Michelle Caswell, Alda Allina Migoni, and Noah Geraci, "What We Do Crosses over to Activism: The Politics and Practice of Community Archives," *The Public Historian*, Vol. 40, No.2, May 2018, 69–95. See Howard Zinn, "Secrecy, Archives and the Public Interest," *Midwest Archivist*, 2, No. 2, 1977, 14–26.

39. Malia Wollan, "65 Years Later, a Memorial Gives Names to Crash Victims," *New York Times*, September 3, 2013; Tim Z. Hernandez, *All They Will Call You*, The University of Arizona Press, 2017.

40. Andrew Flinn and Mary Stevens, "'It Is Noh Mistri, Wi Mekin History': Telling Our Own Story: Independent and Community Archives in the U.K., Challenging and Subverting the Mainstream," in Jeannette Bastian and Ben Alexander, eds. *Community Archives: The Shaping of Memory* (London: Facet, 2009), 3–4.

PART I

In Practice

Collecting and Interpreting
the History for the Public

In *Nearby History*, Daniel Kyvig and Myron Marty note, ". . . . nearby history has a further intangible appeal that may be its most notable quality. The emotional rewards of learning about a past that has plainly and directly affected one's own life cannot be duplicated by any other type of historical inquiry."[1] Purposeful collecting and interpretation bring such stories into the foreground where they can function as rhetorical frames that select, highlight, and organize information in a familiar and easy-to-follow format.[2]

This section opens with Lou Martin's essay on establishing the West Virginia Mine Wars Museum. He explores the significance a historical site can hold for local and regional populations. An important center of mineworker organizing in the late nineteenth and early twentieth centuries, the Matewan storefront museum opened to help residents reclaim their history. After its grand opening, Chuck Keeney, a Museum board member and great-grandson of District 17 United Mineworkers president Frank Keeney, told a reporter that the coal industry did not need to use force anymore because they controlled the radio, the news, and the schools. "When a region or a country doesn't know its own history, it's like a person with Alzheimer's. . . . When people don't know who they are, they become much easier to manipulate. This Museum is our own form of reclamation." Keeney continued, "It's cultural or identity reclamation."[3] Amanda Gustin, Karen Lane, and Scott McLaughlin demonstrate how a collaborative partnership in Barre, Vermont, produced local stories at the intersection of industrial, labor, and immigration history. Deeply tied to place, the chapter explores the myriad challenges that confront multiple nonprofits working within a small community and from quite distinct vantage points.

In some cases, competing stories must be managed to engage audiences whose memories of the past lie well outside the conflict framework that tends to dominate much of labor history. Rebecca Bush explores the work of sustaining a nonprofit organization and creating meaningful exhibits in her essay on mills and millwork in Columbus, Georgia. A challenge is that many residents "recall mill owners as civic leaders who set the tone for a vibrant culture of local philanthropy," while simultaneously others "recognize the questionable tactics that allowed them to accrue the wealth that made such charitable giving possible." With support often received from state and local governments and family foundations, balancing storytelling becomes politically and financially practical and essential.

The resonance of stories is enhanced when embedded in physical locations that activate place memory. Indeed, memory scholars Greg Dickinson, Carole Blair, and Brian Ott note that "place has survived as a recognized memory apparatus perhaps longer than any other."[4] For the one-hundredth anniversary of the 1912 Bread & Roses Strike in Lawrence, MA, the exhibit located on the top floor of the Everett Mill was such a space. Kathleen Flynn, Susan Grabski, and Jim Beauchesne describe how the mill's physical spaces were as much a part of their exhibit as the artifacts, images, and words. Physical structures like the Everett Mill contain intentionally and unintentionally encoded memories. These memories may speak to insiders who share a collective past, in this case, the experience of industrial labor in a manufacturing economy, or they can represent shared pasts to outsiders who might be interested in knowing about them in the present.[5]

Many sites treated herein have connections to manufacturing. In a special issue of *The Public Historian* focused on deindustrialization Stefan Berger and Christian Wicke ask:

> Against the dramatic effects plant closures had around coalfields, steel mills, shipyards, car factories, and other heavy industries, it remains to be fully understood what deindustrialization has done to collective memory and identity. How have large-scale deindustrialization processes since the second half of the twentieth century affected public representations of the past?[6]

As the U.S. transitioned to a service economy, the nature of manufacturing work is increasingly unfamiliar. The challenge for industrial sites is somehow to speak in a way that resonates with people who have no frame of reference for such labor. One way to achieve this is by the activation of visual memory. Still photos, video and film clips, maps, and other visual artifacts facilitate individual and community engagement with labor's past by showing long-gone people, places, and objects in a new light. In their essay on the Loray Mill, Elijah Gaddis and Karen Sieber recount how the University of North Carolina at Chapel Hill Digital Innovation Lab transformed "cold and boring" census records into a vital and engaging visual representation of mill village life. "With a detailed pin for every person on a digitized Sanborn Fire Insurance map," they note, "the map took on life, visibly highlighting the number of people packed into the house, or the average age and sex and race of certain mill jobs, from the janitors and draymen to the spinners and carders."

Katrina Windon's essay on the Elaine Massacre describes how the University of Arkansas Archives took specific steps to contextualize and tell the story of the massacre so that audiences could gain an understanding of the events that preceded and followed it. A crucial part of giving fair play to the Elaine Massacre is "acknowledging the organizing efforts, agency, and legacy of those Phillips County laborers" involved while placing the story within the long history of the civil rights and labor justice movements.[7] Archivist Conor Casey makes a case for purposeful collecting. "Social power and implicit bias influence the writing and framing of history," Casey notes, and "the creation of archives that enable that history." Purposeful collecting remedies omissions to address such representation gaps.[8]

Notes

1. Daniel Kyvig and Myron Marty, *Nearby History: Exploring the Past Around You* (Lanham, MD: AltaMira Press, 2010), 14.

2. Kieran Egan argues that anyone can acquire historical knowledge when presented in an age-appropriate story format. See Kieran Egan, "Accumulating History," *History and Theory: Studies in The Philosophy of History* 22, No. 4 (December 1983), 66–80; and Egan, *Teaching as Story Telling: An Alternative Approach to Teaching and Curriculum in the Elementary School* (Chicago: University of Chicago Press, 1989). The emotional impact of stories in various educational settings is explored in M. Vayanou, M. Karvounis, A. Katifori, M. Kyriakidi, M. Roussou, Y. Ioannidis, The CHESS project: adaptive personalized storytelling experiences in museums, In V. Dimitrova, T. Kuflik, D. Chin, F. Ricci, P. Dolog, G. J. Houben (editors), "The 22nd conference on user modeling, adaptation and personalization (UMAP), Project Synergy Workshop," 2014, Springer, 15–18; Ivor F. Goodson, Gert J. J. Biesta, and Mi-

chael Tedder, and Norma Adair, *Narrative Learning* (London: Routledge, 2010). On place-making, see Lynda H. Schneekloth and Robert G. Shibley, *Placemaking: The Art and Practice of Building Communities* (New York: Wiley, 1995); Stephen Ward, Selling *Places: The Marketing and Promotion of Towns and Cities, 1850–2000* (New York: Routledge, 1998); Cathy Stanton, *The Lowell Experiment: Public History in a Postindustrial City* (Amherst: University of Massachusetts Press, 2006).

3. "Rednecks Symbolize Solidarity: West Virginia Mine Wars Museum Reclaims Union Identity," *Counterpunch.org.* https://www.counterpunch.org/2015/08/10/rednecks -symbolize-solidarity-w-va-mine-wars-museum-reclaims-union-identity/.

4. Greg Dickinson, Carole Blair, and Brian L. Ott, *Places of Public Memory: The Rhetoric of Museums and Memorials* (Tuscaloosa: University of Alabama Press, 2010), 24.

5. Dolores Hayden, *The Power of Place: Urban Landscapes as Public History* (Cambridge: MIT Press, 1997), 46. The Woonsocket, Rhode Island Museum of Work & Culture represents an example of a place-based historical space. Operated by the Rhode Island Historical Society, the stories of French Canadians who left Quebec's farms for New England factories get told, including the history of labor organizing in the 1930s.

6. Stefan Berger and Christian Wicke, "Deindustrialization, Heritage, and Representations of Identity," *The Public Historian*, Vol. 39, No. 4, 2017, 10–20, 11.

7. Cathy Stanton, "Performing the Postindustrial: The Limits of Radical History in Lowell, Massachusetts," *Radical History Review*, 98 (Spring 2007) 81–96, 83.

8. Na Li, "Whose History, Whose Memory? A Culturally Sensitive Narrative Approach," in Page and Miller, *Bending the Future: Fifty Ideas for the Next Fifty Years of Historic Preservation in the United States* (Amherst: University of Massachusetts Press, 2016), 137–138. Casey's and Li's points receive amplification in Bill Adair, Benjamin Fine, and Laura Koloski, eds. *Letting Go? Sharing Historical Authority in a User-Generated World* (Philadelphia: The Pew Center for Arts & Heritage, 2007). See therein Steve Zeitlin, "'Where Are the Best Stories? Where Is My Story—Participation and Curation in a New Media Age," 34–43; and Deborah Schwartz and Bill Adair, "Community as Curator: A Case Study at the Brooklyn Historical Society," 112–123. An example of a purposeful collection is the South Asian American Digital Archive. See Michelle Caswell and Samip Mallick, "Collecting the Easily Missed Stories: Digital Participatory Microhistory and the South Asian American Digital Archive," *Archives and Manuscripts*, Vol. 42, No. 1, 2014, 73–86. Among the many things they do, the archive organizes what they term "digital participatory microhistory projects that encourage community members to create new records documenting their experiences." See also Cinnamon Catlin-Legutko, "We Must Decolonize Our Museums."

CHAPTER 1

Public Memory and the West Virginia Mine Wars Museum

LOU MARTIN

Introduction

On May 16, 2015, the West Virginia Mine Wars Museum opened in a 500-square-foot storefront in Matewan. Featuring permanent exhibits about life in company towns, strikes, and gun battles, the museum attempts to capture the major events of coal miners' efforts to unionize the state's southern counties during the first two decades of the twentieth century. More than 500 visitors crowded into the museum during the grand opening and gathered out on the sidewalk. After the air conditioner broke, the crowd inside listened carefully to speakers in stifling heat. Cecil Roberts, the United Mine Workers of America (UMWA) president, told the audience, "I happen to think that what we're doing here today is extremely important because I never read about Ludlow, I never read about Paint Creek, and I never read about Cabin Creek in my history books. And young people today, they don't either." With retired miners from UMWA Local 1440 standing by his side, he said, "I submit to you that it is time for working folks not only to stand up and fight back and keep the middle class . . . it's time to stop the millionaires and the billionaires telling us what our kids can read and learn in the schools."[1]

Coal mining has dominated the history of Matewan and much of southern West Virginia for more than a century, but the industry has left a mixed legacy. Almost everybody remembers when coal was king, and local businesses thrived, miners could afford to send their kids to college, and community ties were strong. Since the 1980s, employment has declined, and Matewan's county has lost about a third of its population. Thousands continue to work in the industry, and thousands more are retired miners, but coal companies have

FIGURE 1.1. Front of Original West Virginia Mine Wars Museum. Credit: West Virginia Mine Wars Museum staff, 2015.

used bankruptcy filings to shed pension and healthcare obligations. Adding to retirees' troubles, the government funds to cover "orphaned" pensions and retirees' healthcare have been in danger of running out multiple times. Recent years have witnessed increasing poverty levels, political corruption scandals, and a drug epidemic fueled by pharmaceutical manufacturers. Finally, some residents have had to bear the industry's environmental burdens, experiencing intensified flooding off old strip mines, toxic runoff, and groundwater pollution.[2]

Assessing coal's impact on residents is complicated and made even more so by competing narratives. In the last two decades, the West Virginia Coal Association has sponsored a public relations campaign that portrays the industry as an embattled jobs-provider. The Association touts the role mining jobs have played in community life, vilifies environmental regulators and their activist allies, and ignores the positive influence the UMWA has had on wages, benefits, and mine safety. Simultaneously, many retirees feel abandoned by companies that profited handsomely from their labor over the years. The president of UMWA Local 1440 in Matewan recently said that the companies "raped" the area and left. He continued, "We're left here trying to rebuild our community and everything, and they're gone."[3] The International Office of the UMWA has further complicated discourse by sometimes siding with coal companies in recent battles against environmental regulations in hopes of keeping struggling mines in business, and other times by condemning companies for failing to meet pension and healthcare obligations and ignoring unsafe working conditions.

The public memory of the Mine Wars has been similarly complicated. It represents a painful past of violence, division, radical critiques of capitalism, and unconstitutional state actions. Given the tough times in the area, it may not seem like a past that residents would want to preserve, but thousands, especially the members of UMWA Local 1440, have supported and celebrated the museum. The museum opened intending to help residents reclaim their history while contributing to heritage tourism to the area. Many retirees and their family members see the Mine Wars as a significant chapter in the nation's history and want to preserve the memory of past generations' sacrifice and struggles, especially as some towns and a way of life are fading away. In its efforts to preserve and interpret this history, the museum has encouraged conversations filled with both pride and pain about the past in a time when working families are fighting to keep rights and benefits won a century ago.[4]

Matewan and the Mine Wars

Matewan, a town of 500 residents in southern West Virginia, sits on the banks of Tug Fork River in Mingo County. Mountains covered with hardwood forests rise high above the county's roads and valleys where rusty coal tipples and active strip mines act as powerful reminders of coal's past and present. Mingo County was formed in 1895, shortly after the Norfolk & Western Railroad extended a line into the county, and a flurry of economic and political activity followed. Its population grew from 6,000 in 1895 to 26,000 by 1920. The most widely known event in the county's history occurred on May 19, 1920, during a strike for union recognition, when Matewan's chief of police, Sid Hatfield, deputized several miners and led them into a battle with thirteen mine guards from the Baldwin-Felts Detective Agency. The shootout left ten people dead, including seven mine guards, two miners, and the town's mayor. Newspapers across the nation carried stories about what came to be known as the "Matewan Massacre."[5]

For national newspapers and the reading public, the battle in Matewan reinforced an image of lawless hillbillies in the land of the Hatfields and Mc-

Coys, but for coal miners and their families, Matewan came to represent a key event in the West Virginia Mine Wars. It was a rare moment when local law enforcement joined the miners to outgun the coal operators and their hired men. The brave Sid Hatfield—the man who would not be intimidated by the hated Baldwin-Felts agents—became a hero to miners everywhere. When Hatfield was murdered on the courthouse steps in neighboring McDowell County a year later, it spurred miners across the region to action. When the Mingo County miners' strike for recognition entered its second year, the state and county governments mobilized against it, declaring martial law, jailing union supporters, and raiding tent colonies to break the strike.

Hatfield's murder was the last straw for thousands of miners in union territory near Charleston's state capital, and they took up arms, tied red bandannas around their necks, and began marching toward Mingo County to aid the strikers. Most miners already owned red bandannas, and tying them around their neck let fellow miners know which side they were on, and they became a symbol of their solidarity. Fifty miles south of Charleston, the "redneck army," as they became known, encountered some three thousand militiamen and deputies at Blair Mountain. A five-day battle ensued until the U.S. Army arrived, and the miners either surrendered or retreated into the hills. The UMWA drive broken, thousands of families remembered the heroism of Hatfield, the sacrifices of miners and their families, the gunfire on Blair Mountain, and the lengths to which coal companies went to prevent unionization.[6]

In 1933, a few months after Congress passed the National Industrial Recovery Act, which recognized workers' rights to organize and bargain collectively, tens of thousands of miners, who now had the support of federal law, flocked to the UMWA in the Mountain State. Those who had lived through the Mine Wars became some of its most loyal members. During the 1950s, mechanization of mining led to layoffs and shutdowns throughout the state, but those who kept their jobs enjoyed better wages and benefits, job security, a stronger voice in working conditions, and influence over county and even state politics. The UMWA became a powerful institution in places that had once been company towns. Many in southern West Virginia have fond memories of the 1950s, 1960s, and 1970s, a time of relative prosperity built on union paychecks, won by the Mine Wars generation's sacrifices.[7]

Public Memory and the Mine Wars

In recent decades, historians have turned their attention to what they have termed "public memory," a community's or society's collective interpretation of historical events. Communication scholars Brian Ott, Carole Blair, and

Greg Dickinson have noted that remembering the past in public is complicated and contentious because it "narrates shared identities," is activated by "present concerns, issues, or anxieties," and is partial and partisan.[8] While memorials or commemorations provide interpretations—which are often the official narratives—the public's understanding of the past actually emerges from "the intersection of official and vernacular cultural expressions," according to historian John Bodnar. He observes that authorities who create official histories typically come from the ranks of middle-class professionals and promote a nationalistic culture. Conversely, grassroots efforts are often led by working-class residents with a vested interest in preserving the history whose interpretations of the past are grounded in lived experience in "small-scale communities." The result is an "argument about the interpretation of reality." The elite have significant advantages in shaping public memory, authoring official histories, and deploying powerful symbols and language to "foster patriotism and civic duty and ordinary people continue to accept, reformulate, and ignore such messages."[9] Grassroots preservationists usually have fewer resources to present their competing interpretations. They also tend to draw on a different array of symbols, not those that celebrate the elite but those of working-class struggle and sacrifice. Such symbols may not have a ready audience but come closer to reflecting working families' lived experiences.

Such contests between elite and grassroots interpretations of the past have often played out in efforts to shape the public memory of important events in U.S. labor history. As Jim Beauchesne, Kathleen S. Flynn, and Susan Grabski observe in chapter three on the Bread and Roses Strike of 1912, local elites in Lawrence, Massachusetts, suppressed important aspects of the strike's history, instead crafting an "official story" that built directly on the elite's response in 1912, an antistrike "God and Country" demonstration. For the 50th anniversary of the strike, city leaders held a "God and Country" parade and perpetuated a version of events that omitted working-class perspectives and experiences. Similarly, archivist Katrina Windon reveals the power struggles that shaped the public memory of the Elaine Massacre, a rampage by antiunion white supremacists in Arkansas that left hundreds of African Americans dead. One of the state's U.S. senators made statements in Congress that framed the violence as the result of a planned uprising by radical sharecroppers. When the *New York Times* reprinted the statements, it gave credence to an elite portrayal of events that persisted for decades. More recent efforts, including an exhibit at the University of Arkansas Special Collections, (see Windon, chapter six) have attempted to recover the history of sharecroppers organizing to demand fair prices for their cotton and an end to debt peonage, which was also a challenge to white supremacy.

Such contests have also shaped the public memory of the West Virginia Mine Wars. In some ways, these struggles have been an extension of the competing narratives over the coal industry's role in Appalachian communities for more than a century. Beginning in the 1880s, coal company executives and state officials described the industrialization of mountainous, rural sections of the state as a great achievement that would usher in a new era of civilization and progress. In his 1897 inaugural address, Governor George Atkinson declared, "Instead of fewer corporations in West Virginia, we need more of them . . . to aid us in the development of our almost inexhaustible natural resources." He also framed critics as opponents of progress who cried "down with rich men and corporations." Atkinson continued, "Such talk is anarchy, and anarchy will never secure an enduring foothold in our 'Switzerland of America.'"[10] In the early 1900s, one newspaper editor listed the "accomplishments of old king coal": new towns and cities, the construction of railroads, and the new commerce with distant cities.[11] In 1921, a circuit judge in southern West Virginia told a group of U.S. senators, "If you take our coal from us, we shall go back to the days of bobcats and wilderness. Coal is our existence."[12]

During the unionization efforts between 1912 and 1921, West Virginia mine operators routinely portrayed striking miners as radicals bent on the destruction of the American government and society. After the Paint Creek-Cabin Creek Strike of 1912–1913, one official said that this "armed revolution in West Virginia" had partly succeeded because companies failed to coordinate their defense of law and order. A few years later, Mingo County operators declared that the UMWA was "unlawful per se, revolutionary in character, and a menace to the free institutions of this country." After the 1921 Battle of Blair Mountain, a Logan County operator claimed that the UMWA wanted "control of a necessity of life" to "establish a soviet government."[13]

Famed journalist Boyden Sparkes made his way to the Blair Mountain battle site, only to be shot in the leg by the state police and held—along with other reporters—by the county sheriff, who prohibited them from writing stories without his approval. According to historian Chuck Keeney, this was the beginning of a decades-long effort by state and local officials to shape the public memory of the Mine Wars. In 1939, the governor demanded that references to Blair Mountain be removed from the Works Progress Administration's *West Virginia Guide*. When the state added West Virginia history to the public school curriculum that same decade, officials systematically omitted the Mine Wars from textbooks. In 1972, when the state adopted a new textbook, it contained only one paragraph devoted to the Battle of Blair Mountain.[14]

Perhaps surprisingly, through the 1960s, the United Mine Workers also made no apparent effort to memorialize the Mine Wars or the Battle of Blair

Mountain. President John L. Lewis built the UMWA into one of the most powerful unions in the nation, and part of his strategy was to ensure unity of action by demanding complete loyalty from local officers. In 1930, Frank Keeney, the one-time UMWA District 17 president who helped organize the 1921 Miners' March, became part of a rival union, the West Virginia Mine Workers Union.[15] On the battle's tenth anniversary, the *United Mine Workers Journal* did not mention the historic battle and instead chastised Keeney for forming a "scab dual outfit."[16] The UMWA's official history, published in 1950, makes no mention of the 1919–1921 unionization drive in southern West Virginia, writing only that these "were hard, lean years for the UMWA and for John L. Lewis."[17]

Rediscovery, Decline, and Division

Beginning in the late 1960s, as West Virginians organized to tackle social issues such as corruption in the UMWA leadership, environmental degradation, political corruption in county governments, and the lack of healthcare for miners with Black Lung disease, they took new pride in their state and Appalachian identity. Rediscovering the region's distinctive histories became part of this "reawakening," including rediscovering the Mine Wars.[18] In 1976, John Alexander Williams wrote a new history of West Virginia for a bicentennial series supported by the National Endowment for the Humanities. In stark contrast to the 1939 WPA guide, this government-funded history includes an entire chapter on the Mine Wars as well as the economic exploitation that fueled them. In the book's last paragraph, Williams highlights the distortions of history that had been common in the state's schoolbooks, labeling it the "'Soviet Encyclopedia' approach to local history" because the books were filled with boasts and trivia and ignored much more significant albeit painful events.[19] In 1981, David Corbin's *Life, Work, and Rebellion in the Coal Fields: The Southern West Virginia Miners, 1880–1922* became the first academic history focused solely on the Mine Wars and their causes. Multiple books and even the independent film *Matewan* followed. In 1989 and 1990, Matewan hosted an oral history project funded by the West Virginia Humanities Council, which preserved first-hand accounts of the 1920 battle in the town and many other aspects of the community's history.[20]

While many were rediscovering Matewan's history, Mingo County residents were entering a painful chapter in their history. In the early 1980s, the A. T. Massey coal company, headquartered in Richmond, Virginia, began an assault on the UMWA that proved devastating. In 1981, the company thwarted a unionization campaign at its Elk Run complex despite the union's all-out effort that resulted in dozens of arrests. In 1984, Massey refused to sign contracts for its subsidiaries, precipitating the longest authorized strike in the union's history. Local manager Don Blankenship intensified the company's strikebreaking efforts by using video surveillance, hiring armed guards who patrolled with attack dogs, and recruiting nonunion truck drivers to barrel through picket lines. Much of the conflict unfolded in Mingo County, leaving scars on the communities for decades to come.[21]

The defeat at the Massey mines signaled a change of fortunes for the union, and its membership began a steady decline in Kentucky and West Virginia. In the late 1970s, the percentage of U.S. miners who belonged to the union stood at 50 percent, then declined to 44 percent in the early 1980s, and fell to less than 22 percent by 2012.[22] The decline in union membership coincided with more mechanization, especially as companies shifted to surface mining,[23] and the number of miners in West Virginia dropped from 62,000 in 1978 to 35,000 just five years later. A steady decline followed, and by the early 2000s, only 15,000 miners remained.[24]

Along with the decline in employment and union membership, residents faced other hardships, such as loss of community spaces and institutions, decreased social capital, and environmental burdens from mountaintop removal—a surface mining method that levels mountains with high explosives. Some residents endured air pollution, groundwater pollution, intensified flooding, and the growth of massive waste impoundments—some holding as many as 3 billion gallons of coal slurry—near their homes.[25] Beginning in the 1990s, residents most directly affected by the impacts of mining sued the companies and regulatory agencies and organized a grassroots campaign to raise awareness and gain allies. The coal industry also mobilized with a new public relations campaign that defined coal companies as "local" and environmentalists as "outsiders" who knew little about miners' "way of life." In 2002, the West Virginia Coal Association created the Friends of Coal to have supporters display Friends of Coal stickers on businesses, trucks, homes, and helmets. After the 2008 election of Barack Obama, the campaign developed the "war on coal" rhetoric, which included all the previous elements—outsider environmentalists, government overreach, and job loss—but also highlighted the powerlessness of miners and their families. Public hearings over mining permits became increasingly contentious, and environmental activists, especially local ones, received threats of violence.[26] In a 2012 speech in the U.S. Senate, Jay Rockefeller criticized the industry for its "carefully orchestrated messages" that struck "fear in the hearts of West Virginians."[27]

The environmental conflicts represented another round of competing narratives about the industry's role in the region and mirrored discourse from decades earlier. The various threads of this extended discourse—the rediscoveries of the Mine Wars, the union's decline, jobs and the mechanization of mining, increased strip mining, and environmental degradation—all intersected at Blair Mountain.[28] In the 1990s, multiple mountaintop removal operations began around the mountain over community members and historians' objections. In 2009, a team of historians, archaeologists, and residents succeeded in getting the battlefield temporarily placed on the National Register, but coal industry attorneys quickly challenged the listing in court and won.[29] One West Virginian who has inspired hundreds with Blair Mountain's history, Wilma Lee Steele, told a group of young environmental activists about the 1921 battle and the history of resistance in Appalachia and gave red bandannas to the group, encouraging them to embody the spirit of Blair Mountain.

In 2011, those activists joined forces with the historians and archaeologists to reenact the miners' march, this time protesting the imminent destruction of the mountain and calling for a more sustainable economy in southern West Virginia. These marchers covered 50 miles over six days, garnered considerable local and national news media attention, inspired local supporters, and sparked angry counter-protests. On the sixth day, about 1,000 marchers rallied on the mountaintop, listened to speeches, and sang labor songs. A month later, on Labor Day, the Blair Mountain Community Center and Museum opened in Blair to organize opposition to the mining permits and share artifacts from the mountain with tour groups. Reportedly, continued opposition from local, nonunion miners using intimidation and vandalism exacerbated disagreements within the organization and ultimately led to the center's closure.

Identity Reclamation

In the fall of 2013, I was one of several people that began meeting in Matewan—a town that had embraced its history by reenacting the Battle of Matewan every year—and we began discussing opening a museum dedicated to preserving and interpreting the events of the Mine Wars. Over the next year and a half, we registered as a nonprofit organization and rented a storefront. Wilma Steele and Kenneth King—who are also founding board members—brought together their artifact collections. Next, we recruited an artist named Shaun Slifer, a participant in the 2011 march, to design permanent exhibits. With funding from the National Coal Heritage Area Authority and the West Virginia Humanities Council, donations from some two hundred individuals, and several hundred hours of volunteer work, we transformed the empty storefront into a museum.

Incredibly, the empty storefront we rented was in a line of red brick buildings next to the railroad tracks where the 1920 battle between Sid Hatfield and the Baldwin-Felts agents had taken place. On the back of one of the buildings, visitors can still see where bullets struck the brick wall facing the tracks. Inside, the space was about twenty feet wide by thirty feet long and appeared to have been empty for a very long time. UMWA Local 1440 members, along with some volunteers, cleaned the space and discovered that the floor, walls, and ceiling all needed repairs.

While a general contractor got to work on the repairs, the board tried to envision the finished museum. Several of the founding board members had participated in the 2011 march and well understood the conflicts in coalfield communities over the issue of mountaintop removal. We wanted the museum to be a place where people from all backgrounds—resident and visitor, union and nonunion—would be welcome to learn, discuss, and commemorate the history of the Mine Wars. We decided that the museum should strive above all for accuracy but that the exhibits should also be an opportunity for coalfield residents to tell their history. Toward that end, we held an open house in November 2014 to share our ideas for exhibits, artifacts and photographs, color schemes, and even carpet samples and get feedback from the community. We collected feedback in conversation and on suggestion cards and were encouraged that community members wanted a museum that explored company town life with all its exploitation and discussed the struggle to unionize with all its complexities, conflict, and violence. Exhibit designer Shaun Slifer recalled, "I was careful. I feel like I spent months listening, but also reading, absorbing." Having worked as a museum professional for several years, he was used to being given exact specifications for exhibits, but at the Mine Wars Museum, the team consisted of teachers, mine workers, and a community organizer. He said, "I had one way I knew to do things, and creating this museum was an incredible exercise in compromise, trust, telling a story 'with' people, not for them."[30]

In the end, the permanent exhibits were laid out clockwise around a center partition wall. The walls were light gray, the carpet a dark gray, and the room had bright red accent walls and trim. Visitors would enter an exhibit on coal camp life before entering an exhibit on the Paint Creek-Cabin Creek Strike of 1912–1913. The exhibit included a replica of a canvass tent, dramatizing the conditions that striking miners and their families endured after being evicted from company housing. Other exhibits featuring artifacts, photographs, interview audio, and film strips focused on the Battle of Matewan, the Miners' March of 1921, and the Battle of Blair Mountain.

After the grand opening, Chuck Keeney, a board member and great-grandson of District 17 president Frank Keeney, told one reporter that the coal industry did not need to use force anymore because they controlled the radio, the news, and the schools. "When a region or a country doesn't know its own history, it's like a person with Alzheimer's. . . . When people don't know who they are, they become much easier to manipulate. This museum is our own form of reclamation." He continued, "It's cultural or identity reclamation."[31] Wilma Steele added that what made her want to be involved was that "all these immigrants from all these different countries" who had been divided then tied on red bandannas, marched, and "became a brotherhood." She said that she hoped the museum would become a place where people throughout the coalfields can come to reclaim their identity and "tell our history."[32]

In many ways, this history challenges the simple and celebratory narratives that the industry and state leaders had promoted for more than a century. The museum's permanent exhibits open with a poem by Carl Sandburg titled "The Company Town":

> You live in a company house
> You go to a company school
> You work for this company,
> according to company rules.
> You all drink company water,
> and all use company lights,
> The company preacher teaches us
> what the company thinks is right.

This poem signals to visitors that the museum's exhibits take an unflinching look at the role of power, conscious of the ways that power has shaped the historical narrative. Keeney told one reporter, "We were able to include quotes and facts that a state-sponsored museum wouldn't be able to do."[33] Just as Bodnar argued, the state-sponsored museums in West Virginia attempt to present the history of the state within a broader progress narrative. However, many of the state's actions during the Mine Wars were considered unconstitutional abuses of power, even at the time of the events, contradicting the state's positive framing of events in official accounts.[34] In her review of the Mine Wars Museum, sociologist Suzanne Tallichet wrote, "The exhibits, some of which are interactive, and the museum's community outreach programs involving the area's public schools underscore the notion that what we learn about a place and its people depends on who gets to tell the story."

FIGURE 1.2. Mine Wars Museum interior, West Virginia Mine Museum Staff, 2015.

She pointed out that, in the museum's work, "truth is being told to power so that these painful lessons can be learned and carried into every workplace for generations to come."[35]

Teachers and Hellraisers

Every year, the West Virginia State Legislature hosts History Day, an event in the Capitol rotunda where museums and historical societies from around the state set up tables and displays about the state's history. Usually, legislators talk to one another as they glance at the displays on their way to meetings or lunch. On February 22, 2018, I arrived at the capitol building with two other founding board members, Katey Lauer and Chuck Keeney, to find a very long line of teachers wearing red, waiting to get through the security checkpoint. It was the first day of the 2018 Teachers Strike, and hundreds of teachers and service personnel filled the wide corridors demanding to be heard. Many of them wore red bandannas in the spirit of the 1921 Miners March, and their voices echoed off the marble walls in thunderous chants of "Knock, knock! Who's there? Teachers, teachers, everywhere!" and "Remember in November!"

Mingo County teachers led the way and were among the first in the state to vote to strike. Eric Starr was one of those teachers. A coal miner's son, he had studied the labor history of the coalfields and wore a red bandanna to one of their secret meetings before the strike. "I'm not going back," he told the others. "We've been sold out!"[36] Mingo County teachers helped spark the West Virginia strike, which in turn sparked a national #RedForEd movement as strikes spread to several other states.[37]

During the strike, Mingo County schoolteachers often referenced the long history of labor activism in their area. Brandon Wolford was one of the lead organizers of the teachers' strike in his home county and noted that his great-grandfather had fought in the Mine Wars. The executive director of the West Virginia Education Association, said, "I think it's part of their culture." He continued, "They grew up in a culture of understanding people standing up to their employers to some degree when things go wrong."[38] Katie Endicott, another Mingo County teacher, told the *New York Times*, "We know that we come from these mountains and we are strong and we have pride and we love this state." She added, "We believe the movement was started years ago through the mine wars. We're just reviving the movement that was started years ago."[39]

The teachers strike was still on our minds that September when the West Virginia Mine Wars Museum held its first "Strike Supper," which celebrated the diverse foodways of the coal camps during the Mine Wars and included the first annual Red Bandanna Award Ceremony—so named because of the bandannas the miners wore during the 1921 Miners' March. We created five awards to be given annually. The Hellraiser Award is given to someone who embodies the spirit of the UMWA organizer Mother Jones who did not let threats, gunfire, or jail time stop her; the 2018 award went to Charles "Hawk-eye" Dixon, treasurer of UMWA Local 1440, veteran of many picket lines, and one of the founding board members of the museum. The History Keeper Award goes to an individual who embodies the spirit of Carter G. Woodson, a West Virginia coal miner who later earned a PhD in history and went on to become a dean at West Virginia State College and father of Black History Month. The award went to Gordon Simmons, a United Electrical Workers field representative and long-time president of the West Virginia Labor History Association. In accepting the award, Simmons waved a red bandanna and said that it was a symbol of our past and our future. Other awards went to a long-time African American mayor of Matewan and a historian who leads annual tours of the coalfields.

It was most fitting to give the Rank and File Rebel Award to schoolteachers Emily Comer and Jay O'Neal, two of the core organizers of the statewide teachers' strike who continue to advocate for teachers' rights and for student education in the state. In 2019, the museum is awarding the Red Bandanna Awards to an investigative journalist, a labor historian, and two more teacher-organizers, Katie Endicott and Robin Ellis, both from Mingo County.

The Miners' Struggles Continue

While visitors to the West Virginia Mine Wars Museum are learning about miners and their families' struggles to win union recognition a century ago, current-day miners continue to fight for their rights. Despite Donald Trump's laudatory rhetoric about coal miners during his candidacy and presidency, miners still face several challenges and often without their elected representatives' aid. The UMWA has struggled to maintain its membership in recent years. In 2015, the *Washington Post* reported that the last union coal mine in Kentucky, where "labor battles once raged," was closing.[40] In 2016, the Republican majority in the West Virginia legislature passed a so-called right-to-work law, making it more difficult for unions to remain solvent, easier for companies to decertify unions, and harder for unions to organize workers. Just before the vote, the West Virginia Education Association reminded its members that they might lose rights that were "forged in those struggles fought against privately armed Baldwin-Felts detectives and anti-union propaganda in the state's coalfields."[41]

While "war on coal" and "forgotten men and women" rhetoric resonated with many miners and their families, the Trump administration's actions not only failed to increase coal industry employment significantly, the number of employed miners reached a record low in 2018.[42] Retired miners continue to see their pensions and healthcare benefits endangered by company bankruptcies and Congressional inaction. Furthermore, many miners and their widows continue to be denied Black Lung benefits because the Black Lung Disability Trust Fund has long been underfunded, and recently there has been a sharp increase in the incidence of Black Lung.[43] Some 120 miners dying of Black Lung disease traveled to Washington, D.C., to meet with Kentucky senator Mitch McConnell, who as Senate majority leader, had great influence over which bills came to the floor for a vote. He spoke so briefly with the miners that George Massey of Harlan County, Kentucky, said, "For him to come in for just two minutes was a low-down shame."[44]

On July 1, 2019, Blackjewel LLC filed for bankruptcy, and shortly after that, miners' paychecks bounced, sending many into financial crises. On

July 29, five miners, who were still waiting to get paid for work already done, noticed the company filling railroad cars with its remaining coal reserves and decided to block the tracks to prevent the company from shipping the coal out. As the blockade stretched into weeks, one miner said that it put him "in mind of 'Bloody Harlan,'" Kentucky's own mine war in the 1930s.[45] The blockade lasted two months, and miners were petitioning the federal bankruptcy judge to prioritize their paychecks over other creditors but had to quit the blockade to look for new jobs.

Miners and their families will likely face more such challenges as the industry continues its decline in the region, and they know that. As they enter these battles, the sacrifices of past generations seem to be on their minds, many mentioning them to reporters. Matewan's UMWA Local 1440 is now all retirees, and they have been very active in the battles for pensions, healthcare benefits, Black Lung benefits, and workers' rights. They are steadfast supporters of the West Virginia Mine Wars Museum in part because many believe that preserving the history of those past sacrifices, the history of working-class solidarity in the region, and the role the union played in these communities is critical for charting the course of the next generation into the future.

Conclusion

The West Virginia Mine Wars Museum is part of an ongoing effort to preserve the history of the struggle over unionization in southern West Virginia in the early twentieth century. For much of the twentieth century, this history either has been suppressed or carefully framed by state and industry leaders. The museum's board hopes to lift up working-class voices and allow coalfield residents to make critical decisions about how this history gets told. Furthermore, the museum opened at a time when working families are fighting against wage cuts and fighting to keep their healthcare and pensions. Many draw strength from their state's history of resistance and the fighting spirit of past generations, and they see the preservation of this history as a vital part of an ongoing workers' movement that started many years ago.

Notes

1. *Williamson Daily News*, May 19, 2015. See also Andrew Brown, "Mine Wars Museum Opens with Battle of Matewan Reenactment," *Charleston Gazette-Mail*, May 17, 2015.

2. See Barbara Ellen Smith, "Another Place Is Possible? Labor Geography, Spa-

tial Dispossession, and Gendered Resistance in Central Appalachia," *Annals of the Association of American Geographers*, 105, 2015, 567–582, for an excellent overview of historical changes since the 1970s. *Charleston Gazette-Mail* articles on the other issues include Eric Eyre, "780M Pills, 1,728 Death," December 18, 2016; Kate White, "Mingo Judge Arrested on Federal Charge," August 15, 2013; Ken Ward Jr., "Before Slurry Deal, Records Outlined Massey Pollution," June 9, 2012; and Ward, "Concerns Grow about Coal Industry Pensions, Reclamation," August 9, 2015.

3. https://www.100daysinappalachia.com/2017/04/25/trumps-promise-bring -back-coal-union-miners-say-cant-live-past/.

4. For a full-length study of the West Virginia Mine Wars, see James R. Green, *The Devil Is Here in These Hills: West Virginia's Coal Miners and Their Battle for Freedom* (New York: Grove Atlantic, 2015). For how another mine war is remembered, see Mark Walker, "The Ludlow Massacre: Class, Warfare, and Historical Memory in Southern Colorado," *Historical Archaeology*, Vol. 37, No. 3, Remembering Landscapes of Conflict (2003), 66–80; Ben Mauk, "The Ludlow Massacre Still Matters," *New Yorker*, April 18, 2014.

5. Rebecca Bailey, *Matewan before the Massacre: Politics, Coal, and the Roots of Conflict in a West Virginia Mining Community* (Morgantown: West Virginia University Press, 2008), introduction and chapter 1.

6. Green, *The Devil Is Here in These Hills*, especially chapters 12, 13, and 14.

7. Jerry Bruce Thomas, *An Appalachian New Deal: West Virginia in the Great Depression* (Morgantown: West Virginia University Press, Pb. Edition, 2010), 92–94; Thomas, *An Appalachian Reawakening: West Virginia and the Perils of the New Machine Age, 1945–1972* (Morgantown: West Virginia University Press, 2011). See also Anne Lawrence, *On Dark and Bloody Ground: An Oral History of the UMWA in Central Appalachia, 1920–1935* (Morgantown, WV: West Virginia University Press, 2021).

8. Brian L. Ott, Carole Blair, and Greg Dickinson, eds., *Places of Public Memory: The Rhetoric of Museums and Memorials* (Tuscaloosa: University of Alabama Press, 2010), 6.

9. John Bodnar, *Remaking America: Public Memory, Commemorations, and Patriotism in the Twentieth Century* (Princeton: Princeton University Press, 1993), 13–14, 20.

10. "Inaugural Address of Governor George W. Atkinson," March 4, 1897, http://www .wvculture.org/history/government/governors/atkinsonia.html.

11. Ronald D. Eller, *Miners, Millhands, and Mountaineers: Industrialization of the Appalachian South, 1880–1930* (Knoxville: University of Tennessee Press, 1982), quoted on 130.

12. David Alan Corbin, *Life, Work, and Rebellion in the Coal Fields: The Southern West Virginia Coal Miners, 1880–1922* (Urbana: University of Illinois Press, 1981), 1.

13. Ibid., 106–108.

14. Chuck Keeney, "The Mind Guard System: Mine Wars and the Politics of Memory in West Virginia," *West Virginia History: A Journal of Regional Studies* 12, Spring and Fall 2018, 47–70.

15. Thomas, *An Appalachian New Deal*, 44–46.

16. *UMWJ*, August 1, 1931.

17. Justin McCarthy, "Brief History of the United Mine Workers," *United Mine Workers Journal*, 1950, 11.

18. See Thomas, *Appalachian Reawakening*. See also Shaun Slifer, "So Much to Be Angry About: Appalachian Movement Press, 1969–1979," *Signal: A Journal of International Political Graphics & Culture* 6, 2018.

19. John Alexander Williams, *West Virginia: A History* (Wheeling: West Virginia University Press, 2003), 204–205.

20. For an overview of the oral history project, see the finding aid at Appalachian State University, http://collections.library.appstate.edu/findingaids/ac393.

21. Paul J. Nyden, "The Rise and Fall of Rank-and-File Miner Militancy, 1964–2007," in *The Encyclopedia of Strikes in American History* (New York: Routledge, 2009), 471–480.

22. Kimberly Christensen, "'Dark as a Dungeon': Technological Change and Government Policy in the Deunionization of the American Coal Industry," *Review of Keynesian Economics* 2, Summer 2014, 148.

23. https://www.eia.gov/totalenergy/data/annual/showtext.php?t=ptb0707.

24. http://www.wvminesafety.org/STATS.HTM; http://www.wvminesafety.org/PDFs/2015%20Annual%20Report%20-%20CY.pdf.

25. Smith, "Another Place Is Possible?" 567–582; Shirley Stewart Burns, *Bringing Down the Mountains: The Impact of Mountaintop Removal Surface Coal Mining on Southern West Virginia Communities, 1970–2004* (Morgantown, WV: West Virginia University Press, 2007).

26. Burns, *Bringing Down the Mountains*, chapter 3.

27. http://blogs.wvgazettemail.com/coaltattoo/2012/06/20/rockefeller-coal-must -boldly-embrace-the-future/.

28. For an excellent overview of these issues and Blair Mountain, see Richelle C. Brown, "Power Line: Memory and the March on Blair Mountain," in *Excavating Memory: Sites of Remembering and Forgetting*, eds. Maria Theresia Starzmann and John Roby (Gainesville: University of Florida Press, 2016): 86–107.

29. Brandon Nida and Michael Jessee Adkins, "The Social and Environmental Upheaval of Blair Mountain: A Working-Class Struggle for Unionization and Historic Preservation, (unpublished manuscript, 2010), 11–12.

30. Shaun Slifer to Lou Martin, email, August 29, 2019.

31. "Rednecks Symbolize Solidary: West Virginia Mine Wars Museum Reclaims Union Identity," *Counterpunch.org*. https://www.counterpunch.org/2015/08/10/rednecks-symbolize-solidarity-w-va-mine-wars-museum-reclaims-union-identity/.

32. http://www.wvpublic.org/post/do-you-know-where-word-redneck-comes -mine-wars-museum-opens-revives-lost-labor-history?nopop=1#stream/0.

33. Carolyne Whelan, "King Coal and the West Virginia Mine Wars Museum," *Belt Magazine*, November 10, 2015, 173.

34. For just one example of criticism of the state at the time, see Green, *The Devil Is Here in These Hills*, 153.

35. Suzanne E. Tallichet, "West Virginia Mine Wars Museum," *Journal of Appalachian Studies* 24, Fall 2018, 260–262.

36. Rick Hampson, "'Any talks of striking?': How a West Virginia Teacher's Facebook Post Started a National Movement," *USA Today*, February 20, 2019. https://www.usatoday.com/story/news/education/2019/02/20/teacher-strike-west-virginia-school-closings-education-bill/2848476002/.

37. Valerie Strauss, "Remember the 2018 Teachers Strikes in Republican-led States? Now Legislators in 3 States Are Trying to Retaliate," *Washington Post*, February 1, 2019. https://www.washingtonpost.com/education/2019/02/01/remember-teachers-strikes-republican-led-states-now-legislators-states-are-trying-retaliate/.

38. Campbell Roberston and Jess Bidgood, "'All-In or Nothing': West Virginia's Teacher Strike Was Months in the Making," *New York Times*, March 2, 2018.

39. Jess Bidgood, "'I Live Paycheck to Paycheck': A West Virginia Teacher Explains Why She's on Strike," *New York Times*, March 1, 2018.

40. https://www.washingtonpost.com/business/economy/closure-of-kentuckys-last-unionized-coal-mine-may-be-ironic-sign-of-success/2015/09/05/8c1a1a42–5417–11e5–8c19–0b6825aa4a3a_story.html.

41. https://www.wvea.org/content/what-does-%E2%80%98right-work%E2%80%99-really-mean.

42. https://www.wvpublic.org/post/coal-comeback-coal-new-low-after-two-years-under-trump#stream/0.

43. https://theconversation.com/the-struggle-for-coal-miners-health-care-and-pension-benefits-continues-112906; https://www.npr.org/2019/06/20/734538252/regulators-resist-call-for-action-in-response-to-black-lung-epidemic.

44. https://www.reuters.com/article/us-usa-coal-blacklung/us-coal-miners-discouraged-by-black-lung-meeting-with-mcconnell-idUSKCN1UI18G.

45. https://ohiovalleyresource.org/2019/08/09/bloody-harlan-revisited-black-jewel-miners-draw-on-labor-history-while-facing-uncertain-future/.

CHAPTER 2

Interpreting Barre, Vermont's Granite Industry in All Its Rich Complexity

AMANDA KAY GUSTIN, KAREN LANE,

SCOTT A. McLAUGHLIN

Introduction

Three themes constantly intertwine in Barre, Vermont's history: industry, labor, and immigration. In this chapter, we discuss how three cultural organizations work toward interpreting these themes. We also provide examples of current programming and public history work with a strong community focus. The Vermont Granite Museum, Vermont Historical Society, and Socialist Labor Party Hall are all located within a few miles of each other within the boundaries of Barre City, which itself is only four square miles in size. An urban environment of fewer than 9,000 inhabitants in a profoundly rural state, its deep industrial and labor history offers an entirely different narrative than the typical Vermont story. Barre also contains a wealth of other cultural institutions that contribute to telling the city's story.

In the past, the Aldrich Public Library served the Barre community as its primary cultural center and played an essential role in preserving local history. For example, for many years, the library hosted an annual exhibit of granite art from local sculptors. With the establishment of the visual arts center Studio Place Arts in 2000, the annual exhibit changed location and now reaches a growing audience as a showcase of local art. In addition to these two organizations, the city's labor and granite history are celebrated at the Barre Opera House, the Millstone Trails Association, the Rock of Ages Visitors Center, Hope Cemetery, and through public art installations scattered across the downtown.

Barre's differences are its strengths. Interpreting their unique angle on history has been a boon to the cultural organizations within its borders. In an already deeply community-minded state, learning more about the history of how workers from a wide variety of backgrounds created community has been an inspiration and a rich historical vein to explore.

Most importantly, the complexity of Barre's history relative to its size has allowed multiple cultural institutions to flourish alongside each other. No one organization can hope to capture the entire story. Even a sizable statewide organization such as the Vermont Historical Society cannot succeed without partnership and cooperation with other organizations. The Vermont Granite Museum's close ties to the corporations behind the granite industry and the Granite Cutters' Association and Barre Granite Association have helped it tell a more complete story. Moreover, the Socialist Labor Party Hall is woven deeply into the Barre community, with a passionate volunteer base and popular annual programs.

In writing this chapter, we thought a great deal about the nature of partnerships and collaborations and the challenges faced by multiple nonprofits within a small community. The concept of "ecomuseums" was a useful one. In fact, in some early conversations about Barre's cultural sector, dating to the 1970s and 1980s, the idea of an ecomuseum was discussed, though never formally implemented. The term, originated by Georges Henri Rivière and Hugues de Varine in France, is loosely defined as a museum or institution that welcomes public participation in its activities, is anchored in its community, and contributes to its development. Deeply tied to place, some have suggested that ecomuseums are more appropriately defined by action than by existence. In other words, these spaces are defined by *doing*, not by being.

Peter Davis, Professor Emeritus of Museology at Newcastle University, whose seminal work *Ecomuseums: A Sense of Place* is a deep exploration of the concept, suggests that it is impossible for museums to accurately reflect local history within the bounds of an exhibition or other such projects. In a 2009 article, he wrote, "Ecomuseums and the representation of place," that "place itself lies outside the museum and needs to be experienced to begin to be fully understood."[1] Because the history of labor is one of collective action, of people-centered narratives, and of connecting modern social justice to historical movements, it seems ripe for collaborative, community-based approaches that ecomuseums exemplify. Because the history of Barre itself is so deeply rooted in place, from its granite deposits to its rich patchwork of neighborhoods to its situation within Vermont (a state for which place is a crucial concept in understanding its history), the concept of ecomuseums seems even more useful. Our sincere hope is that in the coming years, local placed-based partnerships deepen and broaden to lead to closer alliances in Barre.

A Brief History of Barre and Its Granite

The town of Barre sits at the headwaters of the Winooski River in central Vermont. Rail access in 1875 opened Barre's granite works to markets across America and transformed the little farm village into a small industrial city. By 1902, 68 granite quarries operated with an annual output of one and a half million tons. Immigrants from Aberdeenshire, Scotland, arrived in Barre, beginning about 1880, bringing a strong commitment to organized labor. Although some of the Scots were skilled granite finishers, their greatest strength was as quarrymen. Skilled artisans from northern Italy were the next to come to Barre, bringing social and political ideals with their roots in the Italian experience. Many were highly educated stone carvers who had studied sculpture and design in the fine arts academies at Milan, Brera, or Carrara.

The confluence of these two ethnic groups with their specialized skills and background in organized labor led to Barre's early unionization. In 1886, the carvers, cutters, and polishers formed the Barre branch of the Granite Cutters' National Union, later the Granite Cutters' International Association. By 1900, the Barre branch became the largest in the U.S. with over 1,000 members. In 1903, the quarrymen, led by the Scots, established the Quarry Workers International Union of North America (QWIU), with Barre serving as the national headquarters.

In 1940, the QWIU joined the United Stone & Allied Products Workers Union, which in 1970 affiliated with the United Steel Workers (USW); today, the USW represents the quarry workers and some of the manufacturing plant jobs. Historians estimate that by 1900, 90 percent of all jobs in the city were organized. Strikes in the Barre granite industry established the nine-hour day by 1890 and prohibited usage of the dusty 'bumper' in 1909. The bumper was a pneumatic surfacer that created tremendous amounts of dust and could break bones if operated improperly. By 1922, however, workers confronted the open shop (the so-called "American Plan"), and in 1933 a significant strike idled 3,000 with the National Guard called in. Throughout the period, unions also organized around other pressing occupational health challenges, the deadliest of which was silicosis, a disease caused by granite dust buildup in a worker's lungs. It took decades for the industry to recognize the severity of the problem and then to implement workplace safety measures to prevent it.

For Barre's labor history to be grasped, it is crucial to understand the city's and region's granite history. Much of the chronicling of Vermont's granite industry was produced with local and regional sightseers in mind. Tourism began during the late 1880s as the industry grew in size due to the arrival of professional quarrymen, granite cutters, and sculptors from throughout North America and Europe. As a result of this infusion of new ideas and labor, the granite manufacturers and quarry companies developed new technologies, processes, and product lines, creating a buzz of interest among residents and tourists to see the work for themselves. After the Sky Route railroad's construction in 1888, which connected the granite sheds and quarries in Barre, tourists occasionally had the opportunity to ride a special train for a small fee from Montpelier or Barre to see the granite quarries on the weekend. Some visitors enjoyed a picnic lunch at the quarry as granite workers talked about what they did and how tools and techniques were rapidly changing in the granite industry. It was an opportunity for visitors to see the industrial landscape being created on Millstone Hill and to understand the massive undertaking it took to quarry granite. Crucially, this interpretation—though done by workers—tended to focus on technology and process rather than the lives of the workers themselves.

As granite manufacturers and quarriers proliferated at the end of the nineteenth century, many began marketing their products and expertise in national trade magazines like *Granite, Granite Marble & Bronze, The Monumental News, The Monument and Cemetery Review,* and *American Stone Trade.* One crucial early outreach effort was an exhibition at the World Columbian Exposition of 1893, which put Barre granite on the world stage. Vermont photographers also created photo postcards of local granite quarries and granite cutters at work in the sheds. The advertising and postcards targeted customers and potential tourists. These works focused on the granite's quality, the owners of quarries and granite plants, the monumental projects they had completed, and the industry's technologies. They described the immense size of quarries and the types of machines used to quarry and process the granite blocks. However, they left out the risks, struggles, failures, and tragedies of those working in the industry.

Although the Great Depression negatively impacted Vermont's granite industry, it did not stop the visitors. In addition to continuing advertisements in national magazines, the *Wells-Lamson Quarrier* and *Rock of Ages* magazines promoted the respective companies' products and images to a broad audience. Visitors received fliers and rock samples of their sites. However, it was not until the 1940s that the first comprehensive interpretative text for the granite industry written for tourists appeared. *The History of Granite,* published by Rock of Ages Corporation, became the most popular way to answer visitors' most basic questions about Vermont's granite and the industry that developed to exploit it.

In the 1950s, Jones Brothers Granite Company and Rock of Ages Corporation became the most significant tourist attractions among Vermont's granite companies. Jones Brothers had a small museum and gift shop at their granite shed and gave away free granite samples to visitors. Rock of Ages had a similar visitor center near their quarry, stocked with booklets, postcards, small granite products, and other granite-related items. These interpretative centers contained exhibits with text, historical and contemporary images, graphics, objects, and dioramas, and answered visitors' common questions. A Rock of Ages promotional flier told visitors they would learn answers to the following questions: "How this marvelous vein of Rock of Ages granite came to be here; how old it is; how long the quarry will last; how the granite is separated and removed; how it is cut to size and shape; how the combinations of Rock of Ages finishes are produced."

Also beginning in the 1950s, granite firms produced short films of the work in the quarries and stone sheds that were distributed to architects, engineers, contractors, and memorial dealers across the globe. They spoke to the quality, speed, ingenuity, and care which Vermont's granite industry provided to clients' requests compared to its competitors. These efforts had a dramatic impact on the number of visitors to Barre. By the fall of 1974, *Barre Life* magazine reported that "nearly 100,000 persons each year travel from all 50 states and many foreign countries to visit Barre's famous granite quarries. In Vermont, where there is much breath-taking scenery, the granite quarries are a top attraction."

The Vermont Granite Museum

After Jones Brothers Company closed in the mid-1970s, Rock of Ages was the only Vermont granite manufacturer with a visitor center and quarry tour. This situation would change after Central Vermont citizens gathered at the Barre Opera House in 1994 to discuss the development of a heritage center that would educate tourists and locals about the historical importance of Barre's granite industry and its people. In 1997, the Jones Brothers granite plant was purchased, and a multimillion-dollar restoration of the building began. The Vermont Granite Museum also acquired the Barre City railroad depot. It was renovated to display temporary exhibits while the heritage center formed. Early exhibits focused mainly on the granite industry's procedures to quarry and shape blocks of granite.

Between 2000 and 2015, the Museum tried several strategies to gain community support as they worked to restore the century-old Jones Brothers granite shed. One strategy included partnering with historians, including Paul Wood, Paul Heller, Andreas Kuehnpast, and Todd Paton, to write research articles about the granite industry's history and publish them in places like *The Barre-Montpelier Times Argus* newspaper. The articles could then become a basis for exhibit content and future comprehensive history of Vermont's granite industry. Articles focused primarily on the industry's tools, procedures, and products and addressed the granite workers' housing and working conditions. Research continues to inform exhibition development at the Vermont Granite Museum, which will become the basis for a book.[2]

At the Museum in 2005, Kim Bent, executive director of Lost Nation Theater in Montpelier, directed *Stone*, an original play he wrote about the early days of Barre's granite industry. The play grew out of interviews with granite workers and their families conducted by Mari Tomasi and Roaldus Richmond between 1938 and 1940 under the auspices of the Federal Writers Project. Although earlier writings like Brayley's *History of the Granite Industry of New England* outlined the lives of sculptors and granite company owners, Tomoasi and Richmond were the first to highlight the lives of ordinary granite workers in Barre and their neighbors and families. Correspondence in the Vermont Historical Society files between the writers in Vermont and the administrators in Washington, D.C., revealed several attempts to publish selected interviews. However, no agreement was reached until a number of the interviews in slightly fictionalized versions were published in Tomasi's *Men against Granite* in 2004. It was this publication that Bent used as a source for his play.[3]

Starting in 2015, the Vermont Granite Museum has had regularly scheduled hours for tours five days a week from May through October at the Jones Brothers Company granite shed. The Museum originally had few collections and little exhibit content to offer visitors within the 27,000-square-foot facility; however, today, it is full of exhibit content and collections. Although the Museum's only paid staff member is its executive director, it has accomplished a great deal thanks to an active volunteer staff of over fifty residents, helping it to become a must-see destination for those sightseeing Vermont. Some volunteers have worked or currently work in the granite industry. These volunteers are a valuable interpretative resource for visitors and other museum volunteers working on exhibits and educational programming. Oral informants have been one of the most significant resources for interpreting the people, places, processes, events, and other vital issues involving Vermont's granite industry.

The exhibits, guided tours, and educational events and programs offered by the Vermont Granite Museum were designed to reach a broad audience and engage people with varying levels of interest in subjects such as art, archaeology, architecture, science, and social, industrial, and labor history. One successful example is the use of museum theater for educational and entertainment purposes. In 2015, the Museum partnered again with Kim Bent and Lost Nation Theater to stage *Stone* in its space. This use of the Museum inspired Pierre Couture of RockFire, LLC, an entertainment company, to create RockFire Heritage Walk, a candlelit walk with a dozen different stages on which actors portray different historical characters that engage audiences in dialogue. Each character is an individual whose life somehow intersected with Barre's granite industry. RockFire Heritage Walk has been an annual event for the past four years.

Partnerships have been instrumental to the success of the Vermont Granite Museum's approach to its interpretative efforts, whether exhibits or educational programming. Museum exhibits are open to the public between May and October. To remain in the public eye, the Vermont Granite Museum partnered with the Vermont Historical Society to host "The Art of Granite" in a gallery space at the Vermont History Center in Barre in 2018. The exhibit explored Vermont's granite sculptors' lives and works and explained how the state became home to several of America's greatest sculptors. They carved artistic works found in the nation's capitals, parks, and cemeteries.

Another collaboration involved the Vermont Granite Museum and the Granite Cutters' Association, the union representing about 300 of Vermont's granite workers. On separate occasions, Matt Peake, the union representative for the Granite Cutters' Association, has presented to youth groups at the Museum about the history and process by which union contracts are created and used in Vermont's granite industry. Peake has also discussed the present and future working conditions and job opportunities in the industry. These presentations provided children with an effective and direct connection to the existing practices in a nearly two-hundred-year-old Vermont industry. The Granite Museum's situation in a former granite shed, its use of former and current granite workers as active volunteers, its deep engagement with the Barre community, and its emphasis on sharing granite history through demonstration, action, and visitor involvement—all tie closely to the ecomuseum concept of doing rather than being.

The Vermont Historical Society

The Vermont Historical Society, founded in 1838, is an independent non-profit that collects, shares, and preserves the state's history. It began mostly as a library and archive, with some collections of geological specimens. With the construction of the third statehouse in Montpelier in 1859, the Historical Society maintained a "cabinet of curiosities" display in a room just outside the legislative chambers.

From its beginnings, history in Vermont has been highly place-based and localized. In 1858, the state legislature passed a law encouraging towns to write their histories. The first of these appeared in 1859, with subsequent volumes added to the Historical Society collections. At the time, the Society was entirely volunteer-run but worked with towns to produce their histories, providing encouragement and some research support. In the early part of the twentieth century, the Society began adding its first object collections, and over the next hundred years added greatly to its collections as it hired professional staff to care for and interpret them.

Though a small state, Vermont has always balanced the tension between centralized narratives and hyperlocal specificity. The Historical Society has often embodied that tension, providing assistance, encouragement, and support to smaller regional organizations, but not always going deeply into local research or collections itself. The state's motto, "Freedom and Unity," is worth remembering when thinking about nearly any aspect of Vermont's history. The Society explored Barre's granite history in the 1980s mainly from an artistic perspective, collaborating with several art galleries and cultural institutions for a small exhibition organized by curator Phil Elwert. The annual Martin Luther King Jr. program, founded by then-director Michael Sherman, also began in the 1980s, focusing on topics that took as their theme Dr. King's work. Over the years, labor history came up more than once.

Still, Barre and its labor history remained underrepresented in the Vermont Historical Society's collections and interpretation until a series of events sparked by the 1992 flood of downtown Montpelier. At the time, the Society's collections were housed where they had been for twenty years, in the basement of the Pavilion building on State Street. The flood, caused by an ice jam on the Winooski River, left the Pavilion stranded, with water pouring down the walls into the basement. Thanks to incredible efforts by staff, volunteers, and passers-by that included a human chain to carry objects out of danger, nothing was lost, but it was evident that the Society needed to find a better space for collections storage.

In September 2000, the Vermont Historical Society purchased the old Spaulding Grade School from the city of Barre for $1.00 and renovated it as a new headquarters. The building, an enormous Richardsonian Romanesque brick edifice built in 1891, had served as the city's high school and then as a middle school, but had been abandoned and in disrepair for the better part of a decade. Like many historic buildings in Barre, it was built at the granite industry's height, for a population and an economy larger than the city's current one. After an extensive two-year multimillion-dollar renovation, the Spaulding building reopened in July 2002 as the Vermont History Center. It housed the administrative offices, collections storage, and research library of the Vermont Historical Society. The space in Montpelier was converted entirely into an exhibition with an overview of the history of Vermont. Due to funding shortfalls, only half of the original renovation plan was completed, leaving approximately 60 percent of the building stabilized, but empty. In 2018, the remaining spaces were renovated for occupancy by the state in partnership with the Vermont Historical Society to be the Vermont Department of Libraries' new headquarters. The Spaulding school's acquisition and renovation saved the building both as an essential part of Barre's history and as a physical landmark. The building sits on a prominent hill overlooking the downtown and is a significant touchstone for residents who remember attending school there. Its conversion to a historical research center has been an excellent case of adaptive reuse.

Collections and Interpretation

With the state's Historical Society headquartered in Barre, several opportunities arose to focus more closely on the city's history and shift interpretation to encompass more of the community's history rather than a more top-down review of just the granite industry. This shift mirrors the Vermont Granite Museum's trajectory from an economic and process-based celebration of the companies and great men of granite to a more people-focused and more complicated narrative.

The reinstallation of a significant new exhibition encompassing the entire sweep of Vermont history at the Vermont History Museum in the Pavilion space in Montpelier was an early opportunity to inject more labor history into the story. The space interpreting early-twentieth-century Vermont industries was designed to look like an early granite shed, and labels explicitly charted Barre's multicultural growth. At the end of the exhibition, oral history listening stations opened up individual stories to visitors, including a recorded interview with U.S. Senator Patrick Leahy, which mentions his Italian stoneworker grandparents.

Once the Museum in Montpelier opened, the focus turned in Barre to new temporary exhibition galleries. Of three new galleries, one focused exclusively on Barre. Titled "The Emergence of the Granite City, 1890–1940," the exhibition borrowed extensively from the Barre History Collection of the Aldrich Library, the city's public library, and explicitly presented the history of a city with a lively multicultural population. One section of the exhibition chronicled Barre's labor history from the Socialist Labor Party Hall's construction to the unionization and strikes among granite workers. Among the objects on display was a "bozo" slide whistle used during the 1922 granite strike, which the donor's grandfather used to blow derisively at strikebreakers. Text and photographs showed that strike and others, from the viewpoint of management and the union. The Barre exhibition closed in spring 2018. Before its closing, the Vermont Historical Society reached an agreement with the Aldrich Library to accession the entirety of the Barre History Collection.[4]

The collection, which documents three centuries of Barre history, is an incredible resource of artifacts and archives that will serve to represent the history of Barre and the history of labor in the future. It has already served researchers, and objects from it were integrated into other exhibitions created by the Vermont Historical Society. The Society's location in Barre has also opened the door to collaboration with other cultural organizations in the city, such as the Vermont Granite Museum and the Socialist Labor Party Hall. Now that the exhibition has closed, the Society's local focus is on community programming and outreach. The annual Barre Heritage Days celebration is a significant event with hundreds of visitors to the building and the library. While the interpretation of Vermont's history writ large and Barre's history specifically followed somewhat typical historiographical patterns, the Vermont Historical Society is excited to continue the shift toward people-centered history in the twenty-first century.

The Socialist Labor Party Hall

On the evening of November 28, 1900, nearly 700 people attended the dedication of the new Socialist Labor Party Hall on Granite Street. The mostly Italian-born audience first heard a speech, "What Is Socialism," by Camillo Cianfarra, editor of *Il Proletario*, the New York City Italian weekly paper of the Socialist Labor Party (SLP), then the workers in the Hall danced until the early morning hours. Many Barre Italian colony residents had decided that the town needed a meeting place for its branch of the Party. Founded as the Workingmen's Party in 1876, the SLP originated as a "multiethnic, immigrant working-class coalition." By 1900, under the leadership of Daniel DeLeon, SLP factional disputes had diminished the national role of the Party. The creation in 1901 of the Eugene Debs-led Socialist Party further eroded SLP influence, but it retained strength in certain localities such as Barre. Many of the Hall's adherents joined the Federazione Socialista Italiana del Nord America (FSI), founded in 1902, as well as the Industrial Workers of the World (IWW) founded in 1905.[5]

In its century-plus of history, the Hall has held an array of events and is now a historic landmark itself. It is a place that has created, recorded, and interpreted history. In 1912, the bonds of friendship between Barre and Lawrence, Massachusetts, provided support for the striking woolen mill workers of the Bread & Roses Strike. An invitation from sympathizers in Barre to house some of the strikers' children during the strike was accepted, and 35 Lawrence children made their way to Barre by train. A banquet and celebration for the visitors at the Socialist Labor Party Hall commenced, with the children sheltered by local families through the remainder of the strike. The following year, strike leader Arturo Giovannitti visited the Hall to thank the community for their support of the strike. In the 1920s, the Hall served as a focal point for community concern about the fate of Italian immigrants Nicola Sacco and Bartolomeo Vanzetti. Fundraisers held at the Labor Hall aided the defense for the men who were accused of robbery and murder in Massachusetts and awaited execution. Supporters from Barre traveled to Boston to attend their funeral.[6]

Other well-known labor leaders and activists besides Giovannitti visited Barre over the years. Luigi Galleani, considered the leading Italian anarchist in America, found a haven in Barre, and in 1903, he began to publish *Cronaca Sovversiva*, "one of the most important and ably edited periodicals in the history of the anarchist movement." Galleani maintained its presence in Barre until 1912, when he relocated to Lynn, Massachusetts. Barre welcomed other leading anarchists as lecturers and guests: Emma Goldman visited the city in February 1907 and appeared with Galleani before 500 people at the Barre Opera House. From 1900 to 1935, Barre was a locus for the continuous exchange of ideas by prominent labor and political leaders, including Eugene Debs, Edmondo Rossoni, Joseph Ettor, William "Big Bill" Haywood, and Mary Harris "Mother" Jones. Sold to the Washington Fruit Company in 1936, for the next 58 years, the Hall's heritage faded from memory.

Historic Preservation

Tragedy struck the Socialist Labor Party Hall in October 1994 when its attic contents got hauled away to a landfill. Desperate efforts to retrieve the dozens of boxes of papers failed. The event led to the campaign to purchase and preserve the Labor Hall. Support for the preservation of the Socialist Labor Party Hall came from many sources, including the City of Barre, Senator Patrick Leahy, the Vermont Housing & Conservation Board, and many labor unions. The Granite Cutters' Association, which once had its national union office in the building, contributed $5,000. The United Association of Plumbers and Pipe Fitters, Local 693, put in a heating system, and apprentices installed new bathrooms. Apprentices from Local 300 of the International Brotherhood of Electrical Workers rewired the Hall, donating $5,000 for the apprentices' needed supplies. The Societa di Mutuo Soccorso of Barre held fundraising dinners on behalf of the effort, and volunteers from the community helped out at monthly workdays.

The time was right for the effort in one crucial way. The U.S. Department of the Interior had contracted with Chicago's Newberry Library to conduct a Theme Study in Labor History for the National Park Service. The study aimed to identify and nominate up to 20 sites associated with U.S. labor history to become National Historic Landmarks. Preparing the application was the work of many months and involved scholars from across the country working closely with local historians and community advocates. Formal notification from the National Park Service granting the Socialist Labor Party Hall status as a National Historic Landmark arrived in May 2000. The Grand Reopening of the Labor Hall took place on Labor Day 2000, almost exactly a century from the day the Hall was dedicated.

With the Socialist Labor Party Hall rescued from demolition, everyone agreed that the critical artifact to be preserved would be the Labor Hall itself. Given its history of flooding and the limited space for storage, it was decided that only artifacts and documents with a direct connection to the Labor Hall itself should be collected and preserved in the building. What was more critical was recapturing and celebrating the original programs and activities for which the Hall was built—the lectures, celebrations, banquets, weddings, dances, and fundraising events for causes important to the community. While the Labor Hall is available for rent to families and community groups, its organization holds public events that reflect the history and heritage of the community of immigrants who labored to build the building to serve as the embodiment of their political philosophy.

FIGURES 2.1 AND 2.2. Primo Maggio 1904 and 2004. May 1, 2004 celebration at the Socialist Labor Party Hall to commemorate the centennial of Primo Maggio, 1904. The 1904 photo is the gift of Mario Barberi. The 2004 photo is by Jim Eaton. Both are from the collection of the Barre Historical Society, Barre, Vermont.

Through lectures and related films, the Hall serves a crucial role as a center for labor education, a place where the labor movement's history is discussed and debated. Here, working-class history comes to life for the community through dedicated scholars' knowledge and expertise. By relating the presentations offered during Primo Maggio celebrations to the conditions faced by organized labor today, the Hall plays a role in broadening and deepening citizens' awareness of the forces that shape our economy and our lives in the past and the present. Thus could Barre locals both learn about the Hall's history of community-focused events and also participate in them in the present day, in a direct line of connection and re-creation that again relocates the emphasis from simply being to doing that has proven so crucial to the city's cultural organizations.

Reinvention and Community Programming

In 1901, soon after the Labor Hall opened its doors, a cooperative grocery store was established. It was the first of its kind in New England to serve mainly Italians and soon became the city's largest grocery store. The demand for fresh-baked bread from the coop was soon so high that in 1913, the Union Cooperative Store Bakery was built behind the Labor Hall to provide more loaves. In recent years, Barre residents and Labor Hall members worked to re-create that original bakery in its same location behind the main Hall. Coordinated by Project Director Carolyn Shapiro, restoration of the original building was a community effort involving master craftspeople, young apprentices, and community volunteers. Each work session included hands-on learning and reflections and lessons on the history of bricklaying, carpentry, plumbing, or electrical work. Each step of construction complied with adaptive reuse principles, and students learned about historic preservation while they used modern techniques. Known as "Rise Up Bakery," the old building houses a large brick oven, which provides area high school students and adults an opportunity to learn the art of wood-fired baking. The bakery's business model is one of education and sustainability from the ground up, and it partners with local businesses and farms to follow a farm-to-table model. After years of fund-raising and work, the bakery opened on December 15, 2018.

From its earliest days, the Labor Hall was the site for the annual May 1 celebration of International Workers' Day or *Primo Maggio*, commemorating the 1886 Haymarket Massacre in Chicago. Annual festivities included banquets, dancing, plays, lectures, and parades. The May 1 holiday, revived in 2004, is again an annual event at the Hall. Each year, the celebration's main event is a presentation by a scholar knowledgeable about an aspect of Hall history. These scholars have included Paul Buhle, Rudolph Vecoli, Nunzio Pernicone, Ilaria Brancoli-Busdraghi, Sean Sayers, Mary Anne Trasciatti, Dennis Montagna, Senator Bernard Sanders, Rachel Donaldson, and film-makers Peter Miller and Randy Croce.

Connections remain across a century between Barre and Lawrence. On February 8, 1912, more than 350 citizens attended a gathering at the Socialist Labor Party Hall to pledge their unanimous support for Lawrence's striking textile workers. Further meetings and events followed to raise funds for the strike, and hundreds of dollars were sent from Barre to Lawrence to support the strikers. Workers speaking in English and Italian, many of them members of the Industrial Workers of the World, adopted a resolution pledging that "We in mass meeting tender the workers of Lawrence our heartfelt sympathy in the sad condition capital has placed them in, and pledge them our moral and financial assistance in the heroic struggle they are making for mere existence." An invitation was offered to house Lawrence strikers' children for the duration of their battle with the city's woolen mills.

Decades later, the power of human connections emerged when on Labor Day, 1997, members of the Barre Historical Society traveled to Lawrence to attend the annual Bread and Roses Festival. Taking with them a large photograph of Lawrence strikers' children posed on the Socialist Labor Party Hall steps on February 15, 1912, they asked, "Can you identify any of these children?" Sure enough, an elderly gentleman emerged from the crowd and pointed to his father, Angelo Savinelli, in the photo. "That's my father!" said Salvatore "Sully" Savinelli, who at age 4 in 1912 accompanied his father on the trip to Barre with the other Lawrence children. Mr. Savinelli returned to Barre in July 2002 as Parade Marshall for the Barre Homecoming Parade, representing the City of Lawrence and the Bread & Roses Strike. He proudly wore a pin representing the Socialist Labor Party Hall. Shirley LaFontain, whose parents came to Barre from Lawrence in 1912, attended the Socialist Labor Party Hall's Grand Reopening on September 2, 2000. She spoke of the warm reception given to her relatives by Barre residents and had her photograph taken on the steps just as the children did in 1912.

In 2006, renowned author Katherine Paterson, a longtime resident of Barre, published a children's book about the storied 1912 strike, after seeing photographs of the children of strikers from Lawrence standing on the steps of the Socialist Labor Party Hall. The work of fiction for young people is based on the true story of the "children's exodus" to Barre. To launch the publication of *Bread and Roses, Too*, there was a celebration at the Socialist Labor Party Hall. A reenactment of the arrival of the children from Lawrence at the railroad station included a march to retrace the route to the Hall the children took in 1912. Inside the Hall, young thespians enacted scenes from Paterson's novel, heard "The Internationale" and other songs sung by the strikers during the strike, and met the author. Chosen as the statewide Vermont Reads book of 2018 by the Vermont Humanities Council, *Bread and Roses, Too* has been read by children and adults in schools and libraries across Vermont during the year, and busloads of visitors have come to see firsthand the place where the Lawrence children were welcomed to Barre on a cold day over a century ago.

As discussed in chapter three, the Lawrence Heritage State Park and the Lawrence History Center organized similar events during their yearlong efforts to interpret the 1912 strike for new audiences. Indeed, Paterson received the Bread & Roses Heritage Festival's 2019 Hall of Fame Award for her book. Every year since 1997, members of the Barre Historical Society have attended the Bread & Roses Festival in Lawrence, bringing the latest news from the Socialist Labor Party Hall and honoring the ties of friendship and historical memory that bind the two communities. At the 2012 Festival, Barre Historical Society President Chet Briggs and his wife Karen Lane received its annual Hall of Fame Award. A further connection concerns 1912 striker Anna LoPizzo. An Italian immigrant, she was struck by a policeman's bullet while watching a confrontation between security forces and strikers. The first martyr of the strike, her grave had no marker until officers of the Granite Cutters Union reached out to Granite Industries of Vermont, a Barre granite manufacturer, who donated a gravestone of Barre granite which reads, "Anna LoPizzo. Killed during the Bread and Roses Strike, January 29, 1912. Age 34." Above her name is a rose and a sheaf of wheat. Historical ties remain strong. The strong ties of community exemplified by the Labor Hall are therefore not limited to Barre, but also extend to other sites in the history of labor, suggesting the possibility of opening the ecomuseum definition to include sites linked by philosophy and theme, rather than just by location.

The Socialist Labor Party Hall remains connected to the contemporary labor movement through participation in various union organizations and hosting meetings such as the annual Committee on Political Education Conference of the Vermont State Labor Council AFL-CIO, the Vermont State Employees' Association Council, the Vermont Workers Center, the International Alliance of Theatrical Stage Employees, Local 919, and many other groups. Additional programming at the Hall focuses on Barre's immigrant communities, labor history and activism, and the power of community. Bread and Puppet Theater from Glover, Vermont, performs annually at the Hall. The building has hosted labor history films, often with appearances by the filmmakers, concerts and community gatherings, and Labor Day events. Operated by an all-volunteer board with no paid staff, the Socialist Labor Party Hall has been a community center for Barre for nearly 120 years, and plans are for this historic landmark to continue serving in that way into the future.

Layers of History

Many museums and historic sites purport to tell the story of a place or a movement. However, in Barre, the history of place is inextricable from the history of the labor movement. In the most basic sense, the work of the granite industry was made possible by the place itself, the deposits of stone in the hills, and the quarries and sheds that grew up to exploit that resource. Though the industry has changed, it cannot ever escape its tie to place, and the layers of history in Barre attest to the complexities and richness of its labor story. As museums and historic sites have evolved their interpretation over the last century, they have opened their doors and welcomed in a more communally minded sense of history, and that opening has been crucial for the advancement of Barre's story. For such a small community, large for Vermont, but tiny for nearly anywhere else in America, to support so many cultural institutions that weave together such an all-encompassing story requires continual delicate rebalancing, focused cooperation, and thoughtful communication.

The ecomuseum concept focuses less on a specific model and specific mode of practice and more on the process of a community-minded development of a shared historical narrative. It is a useful lens to examine Barre's various cultural institutions, their ties to one another, and how they weave Barre's history into its present. Though, as mentioned, there was no formal development of the idea of an ecomuseum, it proved to be the unconscious model for the growth and improvement of Barre's cultural sector in the late twentieth and early twenty-first centuries. Those institutions have learned to share authority over the historical narrative with a community that continually develops its own story. Barre's historic places have participated in this back-and-forth for decades. None of the three institutions represented in this chapter could thrive without their community's active support and involvement, whether hyper-local or statewide. Sharing that authority allows for a more extensive representation of voices within the narrative. Though this is sometimes a contentious process, the result is a more robust sense of history and place.

Notes

1. Peter Davis, "Ecomuseums and the Representation of Place," *Rivista Geografica Italiana*, 2009, 116, 483–503; Davis, *Ecomuseums: A Sense of Place* (London: Leicester University Press, 1999).

2. Paul Wood, "Tools and Machinery of the Granite Industry," *The Chronicle of the Early American Industries Association*, Vol. 59, No. 2, 3, 4, 2006, and Vol. 60, No. 1, 2007; Paul Wood, "Horses, Oxen and Granite," *Barre Montpelier Times Argus*, January 7, 2008; Paul Heller, *Granite City Tales: Writings on the History of Barre, Vermont* (Scotts Valley, CA: CreateSpace Independent Publishing Platform, 2012); Andreas Kuehnpast, "The world's largest derrick," *The Barre-Montpelier Times Argus*, August 4, 2014; Todd Paton, ed., *The Rock of Ages Story* (Barre, VT: Rock of Ages Corp., 1992). For an extensive collection of books, articles, and images covering the history of the granite industry: https://quarriesandbeyond.org/states/vt/vermont-sources.html.

3. Arthur Wellington Brayley, *History of the Granite Industry of New England* (Boston: E. L. Grimes Company, 1913); Alfred Rosa and Mark Wanner, *Men against Granite* (Shelburne, VT: New England Press, 2004).

4. For an introduction to labor history, see David R. Seager, "Granite Workers and the Struggle against Silicosis, 1890–1960," *Labor History*, February, 2001; J. Costello and W. G. Graham, "Vermont Granite Workers' Mortality Study," *American Journal of Industrial Medicine*, Vol. 13 (4), 1988, 483–497; Douglas S Lertola and Mary H Fregosi, "The Vermont Marble Company Strike of 1935–1936," *Rutland Historical Society Quarterly*, Vol. 32, No. 3, 2002; Wendy Richardson, "'The Curse of Our Trade': Occupational Disease in a Vermont Granite Town," *The Proceedings of the Vermont Historical Society*, Vol. 60, No. 1, 1992, 5–28.

5. For a brief history of the Labor Hall and the region's labor history, see Karen Lane, ttps://oldlaborhall.org/history/; Woodsmoke Productions and Vermont Historical Society, "The Anarchist Movement in Barre, 1920," *The Green Mountain Chronicles* radio broadcast https://vermonthistory.org/anarchist-movement-in-barre-1920; Andrew Douglas Hoyt, *And They Called Them "Galleanisti": The Rise of the Cronaca Sovversiva and the Formation of America's Most Infamous Anarchist Faction (1895–1912)*, PhD Dissertation, University of Minnesota, 2018; Paul Demers, "Labor and the Social Relations of the Granite Industry in Barre," BA Thesis, Goddard College, 1974; Stephen J. Randall, "Life, Labor and Death in an Industrial City: The Occupational Health of Barre Vermont, Granite Workers, 1870–1940," *Canadian Review of American Studies* 22, 1991, 195–209; Maartje Melchiors, *Barre: History of a Vermont Granite Town*, https://www.uvm.edu/landscape/learn/Downloads/scrapbooks/barre_history.pdf; Robin Hazard Ray, "No License to Serve: Prohibition, Anarchists, and the Italian-American Widows of Barre, Vermont, 1900–1920," *Italian Americana*, Vol. 29, No. 1, Winter 2011, 5–22; "Old Labor Hall, Barre, Vermont: Preserving a Working Class Icon" in *Labor's Heritage, the Quarterly of the George Meany Memorial Archives*, Vol. 10, No 3, Spring/Summer 1999. Richard Hathaway, "The Granite Workers of

Barre, 1880–1940" in *We Vermonters: Perspectives on the Past*, Michael Sherman, ed. (Montpelier, VT: Vermont Historical Society, 1992); "Rudolph Vecoli, "Primo Maggio: May Day Observances Among Italian Immigrant Workers, 1890–1920," *Labor's Heritage*, Vol. 7, No. 4, Spring 1996.

6. For recent scholarship on the 1912 strike and the children's exodus to Barre and other East Coast cities, see Robert Forrant and Jurg Siegenthaler, Eds. *The Great Lawrence Textile Strike of 1912: New Scholarship on the Bread & Roses Strike* (Oxfordshire, UK: Routledge, 2014).

CHAPTER 3

Lawrence, Massachusetts, and the 1912 Bread & Roses Strike at Street Level

Interpretation Over Time

JIM BEAUCHESNE, KATHLEEN S. FLYNN,
SUSAN GRABSKI

Introduction

Telling the 1912 Bread and Roses Strike story in Lawrence, Massachusetts, to its 2012 resident population was critically important to those seeking to commemorate the event. The city is now comprised mostly of immigrants from areas of the world with different languages and cultures than those of the previous European immigrants. Residents now work in very different industries with seemingly no direct connection to the city's labor past. However, the parallels between the lives of workers then and now are indeed many. Moreover, the city holds the memory of the 1912 strike in its many prominent red brick mill buildings where workers toiled, the streets that militia patrolled and where workers picketed, and in various common spaces where strikers gathered to organize their efforts. While making the connection between 1912 and 2012 resonate was challenging, the "place" would provide a road map and living museum for two major historical organizations in Lawrence, along with their collaborators, to walk the past into the present in a meaningful way.[1]

The Lawrence Heritage State Park (LHSP) and the Lawrence History Center (LHC) took the lead in telling this story, offering numerous events, often in locations where significant strike activities occurred. Many of these events were participatory in order to engage a broad audience. Several chapters in this volume discuss outcomes similar to those that arose in the Lawrence yearlong celebration. In chapter three, Gustin, Lane, and McLaughlin describe Barre, Vermont's experience of strength through partnerships. Bush (chapter four) and Windon (chapter six) describe the difficulties in interpreting complex events, especially when balancing multiple perspectives and competing memories.

Walking the Past into the Present

Incorporated in 1847, Lawrence, Massachusetts, was carved out of two existing towns, Andover and Methuen, on either side of the Merrimack River. The final and most ambitious of New England's planned textile-manufacturing cities, the Essex Company, built a dam and canals on the Merrimack River to provide waterpower for the textile mills it also constructed. Less than 40 years after the Essex Company's 1845 incorporation, 338,100 spindles, 9,057 looms, and 10,200 employees wove two million yards of worsted wool a week—25 percent of the nation's worsted wool output. The city's population grew by approximately 14,000 per decade. In 1912, just over half of its population was foreign-born, including immigrants from Ireland, Italy, Lithuania, Poland, Russia, Syria, Lebanon, and Turkey. According to the 2010 federal census, Lawrence is home to 78,197 residents. One of the poorest, youngest, and most heavily Latino cities in New England, 27 percent of residents live below the poverty level, 47 percent are below the age of 25, 73 percent are Latino, 74 percent speak a language other than English at home, and 36 percent are foreign-born.

Following the Second World War, most of the city's textile mills closed. Suburbanization, urban disinvestment, and immigration from predominantly Puerto Rico, Cuba, and the Dominican Republic followed. The Lawrence economy became based on Latinx-owned businesses and family-owned establishments serving the Latinx community. The city's bilingual and bicultural social services providers coalesced to provide health, education, and employment services to Latinx families. By the early 2000s, Lawrence had become New England's first Latinx majority city.[2]

One of the city's most significant historical events is the Great Lawrence Textile Strike of 1912, known to many as the "Bread & Roses Strike." It stands as one of a handful of significant events in working-class history. The 1912 Strike ended with a memorable and compelling victory for the mostly immigrant workforce and the Industrial Workers of the World (IWW). The walkout began on January 11, 1912, sparked by a wage cut when Massachusetts' legal workweek went from 56 to 54 hours for women and children. Simmering resentments over nearly every aspect of workers' lives came to a boil when over 20,000 workers walked away from their machines. Mostly peaceful, the strike lasted nine weeks, concluding on March 14, 1912.

Local elites, including leaders of the Catholic Church, organized a "Citizens Committee" to oppose the strike and the IWW's presence and continued their efforts in the months after the March settlement. Their campaign climaxed seven months later when in October of 1912, they organized a grand "For God and Country" parade that forced rank-and-file workers to choose between support for what the strike represented or possible loss of employment. Soon the IWW's presence in the city dissipated, and the "redemption" of Lawrence through the "God and Country" parade became the official strike narrative. That version of events suppressed aspects of the strike story and demonized its leaders and activists as radicals and godless communists. Just as occurred in West Virginia concerning the history of the mine wars (chapter one), Lawrence and Massachusetts leaders objected to the pro-strike treatment in the Works Progress Administration's *Massachusetts Guide*, and forced the publication of a censored second edition. In 1962, at the 50th anniversary of the strike, city leaders organized a massive "God and Country" parade, further reinforcing this antistrike narrative.[3]

However, amid the social and intellectual upheavals of the 1960s and 1970s, cracks appeared. Renowned labor artist Ralph Fasanella spent three years in Lawrence creating eighteen paintings, three focused on the 1912 strike. His "Lawrence 1912: The Bread and Roses Strike," hangs permanently in the Lawrence Heritage State Park, and an exhibition of paintings titled "Fasanella's Lawrence" graced the Park's gallery during 2013. Almost simultaneous to Fasanella's sojourn, *Village Voice* journalist Paul Cowan visited Lawrence and then wrote about the suppression of the strike story, calling it a "town's amnesia." This is eerily similar to Chuck Keeney's description of the regional "Alzheimer's" following the West Virginia Mine Wars (chapter one), or John Salmond's "collective amnesia" in Gastonia, NC (chapter four). These became the initial openings to tell a very different story about the 1912 strike.

Two Historical Organizations Form

In the late 1970s and early 1980s, a revival of interest in local history, fueled in part by the nation's Bicentennial (a la Matewan, WV, chapter one), led to the creation of two organizations, the Lawrence Heritage State Park (LHSP) and the Lawrence History Center (LHC). The State Park, developed under Massachusetts' Heritage Parks program, marked a pioneering effort to create urban parks in several declining industrial cities. With car-oriented and demolition-centric urban renewal increasingly discredited, Heritage Parks, it was imagined, could be catalysts for revitalization by modeling downtown reinvestment and preservation. Governor Michael Dukakis formed the Parks with Visitor Centers that featured exhibits focused on local history and culture. The Massachusetts Department of Environmental Management (DEM) planned the Parks with community input. An advisory committee that included representatives from the Mayor's office, members of the local historical community, and the Lawrence History Center—then known as the Immigrant City Archives—met with consultants and exhibit designers hired by DEM to create a Visitors Center in a place that once housed mostly young female workers. The LHSP soon occupied a former worker boardinghouse along the North Canal in the heart of the old mill district, now dominated by partially filled enormous red-brick mill buildings with a desultory mix of sweatshops and warehouse space.

At the outset, the Lawrence History Center (LHC), founded as the Immigrant City Archives in 1978 by German immigrant Eartha Dengler, had a specific mission to collect, preserve, share, and animate the history and heritage of Lawrence and its people. Its first archival collection consisted of stories of women immigrants. In 2021, its most extensive collection is the Essex Company records that meticulously document Lawrence's construction. Other collections include well over 35,000 photographs and glass plate negatives, 800 digitally mastered oral histories with accounts dating back to the 1912 Strike (including two of Angelo Rocco, a local organizer during 1912), mayoral papers, municipal and church records, newspapers, and an array of records documenting the ethnically diverse history of the city. The History Center uses these materials in physical and online exhibits, educational programming, and research services to the public to foster an understanding of the interaction between the built environment and the lives of ordinary people. In 1992, the LHC moved into the former Essex Company's headquarters, an 1883 complex listed on the National Register of Historic Places.

Although their approaches differ, the Heritage State Park and the History Center collaborate to educate the public about the 1912 Strike. As we show in this essay, the strike's interpretation has evolved. The 'God and Country' paradigm, which vilified militant labor activists and celebrated religion and patriotism, dominated strike storytelling for over fifty years. Challenged by the "bottom-up" approach of the New Social History that emerged in the 1970s, the centennial anniversary offered an opportunity to gather and present more nuanced interpretations of the strike story.

The Lawrence Heritage State Park
Visitor Center Interprets the Strike

When designing the LHSP's first exhibits, creators faced a conundrum. How would they deal with tensions over strike interpretations that had arisen over the years? When the strike story was revived in the 1970s by social historians, journalists, artists, and labor activists, new interpretations of "Bread and Roses" did not sit well with individuals still enamored of the "God and Country" storyline. A 1986 *Eagle-Tribune* letter-writer noted the strike "was, and always has been 'the 1912 Strike' . . . (until) some hotshot public relations writer . . . (re-labeled it) with the ridiculous phrase, 'Bread and Roses'!" The LHSP's designers had to deal with contested interpretations of the strike as the Visitor Center opened.

Much of the Center's floor space is devoted to a permanent exhibit on the history of Lawrence. On the first floor, "Lawrence, Massachusetts—A Planned Industrial City" includes scale models of downtown and the mill district. With the models, accompanying text describes the waves of immigrants who entered the city. Except for a small panel that contains a strike chronology, there is no mention of the Bread & Roses Strike. The panel is at the entrance to a 25-seat theater, where visitors can watch a 20-minute strike documentary, "Collective Voices," created by the Commonwealth Museum at the Massachusetts State Archives and the Massachusetts AFL-CIO.

Organized labor's participation offers a clue to the video's approach to the story. Immigrant workers, oppressed and exploited, rising in resistance and solidarity, win an improbable and stirring victory. However, elements of the larger history disappear. For example, the video elides the American Federation of Labor's opposition to the strike because their radical rival, the Industrial Workers of the World (IWW), led it. One could accuse the AFL-CIO of co-opting the story into its own labor history narrative. Also, the more substantial omission is any reference to the "God and Country" parade, repression, and the blacklisting of strike activists and IWW members. This series of events made it possible to marginalize the strike's history for decades. None of this is mentioned in the video, nor is the struggle between the IWW and the AFL-CIO.

The Visitor Center's large second-floor "City of Workers" exhibit is a chronological history of the region, starting with the pre-Columbian Native American presence in the Merrimack Valley. Included here is a treatment of the 1860 Pemberton Mill collapse and fire that killed 100 workers and injured scores more. There is also a series of newspaper front page mock-ups, with superimposed photos of the twentieth century. For the strike, a mock street scene consists of two storefront windows bracketing a street corner news vendor's booth. Inside the booth, a 10-minute video about the strike plays. In it, a news vendor, hawking papers with the cry "Titanic," which sank a month after the strike, describes the strike as a first-person experience, unlike the more impersonal narrator of the "Collective Voices" video. Nevertheless, it too omits references to the poststrike repression or the decades of suppression and demonization of the history.

Nearby, a backlit panel to the right of the second storefront window constitutes the only non-video depiction of the strike. It offers the work stoppage's essential facts in less than one hundred words and with a series of strike-related images. Notably, there is no mention of the October 1912 antistrike, anti-IWW demonstration, or the strike story's suppression. Thus, the more contentious aspects of the walkout and its aftermath remain invisible to the visitor.[4]

In 1962 the city organized a 50th anniversary, not of the strike itself, but of the God and Country Parade. In this retelling, the IWW remain godless outsiders and radical agitators who duped unsuspecting immigrants into striking. At the height of the Cold War, when organized labor had little use for the class war politics of the IWW, the LNHP's mock newspaper includes a photograph of the 1962 Parade. Thousands of marchers fill city streets, with hundreds of uniformed Catholic school children front and center. Scores of parade watchers line the sidewalks. The photograph's label misleadingly reads:

1962—Thousands Watch:
Commemorative Parade
City Celebrates Anniversary of
1912 Strike; Looks to the Future.

Obviously, the 1962 "God and Country" Parade did not celebrate the anniversary of the 1912 strike. Why did this exhibit panel omit references to the "God and Country" story and misrepresent the 1962 anniversary? It seems likely that exhibit designers and their local advisers feared an adverse reaction from the significant swath of Lawrencians who disagreed with any reinterpretation of the strike as a positive event. For generations educated to consider the 1912 events a shameful episode in city history, the God and Country Parade was deemed worthy of commemoration and reenactment at the 50th anniversary. In fact, the 1962 Parade was fondly remembered twenty years later when Visitor Center planning took place. Exhibit designers settled on a compromise: describe the strike in the more positive way created by new

FIGURE 3.1. Student from the Oliver Partnership School in Lawrence sketching the 1912 Strikers' Monument as part of the 2014 My City is a Museum project. Courtesy of Lawrence History Center.

scholarship while avoiding the 'God and Country' story of repression. This resulted in an uplifting characterization of heroic immigrant ancestors making just demands and winning for themselves and the generations that followed.

In recent years the LHSP interpretive staff has counteracted this shortcoming by acknowledging it and freely interpreting the more complex history. Video options include a locally produced strike documentary that includes the God and Country Parade and the domination of public memory by this paradigm through the early 1980s. During Bread & Roses Strike Walking

Tours, park staff delve into the repression and reinterpretation. The tour ends on the Lawrence Common. There, walkers view the Shattuck flagpole, erected in 1914 to celebrate the God and Country Parade, and the 1912 Strikers' Monument, dedicated in 2012. The bronze monument holds a bas-relief plaque depicting hundreds of strikers pouring out of the mills, framed by a shuttle, yarn, and gear images, symbolic of the textile industry. Two upright bayonets flank the workers, symbolizing the militia's threatening presence. The IWW's insignia acknowledges the critical role they played in leading the strike. Between these two historical markers, Park staff describe the evolution of the 1912 Strike story from a shameful episode best forgotten to a world-renowned event that many of today's Lawrencians regard proudly. Learning this history, tour-goers glimpse how event narratives get framed or forgotten, revised and reinterpreted.

As the LHSP and the LHC got off the ground, the interventions of Fasanella and Cowan, and the encouragement and assistance of New York City–based Moe Foner's Service Employees International Union 1199's "Bread & Roses Cultural Project" led to Lawrence residents organizing "Bread and Roses Day" in May 1980. With the presence of two-thirds of Peter, Paul, and Mary, it became the first public, pro-strike commemorative event in Lawrence in 68 years. In 1985, the Bread and Roses Heritage Committee (BRHC) organized the first Bread and Roses Labor Day Heritage Festival, on the Lawrence Common, the site of numerous 1912 strike rallies. The BRHC commemorated the 75th anniversary of the walkout and declared the period from Labor Day 1986 to Labor Day 1987, the "Year of the Worker." In 1988, "Shifting Gears" organized by Dr. Yilderay Erdener, Scholar-in-Residence at the LHSP, used audio and video to record the experiences of sixty-eight older Lawrencians working in the textile industry. In addition, local historians and labor activists identified and marked the gravesites in Lawrence's Immaculate Conception Cemetery for strikers Anna LoPizzo, John Ramey, and Jonas Smolskas.

The Lawrence History Center and 2012

Unlike the LHSP's permanent exhibit, the Lawrence History Center is less constrained in its ability to support ongoing interpretations of the strike. Its collections document the city's growth and reveal how that trajectory parallels the development of the labor movement: both intersect with the study of immigration, urban planning, industrialization, engineering, and public health. There is a depth of materials for researchers and audiences at all levels of scholarship. Moreover, its proximity to the remaining mills, the North Common, and other strike sites in the walkable historic district, makes the Center ideal for impactful placed-based learning opportunities. The 100th anniversary of the strike presented an excellent opportunity for commemoration and an exploration of the event's impact.

A unique collaboration established the framework for citywide activities. The Bread and Roses Centennial Committee (BRCC), headed by a five-member steering committee including Susan Grabski, LHC executive director, and Jim Beauchesne, LHSP visitor services coordinator, and chaired by University of Massachusetts Lowell history professor Robert Forrant, led the initiative. A website ensured that event information was available to the public. Foundation grants and donations from trade unions supported exhibit construction while a UMass Lowell intern engaged in extensive archival research to create exhibit text. Planners felt that in order to expose a wide range of people— young, old, present-day Lawrencians, Spanish speakers, and people from a distance—to the history of the strike and, more importantly, to become engaged with the larger history of Lawrence and its future, they needed to populate the city's numerous strike-related locations with events, presentations, concerts, art exhibits, and the like to encourage visitors to return a few times during the anniversary year. The goal was for a community dialogue to flourish around the strike's causation, including working and living conditions, social justice, immigration, and the effectiveness of collective action. Residents and visitors could explore how such issues resonate today.

A venue that fostered this exploration, the Lawrence History Center's bilingual exhibit, *Short pay! All out! The Great Lawrence Strike of 1912* inhabited a 3,000-square-foot raw mill space on the Everett Mill's top floor. A cornerstone of the yearlong celebration, located in the very mill where the strike commenced, *Short pay! All out!* described how Lawrence was a community in crisis long before a January 1912 wage reduction. Just as workers struggled in 1912 with low wages, difficult living conditions, and anti-immigrant attitudes, so too did residents in 2012.

For example, in 1910, Lawrence had the eighth highest death rate per 1,000 in the country and the seventh-highest death rate for infants. The Massachusetts Labor Commission found that "the lowest total wages for human living conditions for an individual was $8.28 a week." A third of families in Lawrence earned less than $7.00. The 1912 U.S. Bureau of Labor's *Report on the Strike* noted that weekly rents varied from $1 to $6, but the amount commonly paid in Lawrence was $2 to $3 for a 4-room apartment and $3 to $3.50 for five rooms. Wages did not cover food and family necessities. Life was desperately short for mill workers. Lawyers and clergy had the longest life expectancy at 65.4 years; manufacturers were next at 58.5; for mill operatives, it was 39.6 years. The strike prompted the nation to confront conflict-

FIGURE 3.2. Mural, *Faces of Immigration*, painted by students at the Lawrence Humanities and Leadership Development High School. The large-scale mural was in the Lawrence History Center exhibit, *Short pay! All out!* Courtesy of Lawrence History Center.

ing visions of community identity and struggle, civic culture, immigration, and industrialization. It influenced public policy, helping construct some of the current social safety nets. The exhibit became a lens through which to examine similar current-day issues.[5]

Visitors to the exhibit space became immersed in the strike story through the use of imagery, artifacts, documents, videos, and a stairwell installation that re-created the sounds of the mills for visitors who climbed the stairs, like the workers before them. The noise, personal stories, and incredible multicultural energy of the strike resonated. Quotes in English and Spanish from the Lawrence History Center's oral history collection appeared on exhibit kiosks and walls. Two wall-sized murals created by the Lawrence High School art students reflected life in Lawrence in 1912 and 2012, connecting the city's past and present. A 10-year-old student visitor wrote, "I love the exhibit. I love how there are quotes of the people who participated in the strike. The large murals painted by the high school students showed how the children interpreted their city and the great strike."

Movable exhibit kiosks wove together important themes: What happened? Who makes a community? What makes a community? Why strike? How do we remember? Visitors could contribute their reflections, photographs, artwork, and writing to the exhibit in an available logbook. A student described how the physical space transported her to 1912: "where I am standing is where the people who worked were standing . . . the oil from the machinery is still soaked into the wood floor . . . it makes me so sad that people did not get paid right." A visitor from Boston wrote, "Absolutely beautiful—makes me proud to be union."

On January 12, 2012, to kick off the centennial year, hundreds of union members, students, and community members paraded with signs and U.S. flags to reenact the start of the strike. They marched from the Everett Mill down Common Street to City Hall with a song in the air and their feet on the same streets the strikers marched. *Short pay! All out!* opened immediately afterward to nearly 500 people, including labor, political, and community leaders and hundreds of students from throughout the city. In attendance was 104-year-old Salvatore Savinelli, who, at the time, was likely the last living link to the strike. Salvatore was four years old when he boarded a train bound for Barre, VT, with 35 other children and his father Angelo. Angelo, a member of the Strike Committee, managed a store that distributed food to striking workers on credit since they had no money. The children left the city as part of the February 1912 "children's exodus." Children went to New York City and Philadelphia, where they would be cared for under better circumstances by friends, family members, and union workers. A February 15, 1912, Vermont image shows the children on the Barre Socialist Labor Party Hall steps (chapter two). In the photograph is Angelo Savinelli with a blurred image of a young Salvatore at his side.

The exhibit space hosted lectures, meetings, exhibits, performances, and community gatherings relevant to the strike's themes. Across 2012, well over 5,000 people representing twenty states, the United Kingdom, Italy, Vietnam, Canada, and Australia viewed the exhibit as visitors or attendees at one or more of the seventy-one such programs held in the space. These figures reflect the importance of the subject matter related to the strike and the flexibility of the exhibit layout to accommodate events, meetings, and performances. By offering events related to the strike and/or time period free of charge, LHC sought to draw in different audiences and, at the same time, for them to visit the exhibit space to learn more about the strike's history.

To that end, LHC hosted an exhibit within the strike exhibit, *Follow the Thread*, curated by artist Jackie Cooper, that told the story of Jewish immigrants' involvement and influence in America's garment history. A vintage fashion show highlighted 100 years of fashion and invited local people to model the clothing. Both engaged audiences ranging in age from 4 to 74 who were perhaps less likely to be explicitly interested in labor history.

The Lewis Hine Project: Stories of the Lawrence Children exhibit, by the retired social worker and genealogist Joe Manning, told the stories of what happened to ten Lawrence children photographed by Hine in 1910 and 1911. The exhibit attracted people interested in the history of child labor, photography, genealogy, and—most impactful—descendants of the children profiled:

> We truly enjoyed this interesting step into history. How wonderful to see Grandpa Levesque. It seemed he was with us. We truly appreciate all of the hard work that was put into this project!! Thank you!!
>
> Michael Levesque, Windsor, VT

> As grandchildren of one of the Lawrence children, Leopoldo Andreoli, we are so thrilled and happy to find out about him and the others who had a part of Lawrence history. Thank you very much—your efforts will not be forgotten. Our awareness of our family history has given us a renewed pride.
>
> The Andreoli Family

Engaging the city's youth was considered critical by planners. In turn, *Lawrence Reads*, sponsored by the Lawrence Public Library, brought Lawrencians of all ages into the strike exhibit space to read aloud Katherine Paterson's *Bread and Roses, Too*. Paterson, a popular young adult author from Barre, VT, fictionalized the story of Lawrence children sent to Barre during the strike, making the story more accessible to young people in Lawrence (and everywhere).[6]

To animate locations throughout the mill district, we held the Bread and Roses Centennial Symposium in other historically significant locations within walking distance from the Everett Mill, for example, the Essex Art Center, the Lawrence Heritage State Park, and the Lawrence History Center. This brought attendees out walking on the same streets, breathing the same air, and entering the same buildings that the 1912 strikers would have navigated. The event attracted nearly 300 attendees and featured a keynote address from Richard Trumka, then President of the AFL-CIO, who powerfully emphasized the connections between 1912 and the 2012 labor fight for equity, safety, and fair compensation. Similarly, a symposium panel entitled "Talk to Textile Workers" featured a dozen textile workers from the Lawrence-based Polartec plant who shared their stories. Nearly 500 workers labored at Polartec in 2012. Community leaders were engaged to moderate panel discussions educating present-day key players about the past while facilitating scholarly discussion. An evening concert that featured labor musicians Si Kahn, Karen Brandow, and Charlie King attracted both labor and music enthusiasts to the symposium.

While planners focused on Lawrence's strike story, they also wanted to place the history in a regional context and invite others into the city with broader labor stories. The Maine Mural Project, a reproduction of a 36-foot mural by Maine artist Judy Taylor that was removed in 2011 from the Maine Department of Labor by then-Governor Paul LePage, was brought into the *Short pay! All out!* exhibit space. The mural depicts scenes from Maine's labor history and brought attention to current views on labor from representatives from the Frances Perkins Center and others who participated in a panel discussion at the symposium.

To call attention to current labor action, the Merrimack Valley Central Labor Council AFL-CIO was provided the rare opportunity to convene labor leaders at an actual pivotal strike site for its Annual Legislative Breakfast. Exhibit imagery of 1912 union organizers and strikers surrounded present-day activists like labor's ancestors "fight(ing) like hell for the living."

To round out the year, on November 23, 2012, an original Italian dramatization for the stage based on the writings of Arturo Giovannitti, was performed in the exhibit space. On January 29, 1912, Joseph Caruso, Joseph Ettor, and Giovannitti were arrested for their alleged role in the death of striker Anna LoPizzo. While protesters all over the world marched for the men's freedom, Giovannitti, trade-unionist, and member of the IWW from Molise, Italy, composed several poems in jail. One, titled "The Walker," formed a part of the play's structure. The play also highlighted Giovannitti's "Address to the Jury" delivered November 23, 1912, in a Salem, Massachusetts, courtroom, one hundred years to the day of the 2012 performance to a full house in the Everett Mill.

Activities centering on the 1912 strike continue their reach beyond the centennial year of 2012. For example, Bread and Roses Heritage organizes the Labor Day Festival every year, which attracts thousands of present-day Lawrencians as well as many from the region. Publications including *Lawrence and the 1912 Bread and Roses Strike* by Robert Forrant and Susan Grabski; *The Great Lawrence Textile Strike of 1912: New Scholarship on the Bread & Roses Strike*, edited by Robert Forrant and Jurg Siegenthaler; and *The Great Strike*, a teachers' guide and student workbook curriculum by Small Planet

Communications in Lawrence, impact audiences representing different segments of the population. A Digital Public Library of America (DPLA) exhibition entitled *Bread and Roses Strike of 1912: Two Months in Lawrence, Massachusetts, that Changed Labor History* is available for viewing among other nationally significant exhibits.[7]

Theater Espresso's performance of *American Tapestry: Immigrant Children of the Bread and Roses Strike* based on research at LHC and the Congressional testimony of children who labored in the city's mills is performed annually at the LHSP. Some 6,500 Lawrence public school fifth graders have attended a production since 2010. This original play puts students in the Congressional Committee hearing testimony about the strike. The testimony took place in March 1912 and compelled President Taft to investigate U.S. labor practices. The play asks students to think about the issues the protagonists were forced to confront. Students always seem to remember vividly the testimony of 14-year-old Carmela Teoli, a young woman whose hair got caught in one of the machines. Joseph Cardella, a child during the strike of 1912, recalls this incident in his 1990 oral history with the LHC:

> Si, Esa chica, conozco a sus padres, aquella que quedo atrapada en la correa. Le arranco parte de su cuero cabelludo. Seguridad no era prioridad. La prioridad era la producción.
>
> Yes, that girl, I know her parents, the one who got caught in the belt. Ripped part of her scalp off. Safety wasn't the by-word there. Everything was production.

LHC collections provide myriad opportunities for the study and interpretation of the strike. Essex County Jail Records and Public Health Collections drew the attention of Dr. Christopher Muller, Assistant Professor of Sociology, now at the University of California Berkeley. As the Robert Wood Johnson Foundation Scholar while at Columbia University in 2015, Muller describes the project: "The death and disease records will enable us to study the effects of the 1912 strike on health and mortality throughout the city. The jail records will give us new insights into strike participation as well as the offenses for which strikers were arrested. Combining these records with census records will allow us to study whether neighbors or members of the same ethnic group were arrested and jailed together for strike activity."

Thousands of LHC photographs, strike-related and more current workforce and manufacturing images are available online to the public through the Digital Commonwealth website. In 2016, several of these images appeared in an ABC News piece narrated by George Stephanopoulos, "A Brief History of the U.S. Minimum Wage." The piece begins, "The nation owes much of its minimum wage laws to the industrial workers of Lawrence, Massachusetts."[8]

Social media has also proven an effective way to interpret and disperse the strike story and Lawrence history: LHC has over 5,000 Facebook followers and nearly one thousand on its Instagram page. A related Facebook page, *Bread and Roses 1912–2012*, has over 140,000 followers, expanding its mission from the Lawrence strike to discussing national and international labor history. In 2018, an Instagram-inspired outdoor exhibit was created by artist Lisa Link that interpreted the story of Anna LoPizzo and the strike. It consists of twenty tiles installed along a wooded walking trail taking visitors by surprise at the Heritage Museums and Gardens, Sandwich, MA. The traveling exhibit is now a part of the LHC collection.

What Have We Learned?

Inscribed on the back of the Strikers' Monument on the North Common, immediately across from Lawrence City Hall for all to encounter, is the phrase written by Monument Committee cochairs David Meehan and Jonas Stundzia: "Let the gains of the workers past, be recognized by those who labor today, and preserved for those who toil tomorrow."

Because of the community engagement efforts since the late 1970s, but particularly during the centennial year by both organizations and their partners, we are now seeing greater interest in labor history from present-day Lawrencians. The community is witnessing the passing of the torch of truthful storytelling to the next generation. The Bread and Roses Heritage Committee membership and leadership is increasingly representative of Lawrence's Latinx population. Efforts are underway to engage current populations more effectively. The committee's deft response to COVID-19 pandemic restrictions, which forced the 2020 festival to go virtual, led to the production of a Bread and Roses Virtual Tour in both English and Spanish. The videos are widely available online to residents and educators near and far and will keep the story alive.

Just as the strikers sang songs in what is often referred to as the "singing strike" in 1912, so does the Lawrence High School Girls' Ensemble when they sing James Oppenheim's poem *Bread and Roses* at community events over one hundred years later. The song begins:

> As we go marching, marching, in the beauty of the day,
> A million darkened kitchens, a thousand mill lofts gray,
> Are touched with all the radiance that a sudden sun discloses,

For the people hear us singing: Bread and Roses! Bread and Roses!
As we go marching, marching, we battle too for men,
For they are women's children, and we mother them again.
Our lives shall not be sweated from birth until life closes;
Hearts starve as well as bodies; give us bread, but give us roses.

Inspired by the city's history of organized labor action, Lawrencians are increasingly gaining experience and education that equips them with the skills needed to take on roles in Lawrence as educators, politicians, activists, community organizers, artists, attorneys, and entrepreneurs, and to populate nonprofit boards and committees that push forth the ideals of the immigrant workers that preceded them. At street level in 2020, young people drew clear lines from the labor activities of 1912 to the actions many are taking in response to the COVID-19 pandemic and subsequent racial unrest, for example, gathering on the North Common, building community support networks and fighting for social justice.

In 2021, many of the barriers to resolving the city's 'amnesia' concerning how the strike is remembered no longer exist. With the passage of time and demographic change, a revised, more comprehensive interpretation is more accepted. Of added significance, young people are learning about the strike through programs at LHC and LHSP. They, in turn, share this with their first-generation immigrant parents. This statement was conveyed publicly at a LHC annual meeting in Spanish by the mother of a 5th grade summer program student, translated live into English by her son:

I used to ride the bus around Lawrence with my head down. Soon my son Angell began to ask me to look up as he pointed to different sites around the city. He would say, "Look, Mommy, do you know what happened in that building? Do you know how many people worked in that mill? Did you know that this city has long accepted immigrants like us from all over the world? Now I look up as I travel on the bus and have a greater sense of myself and my new home because of my son.

A new awareness of the Bread and Roses Strike was achieved in the political realm as well. Local leaders cite the importance of Lawrence labor history and collective action when speaking of challenges their constituents face. And its significance was not lost on 2012 U.S. senatorial candidate Elizabeth Warren. She held a rally in the *Short pay! All out!* exhibit space and, eight years later in 2019, launched her presidential campaign just outside the Everett and Stone Mills where the 1912 Strike began.

While the centennial activities commemorating the 1912 Bread and Roses Strike indeed walked labor history purposefully into Lawrence in 2012, the

LHSP and the LHC realize that if these efforts, and those that are ongoing, were to stop, it would be a significant loss to the telling of the broader story of American labor history. If the labor history is not taught to current and future residents, Lawrencians will walk in the footsteps of the 1912 strikers—past the remaining red brick mills (many now converted to upscale apartments, artist's lofts, and mixed-use spaces) and common spaces—but they will not be inspired by the voices of workers who struggled and fought for gains in the city on behalf of subsequent generations. For this reason, the two institutions are working in tandem to continue to teach labor history in Lawrence and to provide ongoing opportunities for historical interpretation and scholarship at all levels. It remains their collective intent to support place-based programming that offers accurate narratives about the 1912 Strike and the many other significant facets of Lawrence history.

Notes

1. Donald Cole, *Immigrant City: Lawrence, Massachusetts 1845–1921* (Chapel Hill: University of North Carolina Press, 1963). For contemporary accounts of Lawrence, see Llana Barber, *Latino City: Immigration and Urban Crisis in Lawrence, Massachusetts, 1945–2000* (Chapel Hill: University of North Carolina Press, 2017).

2. Barber, *Latino City.*

3. Christine Bold, *Writers, Plumbers, and Anarchists: The WPA Writers' Project in Massachusetts* (Amherst: University of Massachusetts Press, 2006); Lisa M. Litterio, "Bread and Roses Strike of 1912: Lawrence, Massachusetts, Immigrants Usher in a New Era of Unity, Labor Gains, and Women's Rights," *Labor's Heritage*, 11, No. 3, 2001, 58–73; Ardis Cameron, *Radicals of the Worst Sort: Laboring Women in Lawrence, Massachusetts, 1860–1912* (Urbana: University of Illinois, 1995).

4. For 1912 strike history, see Dexter Arnold, "A Row of Bricks: Worker Activism in the Merrimack Valley Textile Industry, 1912–1922," PhD diss. (Madison: University of Wisconsin Madison, 1985; Robert Forrant and Jurg Siegenthaler, Eds., *The Great Lawrence Textile Strike of 1912: New Scholarship on the Bread & Roses Strike* (Oxfordshire: Routledge Press, 2014); Cameron, *Radicals of the Worst Sort*; David Goldberg, *A Tale of Three Cities: Labor Organization and Protest in Paterson, Passaic, and Lawrence, 1916–1921* (New Brunswick: Rutgers University Press, 1989); Bruce Watson, *Bread and Roses: Mills, Migrants, and the Struggle for the American Dream* (New York: Penguin Books, 2005).

5. Charles P. Neill, *Report on Strike of Textile Workers in Lawrence, Massachusetts, in 1912* (62 Cong., 2 sess., 1912; United States Congress, House, *The Strike at Lawrence, Mass.: Hearings before the Committee on Rules of the House of Representatives* (62 Cong., 2 sess., March 2–7, 1912).

6. For eyewitness accounts of the strike, see Mary Heaton Vorse, *A Footnote to Folly: Reminiscences of Mary Heaton Vorse* (New York: Farrar & Rinehart, 1935) and Elizabeth Gurley Flynn, *The Rebel Girl: An Autobiography, My First Life (1906–1926)* (New York: International Publishers, 1955).

7. Robert Forrant, Robert and Susan Grabski, *Lawrence and the 1912 Bread and Roses Strike*, (Mt. Pleasant, SC: Arcadia Publishing, 2013); Forrant and Siegenthaler, Eds. *The Great Lawrence Textile Strike.*

8. Lawrence History Center, University of Massachusetts Lowell History Department, "Bread and Roses Strike of 1912: Two Months in Lawrence, Massachusetts, that Changed Labor History," Digital Public Library of America. April 2013. https://dp.la/exhibitions/breadandroses.

CHAPTER 4

"Like a Family" or "A Committee of Half-Starved Human Beings"

Multiple Perspectives in Interpreting Southern Mill Labor History

REBECCA BUSH

Introduction

The history of unions and labor movements in the American South is far from a triumphant one. In contrast to many parts of the Midwest and Northeast, where unions won political power as well as significant rights for workers, the historical trajectory of labor activism in the Southeast has been full of stops and starts with little sustained progress. The labor history of Columbus, Georgia, a community once so defined by its textile mills that business leaders promoted it as the "Lowell of the South," follows the same narrative, marked by a handful of notable moments connected to national movements. In a city where native residents of all socioeconomic levels remember the mills fondly, sharing stories of unionization and resistance can be a delicate proposition. Historically, some people found residing in a mill village to be a reliable and safe way of life, while others fought to upend an existing power structure that they found oppressive. Today, many local residents recall mill owners as civic leaders who set the tone for a vibrant culture of local philanthropy, while others recognize the questionable tactics that allowed them to accrue the wealth that made such charitable giving possible. In a nonprofit setting, where substantial support is often received from state and local governments, as well as family foundations and others with deep community ties, balancing these stories is not only politically and financially practical, but essential.

Using the Columbus Museum as a case study, this chapter considers the value of multiple perspectives in public interpretation of labor history. The museum serves the Chattahoochee River Valley of west-central Georgia and eastern Alabama as a key cultural institution for a metropolitan area of nearly 330,000 people. It is funded by a public-private partnership between the county's K-12 public school district and a 501(c)3 nonprofit corporation, an arrangement that is nearly unique in the United States. As the museum's curator of history since late 2011, I have had the opportunity to examine several different aspects of the city's historic textile industry through temporary and permanent exhibitions. In one permanent installation, visitors hear overwhelmingly positive oral-history reminiscences of mill workers from Columbus's primary mill village while viewing photographs of local child laborers by Lewis Wickes Hine alongside text about the creation of federal child labor laws. Hine's work fits perfectly within the museum's interdisciplinary mission of American art and regional history, offering visitors multiple interpretative avenues through which to consider the images and their implications. In a year-long temporary exhibition, the archival memoirs of labor organizer George Johnston were utilized to examine Operation Dixie in 1946–47. Though Johnston's efforts in Columbus were ultimately unsuccessful, his candid, critical, and sometimes raunchy accounts of his experiences lend a fresh, lively character to stories of encounters with mill security forces and recruitment meetings at mill workers' homes, as well as an outsider's perspective of the community in a rapidly changing postwar society. Finally, the local experiences of a U.S. president help connect local labor activism with an overarching and well-known national story in the museum's permanent history exhibition. Though Columbus contains several extant historic mill buildings in varying stages of adaptive reuse or disrepair, none of these structures are primarily designated for historic site interpretation, meaning that the museum's presentation of mill history and labor activism is the most in-depth account that most visitors will find in the city's public spaces.

Falls and Mills

Columbus's history as a mill town began in its first year of existence. In 1828, Euro-American settlers rushed to settle newly purchased land lots at a rate that startled the community's surveyor and often prevented him from completing his work. Log cabins seemingly sprung up overnight to interrupt his sight line from day to day. In part to feed this growing population, a native Georgian named Seaborn Jones established a grist mill to grind corn for meal and flour. Jones became the first entrepreneur to recognize the power of the Chattahoochee River's waters at the Atlantic Seaboard Fall Line, a geological boundary separating the sedimentary rock of the southern Coastal Plain from the crystalline rocks of the northern Piedmont. Once an oceanic coastline in the Mesozoic Era, today this abrupt change in topography results in dramatic elevation drops and "falls" that become particularly evident in water. Hydropower generated by this American fall line facilitated the development of a bevy of mill towns in the South, including Fredericksburg, Richmond, and Petersburg, Virginia; Greenville, Raleigh, and Fayetteville, North Carolina; Columbia, South Carolina; Augusta, Macon, and Columbus, Georgia; and Opelika, Tallassee, and Tuscaloosa, Alabama.

As the city of Columbus grew, civic leaders realized they needed to establish a plan for development along the Chattahoochee River. In December 1841, city councilors signed a deed to divide the land along the eastern bank of the river into thirty-seven lots, each seventy-two feet wide. They then sold all of the even numbered lots to John H. Howard and Josephus Echols for $100. The deal stipulated that Howard and Echols would construct a dam upstream of Lot 1 in order to provide the power necessary to drive the machinery of potential businesses built on the lots. Howard and Echols followed through with the deal, and business was soon booming along the Chattahoochee. By the 1850s, five mills operated in this small area, producing textiles, lumber, and flour. Many of the men who financed these mills were enslavers, meaning that enslaved African American men most likely provided a substantial amount of labor in construction of these mills and their associated dams.[1]

During the Civil War, Columbus became the Confederacy's second-largest manufacturing center, including the creation of uniform jackets and hats for the military. Columbus newspapers featured frequent advertisements for labor from the city's dozens of industrial establishments, such as a call for twenty or thirty weavers, along with nearly fifty other workers, at the Eagle Manufacturing Company. White farmers and war refugees poured into Columbus to fill some of these new jobs, doubling the city's prewar population, and for the first time African Americans received broad access to manufacturing jobs. The Coweta Falls textile mill contracted with slaveholders to hire out enslaved workers, while the Eagle mill promised "good wages and steady employment" to the area's free Black population. The Eagle also led the way in advertising jobs for "boys and young women," a practice repeated throughout most of Columbus's industrial factories, including the city arsenal and the Confederate Naval Iron Works.[2]

On April 17, 1865, after a brief nighttime skirmish, Union Army forces led by General James Wilson entered Columbus and destroyed the city's manufacturing operations, leaving residences largely untouched. Even as economic devastation gripped the surrounding region after the war, business owners rebuilt Columbus's former mills and quickly developed new ones. In some cases, transplants took the lead, as when George P. Swift rebuilt the Coweta Falls mill formerly owned by John J. Grant. Swift, originally from Massachusetts, had arrived in western Georgia in the 1830s to build mills in Upson County, but his postwar expansion into Muscogee County ultimately secured his family's name in Georgia business history. Other entrepreneurs chose to rebuild in place, such as William H. Young and his Eagle Manufacturing Company. When Young launched his new venture in 1867, he adapted the original name, christening it the Eagle & Phenix Manufacturing Company. The implication was clear: Textile mills, and textile mill labor, would be the catalyst for the city's resurrection from the ashes of war. Young's choice of name proved prophetic. In 1860, his mill had been the second largest in Georgia; by 1878, an expansion of buildings and goods produced made it perhaps the largest in the South. Before long, Columbus boosters marketed the city as "The Lowell of the South" with postcards featuring a skyline of mills and smokestacks. A new generation of white men emerged to finance these manufacturing enterprises, leading to the growing prominence of names that dominate the Columbus geographic and social landscape 150 years later: Jordan, Bradley, Bibb, Illges, Kyle, Spencer, Woodruff.

As these men continued to expand their milling operations, first dozens, then hundreds, of rural white families moved from small farms in Georgia and Alabama to Columbus for the promise of steady work. With more than a dozen mills operating in the city by 1900, the potential for labor activism was high. Although their efforts are now largely forgotten, Columbus workers did organize periodically throughout the late nineteenth and early twentieth centuries. In 1896, weavers at the Eagle & Phenix mill led Columbus's first organized strike to protest a wage cut. Encouraged by news of a successful strike in Augusta on the other side of the state, a weaver named Prince W. Greene organized the city's first union in 1896 and ultimately became the leader of a group of southern laborers who applied to join the American Federation of Labor (AFL). The powerful organization directed the mill workers to join the National Union of Textile Workers, a fledgling group in which the new southerners quickly became a majority.[3] Greene himself served as the union's national president from 1897 to 1900, but his leadership did not produce long-term improvements in Columbus's mills. AFL president Samuel Gompers even visited Columbus in 1895 (the same year as Susan B. Anthony's appearance in the city), but this rare southern trip did not produce any meaningful change in the city's working conditions,

FIGURE 4.1. "At Columbus, Ga. The Lowell of the South." Collection of The Columbus Museum, Georgia, G.2010.14.2.

nor in Gompers' engagement with race and labor. Gompers' service on the executive committee of the National Civic Federation, meant to improve the relationship between management and workers, alongside Columbus mill owner G. Gunby Jordan undoubtedly colored his view of the city's mills and labor conditions.[4]

"The Great Morality"

Columbus's cotton mills provided work for many children and teenagers for more than half a century after the Civil War. Mills occasionally advertised that incoming families must provide a minimum number of workers, or "hands," and the income children provided could make a stark difference in their households. Writing in 1921 about the rise of southern industrialization, economics scholar Broadus Mitchell summarized the prevailing attitude about the use of child labor in the late nineteenth century:

Enough has been said to make it apparent that at the outset the employment of children in the mills, if not absolutely necessary, was practically so, and never excited the least question. Search has failed to reveal one instance of protest against their working, but, on the other hand, cotton manufacturing was hailed as a boon especially because it gave means of livelihood to women and children. Poverty-stricken, the South was mustering every resource to stagger to its feet. All labor power was empirically seized upon; response was eager. At that critical juncture, later results of the employment of children could not be looked to. The great morality then was to go to work. The use of children was not avarice then, but philanthropy; not exploitation, but generosity and cooperation and social-mindedness.[5]

In a footnote to this passage, Mitchell wrote that "[o]f course, the use of children has long since become unnecessary, and has been as cruelly unjust as at first it was natural."[6] As the Fair Labor Standards Act did not provide meaningful federal labor protection for children until 1938, Mitchell's statement would likely have been greeted with consternation by reformers, including Lewis Wickes Hine. Born in 1874, Hine began his professional career as a sociologist and did not seriously engage with photography until he mentored students from New York's Ethical Culture School as they photographed Ellis Island. He began working for the National Child Labor Committee (NCLC) in 1911 to accomplish his goal of wanting "to show things that had to be corrected."[7]

On a trip through the South in 1913, Hine stopped in Columbus and captured nearly three dozen images, almost all of child mill laborers. Children who were not old enough to work in the mills could still find work as "dinner toters," carrying pails of lunch made by their mothers, which were sold to workers for a few cents. These youngest workers appeared on sentimentalized picture postcards of Columbus, depicted as barefoot, with girls wearing colorful dresses, and all carrying wicker baskets on their arms. Hine noted that dinner toters were a visible feature of the city, and their proximity to the mills provided the opportunity to learn machine operating methods surreptitiously before becoming an official employee:

This is carried on more in Columbus than in any other city I know, and by smaller children. Many of them are paid by the week for doing it, and carry, sometimes, ten or more [meals] a day. They go around in the mill, often help tend to machines, which often run at noon, and so learn the work. A teacher told me the mothers expect the children to learn this way, long before they are of proper age.[8]

In a 2012 installation of objects related to childhood in the Columbus Museum's collection, I displayed several of Hine's photographs in both digital and silver gelatin formats with no labels other than their original Hine-penned captions. A nearby panel provided a short summary of the photographer and his work, but Hine's poignant images and straightforward text needed no further explanation. An exhibition tracing the adult lives of ten of Hine's subjects in Lawrence, Massachusetts, discussed in the previous chapter, similarly proves the power of Hine's work across geographic boundaries.

As a documentary photographer, Hine captured hundreds of images, most exhibited and published in venues connected to the NCLC. However, around 1920, Hine made an intriguing change to the name of his studio, discarding "Social Photography by Lewis W. Hine" in favor of "Lewis Wickes Hine, Interpretative Photography." In placing his own name first and choosing to emphasize the interpretative and subjective aspects of his craft, Hine may have anticipated his posthumous induction into the canon of American art photographers. His work now appears in the collections of such major institutions as the J. Paul Getty Museum, the Museum of Modern Art in New York, and the International Center of Photography. Hine's images, then, represent a perfect intersection of the Columbus Museum's multidisciplinary mission of American art and the history of the Chattahoochee Valley: objects that simultaneously display inherent artistic merit while illuminating an element of local history. The museum owns eleven Hine photographs, comprising six images from Columbus and five images from other mill communities across Georgia. A handful of these works are on display in the Chattahoochee Legacy Gallery, which contains a permanent exhibition addressing the 10,000-year history of human habitation in the region. The installation contains a fairly large area giving an overview of mill history, including a cotton gin made locally by the Lummus Cotton Gin Company, once the world's largest independent gin manufacturer, and a terrycloth loom in use as recently as the 1980s. (Sawdust on the concrete floor beneath it continues to catch occasional drops of oil.) Early-twentieth-century images of mill buildings and denim fabric samples from the early 2000s bookend the story of Columbus's one-time textile dominance.

When reinstalling this area in 2014, I chose to position the Hine photographs near a short video of an actor portraying a worker in Bibb City, Columbus's one formal mill village that was its own municipality for more than a century. Company officials purposely chose to locate the mill outside of Columbus city limits to avoid high taxes, union organizers, and "street parades," while workingmen's social clubs organized by management sought to promote "the moral and mental elevation of members."[9] This approach is reflected in the gallery video, in which a middle-aged white woman wearing clean but simple attire speaks approvingly of the company-town atmosphere and rules, both economic and moral, of her community. Some visitors have questioned me about the accuracy of the video, suspecting that it is feel-good pabulum meant to appease wealthy local families who initially gained money and influence through mill ownership. The truth of the video is more complicated than that, however. Its origin predates my arrival in Columbus; I started at the museum in time for the last year of a project to enliven the gallery with the addition of short videos. A previous curator had commissioned Virginia Causey, then a professor of history at Columbus State University (CSU), to write the script for the millworker vignette. Causey, who is not a Columbus native, has spent more than two decades researching the city's history, and labor history in the city's mills is a recurring focus of her lectures and writing. She pulls no punches when discussing the most horrifying incident in Columbus labor history, a nighttime rally in May 1919 that became the culmination of two years of intermittent strikes and union activism at mills across the city:

> A group of nonunion men taunted [union organizer John] Thomas, beating on tin washtubs to drown him out. A bottle struck a union man, knocking him to the ground, and he responded with a stream of invective. Dared to repeat his "blasphemy," he did so "with added vigor, using a more complete description of his assailant." The company men then sprayed an estimated seventy-five bullets into the crowd, killing a World War I veteran and union member and wounding six. A bullet that "ranged down almost the length" of his spine crippled a twelve-year-old bystander. After several minutes of "wholesale shooting," a millhand under owners' orders cut electricity at the Bibb Mill's powerhouse, plunging the panicked crowd into darkness as the shooters escaped. A reporter described it as "the nearest thing to a battle here in years."[10]

Multiple Perspectives Matter

Given her keen awareness of the darker side of mill laborers' interactions with their employers, it may be surprising to learn that Causey authored both that passage and a generally upbeat monologue about the benefits of mill employment. However, Causey based her script on oral histories conducted by a class at Columbus College (the predecessor of CSU) in 1988. Students spoke with forty-two mill workers whose employment record in Columbus's mills spanned collectively from the mid-1930s through the time of their interviews. General impressions of mill work varied greatly based on race, age, and job in the mills, but whites who had worked at the Bibb mill specifically expressed appreciation for Bibb City's tightknit community that felt "like a family," despite restrictions on their ability to organize. At the recommendation of museum leadership in 2010, who then favored a more cautious and traditional approach, Causey drew on these first-person recollections for her script to represent positive experiences in the city's mill villages, though she is well aware of the more troubling aspects of these neighborhoods. The placement of the Hine photographs next to the video, then, presents a counterpoint of grade-school-aged children who labored in the city's mills. Both aspects of the mill experience were true for different people at different times in Columbus's history; thus, as Elijah Gaddis and Karen Sieber elucidate in chapter five in this collection, nuanced interpretation of both perspectives presents visitors with the opportunity to engage with people and their lived experiences before considering specifics of political history. In allowing contrasting or competing experiences to exist side-by-side, museumgoers can experience a variety of viewpoints and draw their own perhaps ambiguous conclusions about the overall experience of laborers. This also meets an ongoing interpretative goal of many history and art museums, including the Columbus Museum, to complicate the traditional historical narrative by focusing on everyday people and not the major power players (or "the companies and great men of granite," as this volume's essay on Barre, Vermont, wonderfully puts it) that still influence so much of our understanding of the past.

These multiple perspectives are particularly vital in a community where there are former millworkers who are just now entering their 60s, and many people carry a certain amount of nostalgia for hearing their parents' and grandparents' memories of mill labor. Sieber and Gaddis note in their examination of Gastonia, North Carolina, that the inability of unions to gain a sustained foothold in the South, as well as relatively recent largescale production in the region, has resulted in more living memory of southern mills as dependable providers of shift labor for many white working-class families. This nostalgia is reflected in two gifts to the Columbus Museum's collection in 2018 from descendants of two couples who worked in Columbus mills from the early 1940s through approximately 1980. The couples (unrelated to each other) both grew up in poor rural areas of the Florida panhandle and moved to Columbus shortly after their marriages as World War II loomed, seeking steady employment in the city's mills. For these families, mill labor provided a reliable income in a sizable town with opportunities, especially for their children, which exceeded the opportunities available in their home communities. The tools of the trade that their descendants donated, then— including a weaver's heddle hook, loom repair tools, and pencils used to test fabric quality—represent the means to achieving the American Dream for themselves and their families. This positivity stands in stark contrast to Lewis Wickes Hine's descriptions of children as young as eight operating dangerous machinery, but both suggest lived truths of those who labored in Columbus mills.

"The one I am most proud of is still 'Union Organizer'"

Not everyone among the 1940s mill employees fully embraced their roles as company men and women, however. In 2015, a temporary exhibition entitled *Troublemakers and Trailblazers* provided the opportunity to spotlight a remarkable collection of personal writings and photographs donated to the Columbus State University Archives and Special Collections by George C. Johnston, a Pennsylvania native who joined Operation Dixie. Spearheaded by the Congress of Industrial Organizations (CIO), Operation Dixie sought to organize laborers, particularly those in the textile industry, in a postwar, modernizing South. Johnston spent less than a year in Georgia, from May 1946 to March 1947, but his time as an acknowledged stranger in a strange land left a deep impression on him. In addition to reminiscing about the foibles and strengths of his fellow organizers, Johnston's unpublished memoir provides a frank outsider's account of the challenges of organizing any of the seven mills in a town as dependent on the industry as Columbus. Though new at organizing, he observed, "I was saying what I meant and meaning what I said, which normally got me in trouble but worked well for me as an organizer." Johnston writes about interactions with the guard who was posted at the entrance to Bibb City as soon as he and his colleagues arrived. Despite being told it was "impossible to organize the Bibb," Johnston once visited a house near the mill and left a pamphlet. The guard immediately followed him and told the home's residents they could expect to find their furniture on the street if they spoke with a labor organizer again. On another occasion, however, Johnston and four fellow organizers snuck into the town and hid just out of view of the guard, who "waved gaily when he saw us waiting for him and drove right on past."[11] In the exhibition, I displayed Johnston's CIO membership card and selected photographs of his colleagues attempting to organize a mill, installed alongside an original Bibb City town ordinance that prohibited picketing and protesting during the General Textile Strike of 1934, suggesting the constant push and pull between union organizers and mill enforcers.

Johnston writes of the cold and sometimes violent receptions he and his fellow organizers often received from the very employees they sought to unionize, but he also shares stories and photographs of the few laborers who were receptive to their crusade and volunteered to help spread the message, even at risk to their own employment and safety. He names them and includes many of their pictures, including Otis McIntyre, or "Mr. Mac," a weaver who was Operation Dixie's most active Columbus recruit; and Alice Price, a young woman who worked in the mills and dated Johnston while helping him recruit for the unions. Perhaps most importantly, Johnston broaches the role of race in labor organizing in the South. Historians often cite Jim Crow laws and social customs as one significant reason for Operation Dixie's ultimate failure, and Johnston makes clear that he both encountered and perpetuated this division in his own work. He writes about the influence of racially inflammatory antiunion rhetoric, noting that although most white employees were not "verbally vicious" toward Black coworkers, their support for segregation meant the organizers "prudently" made no strong push to enroll African Americans in the union.

Despite discussing many white mill workers in his memoir, Johnston mentions only one African American by name at the very end of the document. He praises Dan Cowart as "a remarkable man" and "a quite extraordinary human being," citing his intelligence and willingness to attempt to organize both Black and white mill employees. The most telling statement about the effect of segregation in Operation Dixie, however, is Johnston's offhand comment as he begins writing about Cowart: "Because we knew the sheer stupidity of trying to enroll or even talking to Negroes in Georgia, Dan is the only black man who I really got to know there."[12] The message is clear: Dedicated young Yankee organizers were willing to take on mill police and suspicion of outsiders, but the entrenched nature of the South's racial segregation was perceived as an unwinnable battle. This observation and an accompanying blurry photograph of Johnston and Cowart provides another way to interpret the issue of race in southern mills, a topic seldom discussed beyond the presence of segregated entrances and job opportunities.

In showing selected pages of Johnston's memoir in the *Troublemakers and Trailblazers* exhibition, I was able to put names and faces to the too-often anonymous plural noun of "mill workers." As in the installation of child laborer photographs near a cheerier portrayal of mill life, the images and notes point to tangible dissent against mill employment and labor practices: These are the people who sought better working conditions for themselves and others. Johnston's memoir ends on a bittersweet note, as he notes that his efforts resulted in little permanent change in Columbus. But he also proclaims that "of all the many job titles I have had, the one I am most proud [of] is still, 'Union Organizer.'" The public interpretation of this story suggests a way for working-class people to make a difference. Johnston sometimes displayed

FIGURE 4.2. Operation Dixie organizer Emil Luter (center) passing out leaflets at Muscogee Manufacturing Company in downtown Columbus, 1946. Courtesy of the Columbus State University Archives and Special Collections.

condescension toward southerners he met, but he also made clear his admiration and respect for those who fought to improve their lives. Privileging their stories, then, provides a powerful example of resistance.

Filling the Gaps

Collections like Johnston's are a joy to museum curators who may often be constrained by a lack of visual culture to tell important stories. Just as many artifacts related to eighteenth- and nineteenth-century Black history were once deemed unworthy of preservation by upper-class whites throughout the country, pictures and objects related to working-class labor struggles in the South can be difficult to discover for much the same reasons. Lou Martin's observation in chapter one in this collection that "[t]he elite have significant advantages in shaping public memory" includes decisions made decades

ago—or very recently—about the type of artifacts that museums and historical societies should collect to tell a story of forward progress for the greatest
good. The corresponding erasure of civil unrest and protest in public memory,
whether accidental or intentional, often results in the physical disappearance
of ephemera, photographs, and other artifacts that could directly illustrate and
illuminate these moments. There is no material in the Columbus Museum's
collection to tell the story of the mill strikes of 1896, or 1918–19, or 1934. In fact,
the museum did not acquire its first objects directly related to local strikes or
labor activism until 2020 when it purchased several photographs depicting a
1952 bus drivers' strike. However, unexpected connections can sometimes be
made to other collections and objects. As the result of a 2018 reinstallation of
the twentieth-century section of the museum's permanent history gallery, the
Great Depression is addressed through the lens of President Franklin Roosevelt's frequent visits to his Little White House in Warm Springs, Georgia,
just forty miles from Columbus. Near several artifacts related to the Little
White House, an interpretative panel contains this information:

> During his visits, Roosevelt could see firsthand the effects of the Great
> Depression on the Chattahoochee Valley. Several mills greatly reduced
> operations, but owners like W. C. Bradley committed to keeping businesses
> open to employ as many people as possible. However, these same men
> vigorously opposed many of their workers' requests to unionize for better
> conditions. One group of Columbus workers signed a letter to Roosevelt
> with the phrase, "A Committee of Half-Starved Human Beings Looking to
> You for Help." During the General Textile Strike of 1934, then the largest
> strike in U.S. history, more than 10,000 Columbus workers walked out of
> the mills. After 22 days, the strike ended with most union members fired
> and blacklisted from working in other mills.

This panel addresses several interpretative goals. First and foremost, it
connects a nationally known figure to labor activism and New Deal programs like the National Recovery Administration in the Columbus region.
Secondly, it notes the efforts of local mill owners to keep people employed,
albeit at drastically reduced hours. Mill owner descendants, many of whom
still lead charitable giving lists in the region, speak of pride in their ancestors' philanthropic efforts, which laid the groundwork for many cultural and
health-related organizations (including the Columbus Museum) to thrive in
the city; this text acknowledges that commitment. Its third and final aim,
however, makes clear that mill laborers still faced nearly unprecedented hard-
ship during the Depression and received little relief. Bradley, who owned
substantial portions of the Eagle & Phenix, as well as the Columbus iteration
of the Macon-based Bibb Manufacturing Company, told one federal official

he intended to "discharge every official of the Union found on his plant, or anyone, man or woman, who was active for the Union."[13] The letter referenced in the panel was sent in 1934 and read in part, "Sir, for the sake of humanity, won't you have an investigation made of the pay and working conditions of human beings in the Eagle and Phenix Mill in Columbus, Georgia. . . . There has been no effort made on the part of the Eagle and Phenix Mills to cooperate with you."[14] A promise to reduce worker layoffs actually manifested in underemployment, with workers stating that "only a small portion of their help actually get to work forty hours per week."[15] Though not exactly bold, this installation marks the first known time this history of thwarted labor activism has been explored in a permanent exhibition at the museum. Presenting multiple perspectives—the good and the bad of any individual's life—offers a more politically expedient way to tell these stories.

The same approach can also be applied to examining long-standing community institutions. Mill owner G. Gunby Jordan, at one time president of both the Columbus school board and the Eagle and Phenix, played a key role in establishing Industrial High School, as well as segregated industrial primary schools for white and Black students. Business leaders' aims in establishing the schools were made clear in a 1907 article published in *The World's Work*, a pro-business magazine that frequently warned against the perceived dangers of immigration and labor unions. Recording the words of a school superintendent who insisted that a city like Columbus "must have an army of trained workers" that could be built by "the training of children to properly take the places of life," the author noted the many "economically profitable" jobs that a graduate of Columbus's trade schools might attain. In a telling turn of phrase, the article proudly proclaims that the community is "making finished workers of the school children, its most valuable raw material."[16]

Given the mill ownership positions of many school board members, the aims of this educational program now seem far from altruistic. However, Columbus's vocational high school, the first in the nation, helped create an important alternative to the classical education then designated only for upper-class whites. Students at Industrial High divided their time equally between traditional high-school courses and classes designed to teach skills in machinery, carpentry, or dressmaking, among other trades. Early efforts were deemed successful enough to be the subject of a federal Bureau of Education bulletin in 1913, written by school superintendent Dr. Roland B. Daniel, as well as articles in other national publications. Renamed in 1937 to honor its first booster, today Jordan Vocational High School remains a source of community pride for many local residents, including midcentury white working-class graduates and its contemporary, ethnically diverse student body. Long after closure of the mills and many other manufacturing facilities, enrollment remains high and Jordan High graduates regularly attend area technical colleges and fill vital trade jobs, demonstrating the school's value for students and community members. However, the school's modern success stories cannot be separated from its paternalistic origins that sought to create a school-to-factory assembly line of workers. Acknowledging both of these factors, using museum artifacts such as a copy of the Bureau of Education bulletin and a portrait of Gunby Jordan from *The World's Work*, presents opportunities for discussion about both historical labor conditions and the importance of robust vocational education to the modern workforce.

Additional Interpretative Avenues

Although public history professionals can provide opportunities for members of the general public to broaden their existing viewpoints and historical understanding, there is no guarantee that visitors will take action to do so. In her essay on exhibiting archival material related to the Elaine Massacre in Arkansas, Katrina Windon notes in chapter six that the "ideal" visitor to an exhibition arrives with an open mind and ample "time to read and interpret the exhibit critically." However, interpretation at most museums and historic sites, even in the digital age, remains heavily dependent on visitors' self-directed initiative to read text, whether presented on a traditional static informational panel or a dynamic touchscreen. Public historians and graphic designers can increase the likelihood that audiences will stop and read this interpretative text by limiting word count, writing at an elementary- or middle-school reading level, and providing engaging visual design with graphics and large font sizes. Even when best practices are followed, however, many visitors will choose to skim only the first couple sentences of a label or text panel, while several others will only look at objects and images without reading at all. Thus, without conducting detailed visitor evaluation surveys (a challenging task for many small and mid-size museums), it is difficult to know if presenting multiple perspectives is enough to help general audiences fully grasp the complexity of the past. Visitors who do read the interpretative text may also have strongly engrained family narratives that lead them to instinctively reject ideas that challenge those stories, especially when it comes to showing sympathy for wealthy mill owners or striking laborers, depending on one's background. Still, presenting these multiple perspectives side by side allows museums and historic sites to offer new information to those visitors who are interested and receptive. Engaging graphic design and clear, concise text, as well as first-person accounts drawn from primary sources, can make it more likely that visitors will be drawn to these potentially new narratives and take the time to learn more.

Special programming can also offer other interpretative avenues to tell stories of labor in sometimes unexpected ways. In 2019, the Southeast Region Quilt Study Group met at the Columbus Museum for its annual gathering. Comprised of quilters and quilt enthusiasts from Alabama, Florida, and Georgia, the group maintains a digital presence while meeting once a year in person to examine public and private quilt collections in great detail, providing notes and observations to owners of these collections. The forty participants began their day in Columbus by examining two dozen quilts from the museum's collection, most of which were made in the Chattahoochee Valley. Precise notations about patterns, stitching, and colors provided confirmation or welcome additional information about date and provenance records associated with the quilts, while occasionally opening the door to new questions. After lunch, historian Virginia Causey gave the group a tour of the museum's exhibition areas focused on textile mills, including sections previously discussed in this essay. As Causey embarked on her tour, she noted that the group might notice what was missing from interpretation of the region's mills, alluding to the dearth of information about labor strikes. In contrast to the generally sunny overview of company town life she had written nearly a decade earlier at the behest of previous museum leadership, Causey shared her research about the role of labor activism in Columbus's textile history, connecting the lives and concerns of the people who made fabric with the quilts that group members had just spent two and a half hours poring over. This meeting, as well as a 2016 conference of the West Georgia Textile Heritage Trail at the museum, provide examples of opportunities to share verbally stories of textile mill working conditions and strikes with people who already demonstrate interest in the underlying subject matter. Conor Casey notes in his study of the Labor Archives of Washington (chapter seven) that connecting topical exhibitions and programming with outside groups and conferences "almost always yields a larger audience and a more impactful engagement with [the archives'] collections." In museums and historic sites, public historians know that though visitors may arrive interested in one narrowly defined topic, thoughtful programming and exhibitions can lead them to become curious about interconnected ideas and concepts they had not previously considered.

Befitting the Columbus Museum's multidisciplinary mission, this became especially evident during *The Patient Eye*, a weeklong performance by artist Jonathan VanDyke in 2018. Over the course of forty-eight hours, VanDyke looked intently and silently at sixteen historic quilts from the museum's collection, never allowing his gaze to leave the singular quilt on view at any particular moment. Research visits to the museum led VanDyke to select quilts of predominantly local manufacture, and he also expressed interest in locating fabric remnants from the city's mills, ultimately leading to his creation of an experimental fabric painting made with pieces of denim created at the Swift Manufacturing Company before it shuttered in 2006. VanDyke has explored understandings of labor in his work for years, and among his goals for his performance in Columbus were to explore the idea of looking as labor, as well as attitudes surrounding women's labor and stereotypical "women's work." In doing so, he drew on his experiences as a gay man who sews and who grew up in a household where he remembers his father sewing as much as he remembers his mother "taking on 'handyman' tasks." This subversion of gender norms echoes in the class divide between southern women who toiled near dangerous mill machinery and those who wore the products of their labor. In connecting original contemporary art to historic artifacts, VanDyke offered yet another lens through which museum visitors could consider the heirloom quilts handed down in their own families and the people who made them—both the strangers' hands that created the cloth and the familial hands that stitched that cloth together.[17]

Conclusion

As curators, historic site interpreters, and other public historians seek meaningful ways to present local histories of labor activism, the use of multiple perspectives can offer more accessible entry points. The oral histories of those who considered mill villages to be "like a family" can live alongside the stories of those who wrote letters, held rallies, and organized strikes to protest for better working conditions. Early-twentieth-century mill owners can be examined through dual lenses of formal philanthropic efforts and union suppression activities. Historic artifacts, especially perennially popular ones such as quilts, can be interpreted as useful objects and works of art while also presenting opportunities to talk about the people who made them. The key is to begin to tell these stories, many of which have been too long forgotten. Learning about the successes and struggles of the past, while seeing the faces of those who did so, illuminates working-class history in a way that points to powerful parallels of resistance in the present.

Notes

1. Southern Research, Historic Preservation Consultants, Inc., "Investigations into the Historic Mill Dams on the Chattahoochee River," last modified 2015, http://southres.com/uptowncolumbusdams/whobuiltthedams.php. An excellent list of primary sources related to mill history can be found here.

2. David Williams, *Rich Man's War: Class, Caste, and Confederate Defeat in the Lower Chattahoochee Valley* (Athens: University of Georgia Press, 1998), 65–73.

3. F. Ray Marshall, *Labor in the South* (Cambridge, MA: Harvard University Press, 1967), 35, 81–82.

4. Virginia E. Causey, *Red Clay, White Water, and Blues: A History of Columbus, Georgia* (Athens: University of Georgia Press, 2019), 86–87.

5. Broadus Mitchell, *The Rise of Cotton Mills in the South* (Reprint: Columbia: University of South Carolina Press, 2001), 95.

6. Ibid., 95–96.

7. Quoted in Deborah Dash Moore, *Urban Origins of American Judaism* (Athens: University of Georgia Press, 2014), 126.

8. Lewis Wickes Hine, photographer. "Dinner-Toters" waiting for the gate to open, Columbus Georgia, 1913, April. Photograph. https://www.loc.gov/item/2018675214/.

9. Causey, *Red Clay*, 87.

10. Ibid., 92. A detailed analysis of the labor activism surrounding this strike can be found in Causey's book as well as in Frank J. Byrne, "Wartime Agitation and Postwar Repression: Rev. John A. McCallan and the Columbus Strikes of 1918–1919." *Georgia Historical Quarterly* 81, No. 2 (Summer 1997), 345–69.

11. George C. Johnston, "Operation Dixie: Union Organizing for the CIO in the American South in 1946," unpublished memoir, undated, Folder 7, George Johnston-*Operation Dixie* Collection, MC 272, Columbus State University Archives and Special Collections, Columbus, Georgia.

12. Ibid.

13. Board of Trade of Columbus, Georgia, *Columbus, Georgia: The Place with the Power and the Push*, n.d. [1913]. Georgia Room, Hargrett Library, University of Georgia; National War Labor Relations Board, Case Files, 1918–19, August 21, 1918. National Records Administration, Washington, D.C.

14. Lucille Thornburgh, Roy Wade, Don Rodgers, Bill Winn, and Angie Rodgers, interview by George Stoney and Jamie Stoney, December 29, 1991, The Uprising of '34 Collection, Special Collections and Archives, Georgia State University, http://digitalcollections.library.gsu.edu/cdm/singleitem/collection/uprising/id/222/rec/16.

15. Letter from eighteen employees to Hugh Johnson, August 2, 1933, Eagle and Phenix Mills, general folder #1, E398, RG9, National Archives, Washington, D.C.; quoted in Janet Christine Irons, *Testing the New Deal: The General Textile Strike of 1934 in the American South* (Urbana: University of Illinois Press, 2000), 73.

16. Arthur W. Page, "Training for the Trades: The Next Step in Public School Work," *The World's Work*, February 1907, HathiTrust Digital Library.

17. More information about VanDyke's performance at the Columbus Museum, including artist and curator essays, can be found at the artist's website: www.jonathanvandyke.com.

CHAPTER 5

History, Memory, and Community in the Redeveloped Loray Mill

KAREN SIEBER AND ELIJAH GADDIS

Introduction

The Loray Mill, later the Firestone, is no stranger to labor historians. Lewis Hine photographed child laborers there in 1908, and a deadly National Textile Workers Union-led strike in 1929 made a martyr (and a historian's muse) out of the strike leader and balladeer Ella May.[1] However, for Gastonia, North Carolina, residents, generations removed from the unrest, these individual moments in the mill's history made famous by May, and the "linthead" kids in Hine's photos hardly factor into their understanding of this place. For those who remember the mill, it was the community's lifeblood both economically and socially for nearly a century until it closed in 1993. Locals struggle to reconcile their often positive memories of the place where they lived and worked with the tumultuous history written by professional historians and the erasures of that lived experience brought on by prolonged vacancy and planned upscale redevelopment. The banks and corporations of Charlotte have long loomed in working-class Gastonia. Now, the mill town beckons with small town charm, and the cresting wave of gentrification threatens to engulf the history and memory of the Loray community.

This chapter details the process of interpreting the mill at the moment of its renovation and in the context of its complicated, competing histories and memories. As Lou Martin notes in chapter one of this collection, one of the fundamental struggles of public historical interpretation of labor is the conflict between vernacular memory and written history. Our particular focus here is on our team of public historians' efforts as we sought to bridge that divide and create a community-driven history center in the long-vacant and recently-renovated mill.[2] The project was an attempt to make interpretations that held in tension the Loray's role in national history and local memory. Equally important, we provide a space for community members to tell their own history beyond the famed strikes and amid another revisioning of the mill and its place in the community's past and present. This project suggests how history and memory might serve as equal partners in interpreting the public histories of everyday working life and how we might integrate community and scholarly voices into the linked practices of public and labor history. More than that, it illustrates the space for meaning that opens as communities and scholars work in partnership and collaboration to chart an ongoing and evolving sense of a place's past.

The History of the Loray Mill

Before it even opened, the big mill in West Gastonia was the subject of speculation and anticipation. Early newspaper accounts documented the site selection, initial plans, and naming of the mill with rapt attention. Though textile mills were becoming commonplace in Gastonia—by 1900 the county had several dozen—the Loray was of an entirely different scale. It was to be Gaston County's first "million dollar mill," and it would catapult the town into the ranks of the most important industrial centers in the growing Piedmont textile belt. It was finally named in 1900 right around the time construction began. The peculiar name was a portmanteau of the names of its principal organizers—John Love and George Gray.[3]

When the Loray Mill opened in 1902, it was the largest cotton mill under one roof in the South at just over 300,000 square feet. With 50,000 spindles and 1,600 looms, it rivaled the production output of mills in the dominant New England textile region. As the Loray Mill grew, new workers were brought in from mountain towns and farming communities throughout the surrounding Appalachian region. The mill village expanded to over 400 homes. Large working families lived in these tightly packed houses in the shadow of their monolithic place of work. In its size, scope, and prominence, it was perhaps the best representation of the ambitions of the southern textile mill world. This world was a cocreation of owners and workers, a would-be utopia marked alike by mill-sponsored amenities for workers (schools, churches, and a recreation center), and a kind of surveillance and control made easier by the proximity of the houses to the mill and the insidious intervention of the owners into every aspect of workers' lives.[4]

Those interventions did not go unnoticed. When local funding and management failed, the mill was sold to Rhode Island–based Jenckes Spinning

Company in 1919, and production was switched to woven tire cord to meet the demands of the growing automobile industry. This new, more intensive management and their so-called "stretchout" helped calcify long-standing complaints into a strike later in 1919. More than 750 workers walked off the job in a sign of discontent. Their short-lived initial strike was the first volley in a battle that lasted for the next decade. By 1929, the Communist-led National Textile Workers Union had identified the Loray as a possible foothold into organizing the industrial South. They helped organize a months-long strike for a $20 weekly wage and a 40-hour workweek. When both the police chief (Orville Aderholt,) and local strike leader (Ella May) were killed in a wave of violence and retaliation, the strike gained national attention and local notoriety.[5]

The company worked hard in the years following the strike to rebrand itself, publishing booklets with titles like, "Loray: The Mill with a Purpose," or "Loray, Where the Boss Is the Worker's Friend."[6] Later attempts by unions to gain support among workers ran up against not just strong feelings of paternalism but additional pushback from those fearful of another violent strike. The Firestone Tire and Rubber Company purchased the struggling mill and the boom from WWII sustained worker satisfaction for decades. According to historian John A. Salmond, "for more than fifty years Gastonians developed collective amnesia about the most important single event in the community's history."[7]

Scholars have not fared much better. Other than Salmond's detailed strike monograph, research on the mill is scant, despite its prominence in national labor history. Liston Pope's *Millhands and Preachers* (1942) examined the role of religion in the 1929 strike, from preachers acting as the mouthpieces of the mill owners to the atheist viewpoints of union leaders conflicting with Southern religious values. Even the comprehensive study of southern textile mill life, *Like a Family: The Making of a Southern Cotton Mill World*, focuses mainly on the strike when talking about the Loray Mill.

Cathy Stanton's *The Lowell Experiment: Public History in a Postindustrial City* gives insight into practicing public history in a mill town, and the "perceived tension between history and heritage," in a postindustrial city in the midst of reinventing itself. Stanton was analyzing Lowell National Historic Park after it had been reopened to the public for nearly two decades though, and our work in Gastonia was in its infancy. While both sites serve as anchors of their regions' textile industries and important sites in labor history, there are some major differences between the two. Unlike in New England, unions managed only to make headway in Gastonia for a little over a decade, creating a very different work culture. Most mills in Lowell were closing as production increased in the South, meaning that Gastonians have more recent memories of a booming industry, and thus a stronger sense of nostalgia.[8] As Rebecca Bush notes, this means that locals have "strongly engrained family narratives that lead them to instinctively reject ideas that challenge these stories."[9]

While tourism, cultural programming, and economic benefit may eventually come to the still struggling former mill town, our motivation was to first create opportunities for locals to become invested in preserving the unique history of the Loray Mill and mill village. Historians' focus on the singular violent events of the 1929 strike, and individuals like Ella May, all but erases the stories and positive memories of countless others and hangs like a shadow over the mill. Despite its exploitative and violent past, it remained the economic and social life force of Gastonia for nearly one hundred years until the doors closed in 1993. Everyone in town knew someone who worked at the mill or lived in the surrounding mill village of workers' cottages. The mill's closing created a spatial and conceptual void at the center of the community for two decades as the town deteriorated around it. Thousands moved away. Downtown stores, open for generations, closed one by one. Crime increased, and property values declined. Those who remembered the mill, especially when it was known as Loray, were slowly passing away or moving on.

While Salmond wrote that he encountered an amnesia or suspicion among locals when he was writing his book on the strike in the early 1990s, our experience was that locals were ambivalent. They knew about the 1929 strike— either secondhand or through the repeated scholarly attention—but had a much stronger interest in the rest of the mill's history. Our team at UNC was contacted by the statewide nonprofit Preservation North Carolina in 2013 to explore creating a public and digital history space that would help locals, newcomers, and visitors better understand the mill's long history. Upon joining the project, we began to assess what public history efforts occurred in the decades since the mill's closing, what ephemera did exist, and who was collecting it.

We were curious how the mill was being remembered by locals, especially since developers had recently begun carving out spaces in the long-abandoned mill for loft apartments to lure nearby Charlotte workers. As a partnership developed between UNC, local residents, Preservation North Carolina, North Carolina Digital Heritage Center, Gaston County Museum of Art and History, and the Gaston County Public Library, we knew that true shared authority and a singular vision was unrealistic, but we intended as much as possible to use public knowledge to broaden our understanding of the labor history of the place. We sought to understand working people, not just labor movements. Our goal was not to prove or disprove a thesis or produce a specific tangible outcome but rather to create an evolving space that was digital, physical, and communal, for both history and memory to coexist. We wanted to allow for numerous potential futures depending on locals' continued involvement. In contrast to public historians in the textile town of Lawrence, Massachusetts, we also had a largely clean slate for interpreting the mill's history. We understood that our role as public historians was to interpret both the mill's history and the lengthy process of its history-making.[10] As we quickly realized, the public had begun their own forms of vernacular preservation from the moment the mill closed, and in some cases, long before.

Collective Memory and the Citizen Historians

In the wake of the mill's closure, a variety of former workers, current residents, and community historians sought to preserve its material history and remembered legacy. These vernacular preservation and interpretation techniques reformulated the mill's identity and purpose in and to the area. Its meaning increasingly became one rooted in desire and nostalgia, visions of the past that both celebrated its history and looked forward to the mill's renewal.[11]

Perhaps the most active of this group was Lucy Penegar, a Gastonia resident and ardent preservationist. Penegar had roots in Gastonia, moved to the edge of the village not long after the closure, and advocated almost single-handedly that it be saved from the benign destruction of slow decay. Without familial ties to the mill or village, Penegar was drawn to the mill by the importance that it held in the broader definition of the community. She was perhaps the first to recognize the potential of the building for reuse. Her advocacy (along with her personal maintenance of the mill's grounds) helped keep the structure intact and eventually facilitated its transfer to the nonprofit Preservation North Carolina. Her public historical practice extended beyond interaction with the building's monumental material remains as well.

Early in her volunteer preservation efforts, Penegar began collecting discarded and abandoned material from the mill. Some were old machine parts and molds, remnants of the manufacturing process that had little contemporary use at another factory. The bulk of her collection, though, was of worker-produced artifacts that marked not the official production output of the mill, but the many adaptations and accommodations to the aging machinery and building that workers made over several decades: squat, homemade stools for working on the machinery, wooden benches built for the break area, tags, signs, and notices produced in house. Her collection speaks to the kind of nuanced, quotidian histories of individual workers that the very scale of the building and its significant events seem to obliterate. This assemblage helped preserve the collective ingenuity of the Loray's workforce and gave anonymous testimony to the workers who made, repurposed, or otherwise used these materials. Far removed from the usual collecting strategies of trained historians, this process instead focused on materials of personal and communal significance that would perhaps escape the focus of someone more centered on narratives and historical significance.

Penegar was far from alone in this vernacular public historical practice. Her zeal was matched in many ways by other locals for whom the Loray played a significant part of their identity. Tim Ellis grew up in the adjacent Trenton Mill village but has been a lifelong member at one of the congregations founded with mill money, the Loray Baptist Church. He grew fascinated with the church's history and sought to keep and preserve their extensive records, even as the congregation's numbers continued to falter, particularly after the mill's closure. He still drives in every Sunday for services and zealously guards an archive that has filled to capacity the small basement room allotted to it. There he has records, photographs, and ephemera that help reanimate the central role of religion in the mill village and speak in voluminous detail to the complex relationship between patronage and surveillance. It is perhaps among the largest such collections in North Carolina, though its purpose is less for research than to ensure that there is some tangible remain to mark the fleeting memories of the generations of members.

In both scope and scale, Bill Passmore's collecting efforts exceed each of these two. Passmore is the second generation of a family that worked their entire careers at Loray. His three decades working in the mill began when he was a teenager and were interrupted only for a stint in the military. His mother and father likewise spent long years at the mill and in the surrounding village, moving there in the early 1920s and progressing through the ranks of employment available to each of them. During his own long tenure at Firestone, Passmore became the unofficial documentarian of mill life. Tasked with taking pictures for safety presentations and the company newsletter, he eventually turned his considerable camera skills to representations of working life at the plant. His many hundreds of photographs—taken from the perspective of an insider with virtually unlimited access—are a nearly unprecedented look at the processes and daily tasks of a southern textile mill worker in the late twentieth century. In taking these photographs, he was consciously interested in creating a larger record, recognizing both the many changes in production and employee relations that had occurred since his parents' day and the changes then occurring in his own. It was a documentary effort aimed then

FIGURE 5.1. "Windows Through Time." Image is an interactive compilation of community archival images projected onto a window in the former mill. Photograph credit Will Bosley. Digital Innovation Lab, University of North Carolina at Chapel Hill.

at both capturing the seemingly endangered record of the mill's history and at understanding its present as a period of historical becoming.

His historian's streak extended beyond photographs of the present. During his years of work, he managed to accumulate vast boxes of ephemera, records, and equipment, ranging from a World War II production flag to a pair of brass knuckles, from programs for a 1955 open house to illustrations of equipment parts. His is a nearly comprehensive, if almost entirely unfocused, collection that speaks equally to days spent at work and the many hours of life just outside the walls and fences of the plant's grounds. Like Ellis, his intention was none other than an expression of a seeming necessity to preserve and remember. It is tempting to suggest that his amassed materials were just waiting for an historian to come and make use of them, but that would be to suggest that he did not already have a complex set of interpretations that dictated his process and helped give meaning to his assembled materials. His work, like that of Ellis and Penegar, helps broaden our understanding of the nature of public historical production and challenges practices of preservation and interpretation. Their work as local, community public historians reminds us that our own authority is not only shared but also incomplete without the benefit of community voices that can speak to lived experience.

Passmore is particularly articulate about his feelings toward the Loray, its history, and his memories and perception of the place. In our many hours of informal conversation and slightly more formal interviews, he often expressed happy memories of growing up in the village, playing in the streets and playground, swimming in the pool, visiting with neighbors and chasing after girls in his teenage years. "Everybody was friendly back then," and "it was a good place to live" he once summed up.[12] But what we might classify (or dismiss) as mere nostalgia is complicated by his own working and life history and the way he has come to see it. Recounting the start of his own career at the mill after military service, he talked about moving outside the confines of the village because "during that period of time, the neighborhood just started going away."[13] His meaning is obviously broader than the physical changes in the landscape that accompanied the sale of the village to private owners. But even reflecting at greater length on his own childhood and the legacy of the violent and divisive strikes, he once claimed that it was "almost like the Civil War . . . there were a lot of hurt feelings, even to the day that I left Firestone" three-quarters of a century after the 1929 strike.[14] Certainly both he and many others evinced ready nostalgia for the mill village of their childhoods, but they also bemoaned the mill's absence for its foreclosure of a reasonably good middle-class income. And Passmore, Penegar, Ellis, and countless others expressed both the depth and complexity of their attachment to this place and its history through their own efforts at preserving and interpreting that history.

What we might think of as their vernacular public historical practice pushes the boundaries of both labor and public histories. Though scholars in both subfields have been attentive to the making and use of communal memory, rarely have we focused on it as a form of historical production that might help dictate our own scholarly practice.[15] Memory as an approach has been generative for our fields of study but has chiefly emphasized the distinctions between scholarly and community understandings of the past. In our work on this project, we tried to reverse that trend and relied on community public historical understanding as the basis for our own interpretation. Rather than foregrounding the major events in the mill's labor struggle as historians have for decades, we sought to base our work on the proliferation of material, visual, and experiential evidence of everyday working life at the mill. This complex blending of local memory, history, and academic inquiry is perhaps uniquely suited to public history and its possibility for multiple, even competing, narratives. The experiential nature of well-designed public historical interpretation allows us to theoretically move beyond the strictures of entirely chronological, event-based argumentation to a labor history that is more nuanced, complicated, and ambiguous.

Memory and the Digital Record

In addition to creating a physical space within the mill where visitors and locals could come in contact with the material reminders of the mill that Passmore, Ellis, Penegar, and members of our team collected, we wanted to explore ways in which we could use census records and other digital historical records to help better understand not just the strike and the causes for it, but the lived mill village experience in Gastonia. These records offer unique possibilities for recovering the lives of mill workers, both individual and in the aggregate. For workers in the Loray mill village, many migrating in from poor, rural communities in neighboring Appalachian states, census enumerations and vital records may be the only proof of life they left behind in the world. It became for our project an important counterpoint to the better-documented lives of labor leaders and mill owners. While historic data and government records can seem cold and boring, we looked for ways to use local knowledge and memory to help bring the data to life.

Our team at the University of North Carolina at Chapel Hill's Digital Innovation Lab worked to transcribe, line by line, the census records from 1920 for every resident of the Loray mill village. Far from boring, as the database grew to over 100,000 data points, it began to show us details of the everyday lived experience of mill village life. With a detailed pin for every person on a digitized Sanborn Fire Insurance map, the map took on life, visibly highlighting the number of people packed into the house, or the average age and sex and race of certain mill jobs, from the janitors and draymen to the spinners and carders. It also brought to light conditions we had not imagined, such as the role of chain migration in the village, with residents from certain hometowns settling near each other in the village. Some families we found in records decade after decade, loyal to the mill. Others hopped between local mills based on better wages or conditions.

While this work collecting historical data was a great learning opportunity for undergraduate students working on the project, we wanted to see what new insights about the data could be gained by having locals participate in building our database. Using data dictionaries and detailed step-by-step instructions, we had the public transcribe assigned sections of the neighborhood from the census records. Patty Brooks, who grew up in Gastonia and had familial ties to the mill, quickly deciphered last names in the census that had stumped others on the team or the census taker himself (Gholly, Jolly, Jolley, and Jelly). Passmore contributed to the occupational knowledge of the mill and what various job entries in the census record would have actually been like, whether carders, spinners, or spoolers. While we expected he would have that type of knowledge to contribute, he brought to life work at the mill in ways we had not expected, such as the sounds or smells in different areas of the mill and surrounding neighborhood.

The same integration of community knowledge was true of the digital archive we built. We began the process through a series of conversations, asking community members what kinds of materials they might have and to whom we should speak. These conversations brought us outside of the institutional collections that existed and helped leverage local knowledge, not just of history but of the current contours of the community. This did not entirely mitigate the dangers of assuming one community member speaks for or defines an entire population, but it did make us ever more conscious of those definitional gaps. Indeed, this process reminded us that one of the professional historian's most useful roles in projects like this is to serve as a contextualizing voice to help better animate community narratives.

After collecting, scanning, and returning peoples' accumulated collections, we put them online in an archival collection of around 2,000 images. In particular, we tried to prioritize local categorizations and understandings of the individual items rather than adhering to professional metadata standards. We again turned to informal conversation and surveying, probing our community collaborators about how they would define digital archival objects and their appropriate categories. And we added simple, frequent opportunities to identify or annotate images, either on the web or in person at events in the mill. It has certainly added to our understanding of the mill's history. Some visitors have contributed specific information that deepens our own knowledge of particular items.

While we knew that we had a base of invested residents like Passmore, Ellis, and Penegar, we were curious to see how the rest of the local population would respond to renewed efforts to explore the history of the Loray Mill and village. Over the course of 2016, we had a series of open houses and a grand opening for the history center in which the public at large, many current and former Gastonians, would have an opportunity to interact with the museum exhibits and artifacts as well as the digital archive and map.

Many visitors were eager to find their relatives in our map visualization and/or to figure out who lived in their current home in 1920. While our exhibit may tell them only the age, place of birth, reading and writing capabilities, and profession of the former residents, the fact that there is proof of their ancestor's existence brought comfort to people. The data sparked curiosity and conversation. Who were their neighbors? What was their job like? Where did they move here from? How many people lived in the house? It got people talking about life in the mill, their own neighbors and coworkers, and how things have changed. And, surprisingly, it also got them talking about the strike of 1929.

Several of the names that we tracked in census records were also involved in the strike, like John M. and Iva B. Fulbright. Seeing their names listed in our map visualization humanizes the strikers, with their house full of kids, living down the street from other Fullbright relatives who also worked in the mill. It also helps locals see similarities with their own experiences, a generation or two removed from the strike, as laborers in the mill. Our team could barely keep up with the flow of information coming from attendees looking through what we had come across thus far, identifying mystery people in old employee ID photos, reminiscing about changes in machinery, and chatting with childhood friends about company picnics and ball games.

Toward the end of our second open house in the mill, we offered a showing of a film taken in Gastonia in 1942 by an itinerant filmmaker named H. Lee Waters that we came across in our research. Waters would travel around small-town North Carolina and film snippets of everyday life, returning later to charge the same people he filmed a few cents to watch themselves up on the big screen like a movie star. Our choice of setting up seating for 100 quickly proved comical, as crowds enveloped the seating area and swelled across the former weaving room (see figure 5.2). The crowd sat mesmerized, watching their mothers, uncles, neighbors, and former teachers on the big screen, much as residents did over 70 years earlier during the first showing. Waters cut from classes doing calisthenics to couples cuddling at the movies, some hamming it up for the camera, others shy and giggling. As images of street life or shift changes at the mill came on the screen, people would periodically cry out from the crowd, "There's Mr. Colletta the ice cream man!" or "It's my Uncle Johnnie!" Moviegoers pointed out buildings long ago demolished, and stores, once bustling, now empty for decades. When the lights came on, the room quickly filled with a buzz of passionate conversation. We set out to create a space that sparked conversation and made room for the worker's story beyond the strike, and we knew by looking out into the weaving room that night that we were on the right track.

FIGURES 5.2 AND 5.3. Factory Identification Badges. Badges were a requirement for workers during World War II when the Loray contracted with the defense department. Bill Passmore preserved his parents' badges and allowed their digitization as part of the project. Photograph courtesy of Bill Passmore and Digital Innovation Lab, University of North Carolina at Chapel Hill.

Conclusion

More challenging to quantify is the affective experience of community members engaging with these tangible reminders of history. As we discussed earlier, the town was holding on to their memories and mill artifacts as if in anticipation of our team coming in to build Digital Loray and the history center. The census data was one way people used as an outlet to begin telling their stories. Far from portraying ourselves as conquering hero historians, we suggest that this accumulation of material and knowledge is one that suggests the democratization of public history and the necessity of conceptualizing new forms of praxis that fully integrate communities as interpreters rather than consumers alone. In the nearly three decades since Michael Frisch's articulation of shared authority, the field of public history has experienced a sea change in its conceptualization of its relationship to audience.[16] However rare true shared authority is, we have seen scholars and practitioners alike advocate a number of evolving relationalities between scholar and public. There is a growing recognition that sharing authority means not just a reciprocity of ideas but of approaches as well. James Gardner suggests as much in his critique of the emerging "radical honesty" of American public historical practice. He suggests that we not abdicate our own responsibilities as historians and allow the public to see the history-making process as a "set of facts that they can simply rearrange and share."[17] Indeed, our community interaction with this project taught us that our importance as public historians is in lending our expertise on the practices of history, not its content. For labor history at the intersections of public history, that means taking worker experience seriously and reframing what has been an approach that sometimes elides the quotidian practices of labor in favor of larger events and struggles.

The more we focused on the everyday lived experience for mill families, the more the community became engaged. The overwhelming response to the film, exhibits, and digital visualizations from the open house suggests our success at beginning to bridge the gap between memory and history, and between collective identity and historical understanding. In so doing, we started the process of re-animating workers' experience and forging a public history at the intersection of historical memory and contemporary community. With the mill and surrounding village a construction zone with new residents and businesses moving in, and those with memories of the old days dwindling, it was crucial to create this nucleus or jumping-off point for continued public history work while these windows to the mill's past life are still open.

Unsurprisingly, none of these interpretations came without gentle resistance from our community collaborators. We never experienced the level of pushback Leon Fink writes about in a similar North Carolina mill village, where white racial grievance formed the backbone of local understanding of the past.[18] Our experience was more dictated by the things we were not told, the objects, stories, and people that did not help to shape the collaborative history we tried to tell. Partially this was a result of the vagaries of personal preservation and interest. Individual workers and other community members held on to the material and narrative memories that they experienced and valued. This meant that lots of people were left out of a history that they were not a part of, whether consciously or not. Both of us remember encounters with former workers who failed to understand our fascination with the mill. For them, it was a place they had once worked, often one in a long string of jobs that served for them as a personal history of deindustrialization. Shared authority and collaborative community history were hardly a balm for layoffs and lost opportunity. These personal pasts were part of the history we wanted to convey. Whether or not it worked is still undetermined. The work of community history building is one that is expansive and ongoing, with old workers and new residents each finding usable pasts in the redeveloped mill town. Our professional ethics as public historians dictate that we put collaboration and shared authority at the center of our work. But no amount of collaborative history-making can create interest where there is none or heal the wounds of a worker's career spent rotating through jobs in the declining American textile industry. For now, much of what we have to interpret hardly feels like history. Our hope is that the public history of labor and working people can work to complicate the rapidly redeveloping past and broaden the frame of people who see themselves in it.

Notes

1. Following both contemporary scholarship and her own practice, we refer here to Ella May rather than her more commonly reported name of Ella May Wiggins. By the end of her life, she was long separated from the husband whose last name she had once adopted. Her use of her maiden name is representative in part of her identity as both a worker and feminist, subjectivities that informed her role in the 1929 strike and our understanding of her.

2. As explained later, our working team was comprised of faculty, students, and staff from the Digital Innovation Lab in the College of Arts and Sciences at the University of North Carolina, Chapel Hill. The core team of four people—Julie Davis, Bobby Allen, Karen Sieber, and Elijah Gaddis—worked on this project for its entire duration.

3. Robert Ragan. *The Textile Heritage of Gaston County, North Carolina, 1848–2000: One Hundred Mills and the Men Who Built Them* (Charlotte, NC: R. A. Ragan & Co., 2001); "The Million Dollar Mill," *Newton Enterprise*, September 15, 1899, 1.

4. Jacquelyn Dowd Hall, Christopher B. Daly, Lu Ann Jones, Robert Rodgers Korstad, James L Leloudis, and Mary Murphy, *Like a Family: The Making of a Southern Cotton Mill World* (Chapel Hill, NC: University of North Carolina Press, 1987), 114–182.

5. "The Loray Mill at Gastonia Sold to New Englanders," *Charlotte News*, May 11, 1919, 1; "Loray Spinners Walk Out: Not Satisfied with Boss," *Gastonia Gazette*, July 23, 1919, 1.

6. "The Mill with a Purpose, Where the Boss Is Your Friend: A Pictorial Description of The Loray Mill and Its Environs." (Charlotte, NC: News Printing House, 1929).

7. John Salmond, *Gastonia 1929: The Story of the Loray Mill Strike* (Chapel Hill: The University of North Carolina Press, 1995), 190.

8. Cathy Stanton, *The Lowell Experiment: Public History in a Postindustrial City* (Amherst: University of Massachusetts Press, 2006), 26.

9. See Rebecca Bush, "'Like a Family' or 'A Committee of Half-Starved Human Beings': Multiple Perspectives in Interpreting Southern Mill Labor History," chapter four of this volume.

10. See Jim Beauchesne, Kathleen S. Flynn, and Susan Grabski, "Lawrence, MA, and the 1912 Bread and Roses Strike at Street Level: Interpretation over Time," chapter three of this volume.

11. The broader practice of vernacular preservation should be taken to mean not just a localized reformulation of historic preservation techniques, but rather a broader set of practices aimed at incorporating evolving community understanding of a landscape into practices of historical interpretation. See John D. M. Arnold and Donald Lafreniere, "The persistence of time: vernacular preservation of the postindustrial landscape" *Change Over Time* 7.1 (Spring 2017) 114–133.

12. Bill Passmore, interview by Elijah Gaddis, July 8, 2015.

13. Bill Passmore interview by Greg King, 2013.

14. Bill Passmore, interview by Elijah Gaddis, August 12, 2016.

15. On the intersections of labor history and memory studies, see Sherry Lee Linkon, and John Russo, *Steeltown U.S.A : Work and Memory in Youngstown* (Lawrence: University Press of Kansas, 2002).

16. Michael Frisch, *A Shared Authority: Essays on the Craft and Meaning of Oral and Public History* (Albany: SUNY Press, 1990).

17. Perhaps most characteristic of the recent trends in shared authority is Bill Adair, Benjamin Filene, and Laura Koloski, eds. *Letting Go? Sharing Historical Authority in a User Generated World* (London: Routledge, 2011); James Gardner "Trust, Risk, and Public History: A View from the United States," *Public History Review* 17, 2010, 54.

18. Leon Fink, "When Community Comes Home to Roost: The Southern Milltown as Lost Cause," *Journal of Social History* 40.1 (Autumn 2006): 119–145.

CHAPTER 6

"Cut Off from Fair Play"

Representing Labor Issues in the
Context of the Elaine Massacre

KATRINA WINDON

Introduction

In 2019, Arkansas commemorated the 100th anniversary of what was likely
the state's single deadliest racial conflict, eight days that saw what many
researchers now believe to be more than 200 African Americans killed in
rural Phillips County. The Elaine Massacre, as that event is now known, was
a racially-motivated conflict, and its legacy is often first examined through
that lens. The Massacre was also a labor conflict, however, with roots in the
suppression of sharecropper organization efforts. Many of the barriers faced
by Progressive Farmers and Household Union of America (PFHUA) organizers and members in 1919 no longer exist. Integrated unions and the right
to collective bargaining—though contentious—are now enshrined into law,
with tenant farmers enjoying some legal liability protections. Nevertheless,
antiunion sentiments, like racial inequities, continue to resonate throughout
Arkansas culture and politics. Events and exhibits held across the state to
commemorate the hundredth anniversary of the Massacre varied in format,
scope, and emphasis, from art installations to daylong symposia. However, all
grappled with connections of the events of the Massacre to current cultural
and political realities.

The University of Arkansas, Fayetteville's Special Collections Department,
home to the archival papers of key figures in the conflict like Arkansas Governor Charles Hillman Brough and Prosecutor John Elvis Miller—but not
of any of the victims or their families—opted for a fairly traditional route.
It presented the historical background, including PFHUA organizing ef-

forts, the event itself, the judicial proceedings, initial portrayals of the event, and, finally, the modern-day impacts and ongoing inquiry—in an attempt to provide sufficient but not overwhelming context for a broad audience, most of whom would encounter the exhibit only in passing, rather than as a destination. This chapter explores some of the considerations and challenges involved in interpreting a complex event of this kind, particularly within a resource-constrained exhibit program.

Exhibit Creation

Exhibits are designed with an audience in mind. For the University of Arkansas Special Collections, our desired audience is as universal as our constituency. However, we do acknowledge that the people most likely to view our physical exhibits are those who might regularly walk by our physical exhibit spaces—University of Arkansas students, faculty, staff, and other Special Collections researchers. Due to spatial limitations, we typically do not mount exhibits that are a destination draw for tourists. The Elaine exhibit, for instance, occupied two three-shelf exhibit cases that take up approximately 105 square feet of space in a wide hallway near the main Special Collections reading room. Other Special Collections exhibit spaces include two cases at the entry to the Special Collections reading room, two flat cases in the Special Collections reading room itself, and a vitrine in the middle of the Library's main level. There is nothing in the architecture and furnishings of the library, the landscape of the campus, or even the cultural and physical geography of Fayetteville, to evoke the cotton fields of the Arkansas Delta where Elaine lies, more than 300 miles away, and so our exhibit did not leverage the sense of place, and the grounding in community, described by other contributors to this volume; in this context, the artifacts and exhibit text had to stand alone, or even in tension with their surroundings.

For a typical Special Collections department, exhibits serve not only an educational (and occasionally entertainment) purpose but also a self-promotional one; they are a way for us to let people know what kinds of materials we hold, in the hopes that viewers will later return to do further research and exploration. This approach is particularly true for an exhibit like this one, which highlighted a topic of ongoing historical inquiry and considerable contemporary relevance. The Elaine story is not fully tellable in two exhibit cases. Nor is it one that can be disseminated wholly through archival records. Recognizing that the condensation of extraordinarily complex and contested historical events into broad narratives and short placards cannot do justice to a topic, captions offer citations to source collections, scholarly works, and other fuller resources both in our Special Collections and elsewhere.

In the University of Arkansas Special Collections' exhibit, labor was afforded one shelf out of six. Curatorial considerations surrounding this decision included: is space allotted sufficient to enable an in-depth exploration? (in this case, no); is it proportionate to the importance of the sub-topic within the larger context of the Massacre? (arguably); and does it introduce the topic and include external references sufficiently so that interested viewers can easily seek additional information elsewhere (hopefully)?

In the exhibit, a document that invites men and women to "[j]oin the Progressive Farmers and Household Union of America" notes that "[t]his Union wants to know why it is that laborers cannot control their just earnings which they work for"[1]; the document is drawn from the Charles Hillman Brough Papers, so that the very instrument of labor organization is, due to the traditional archival principle of provenance, arranged and described under the umbrella of a collection whose creator was in a position of power over them. Yet inclusion in an exhibit, drawing records from different sources, can offer recontextualization. Near the promotional flier, a photograph of Phillips County cotton fields illustrates the landscape where many of the Massacre's victims worked.[2] Several pages from a 1976 oral history interview of prosecutor John Elvis Miller include Miller's reflections on sharecroppers and their organizing efforts in Phillips County.[3] Photographs by University of Arkansas professor of rural sociology Dr. Jesse Charlton document examples of tenant farmers' cabins in Phillips County.[4] An exhibit placard references the PFHUA's origins and sharecropper's attempts to gain legal representation and briefly explains to exhibit viewers why these were potentially dangerous steps, with no guarantee of positive results. The exhibit text does not venture into the details of how the PFHUA diverged from a traditional union, merging labor organization and advocacy components with elements of fraternal organizations; nor does it delve into the segregated nature of many traditional unions at the time and prejudices in some industries against African Americans as strikebreakers.[5] Building a complete frame of reference for viewers who have lived only in a post–National Labor Relations Act world in the space a single shelf is not possible, so our focus was on providing essential context. Had the scope of the exhibit been more focused on labor history, we could have drawn from collections like the papers of Southern Tenant Farmers Union organizer Henry Clay East, or the records of the labor education–oriented Commonwealth College, which offer rich potential for future exhibits and programming. For future exhibits, some limitations of physical space may be ameliorated by more investment in supplementary digital resources.

With Viewers in Mind: What Did They See?

An ideal exhibit viewer is open to new information and has the time to read and interpret the exhibit critically. However, because the Elaine exhibit cases were situated in a hallway that serves as a public thoroughfare for the Library, we could not expect that most viewers would read the exhibit either in its entirety or in a linear order. Therefore, it was essential to make sure that the top-level exhibit text for each section included all the main points considered important for viewer understanding, rather than depending on item-level labels for crucial context. For the Elaine exhibit, it was reasonable to assume that many viewers would have minimal firsthand knowledge and experience of unions. Arkansas has been a right-to-work state since the legislature passed one of the nation's first right-to-work laws in 1944. According to the 2018 Bureau of Labor Statistics report, 4.8 percent of employed Arkansans were union members (down from 5.1 percent the year before)—not the lowest in the nation, but certainly in the lower tier.[6] Given the low union density and historically antiunion culture of the state, the exhibit needed additional context about why Phillips sharecroppers might form a union and about the dangers that process entailed for them.

Key to that context was the core rationale for the sharecroppers to create a union—exploitative and inequitable labor practices. While cotton prices in the United States had risen around 400 percent throughout World War I and its immediate aftermath, proportionate profits rarely were passed on to the predominately African American sharecroppers who worked the land of the Arkansas Delta. How white planters oppressed their tenants ranged from exploitative to outright illegal. In 1919, a group of Phillips County sharecroppers visited Little Rock attorney Ulysses S. Bratton, bringing to him claims of cheating, corruption, usury, and debt peonage, through which a planter's acknowledged "profits" would never exceed the sharecropper's expenses, and sharecroppers could be held hostage to the land they worked until their alleged debts got repaid. Bratton agreed to represent the share-croppers. "Never was a bigger fraud perpetrated on any set of people than was perpetrated on those sharecroppers," acknowledged prosecutor John Elvis Miller, decades later.[7]

The legal system offered little hope of redress for many sharecroppers, who saw unionization as another way to band together in advocating for their rights and rightful recompense for their labor. The reaction to worker attempts to unionize was often violent in the early twentieth century, with particularly significant risks for African Americans, who frequently suffered from beatings, whippings, and lynchings. In 1918, organizers Robert L. Hill and V. E. Powell founded the Progressive Farmers and Household Union of America (PFHUA) in Winchester, Arkansas, and began encouraging black sharecroppers around the region to form their own chapters. One of those chapters was the Hoop Spur Lodge in rural Phillips County—about three miles north of the town of Elaine. A shooting that occurred during a meeting of the Hoop Spur lodge left two white men dead and sparked days of violence during which hundreds of African Americans are believed to have been killed by law enforcement, vigilante posses, and federal troops. In the aftermath of the killings, prominent state politicians and newspapers laid the blame for the violence at the feet of African Americans, union members, and Robert L. Hill in particular. This is not because they were at fault (a recent historical study of the event has dismissed the idea of the Massacre as a planned uprising), but because they made convenient scapegoats.[8] The idea of black unionists as inciters of violence fit a prevailing narrative among white citizens at the time, dovetailing both with existing systemic racism and with the ongoing Red Scare, which often conflated union membership with radical communism, even in cases where no such ties existed.[9]

Inserted into the Congressional Record by Arkansas' Senator Thaddeus Caraway is the lie that the Massacre was a planned violent uprising, a lie allegedly substantiated by a *New York World* article by journalist Clair Kenamore, who was not present at the time of the Massacre. Sadly, one did not need to look so far afield for such a narrative; Arkansas' statewide newspapers also endorsed the "planned uprising" frame.[10] One hundred years later, a U. S. House resolution commemorating the Massacre corrected this narrative. The resolution said in part, "[w]hereas the violence erupted when the unionization of sharecroppers was falsely portrayed as a Black insurrection against White landowners." That once-common narrative is, as it happens, the one most heavily represented in Special Collections' primary source records pertaining to the Massacre.[11]

Special Collections Go Public

Special Collections and archival repositories, more so than many museums and galleries, use exhibits as a way to highlight their holdings; loans of items from other institutions are often rare. In such cases, then, exhibits are constrained by the holdings of parent institutions. Our case was no different. The University of Arkansas Special Collections holds a wealth of primary source materials related to the Massacre, but with significant limitations. Heavily weighted toward white accounts of the event, those sources included the words of Charles Hillman Brough, the white Governor of Arkansas who called on the National Guard to quell what he believed to be an uprising; of John Elvis Miller, prosecutor during the initial Elaine trials; and E. M. Allen, the Helena businessman who served as spokesperson of the investigative Committee of Seven.

But, without somehow including the suppressed voices of its victims and accounts of the organizing efforts of laborers, the Elaine Massacre story is incomplete. The University of Arkansas Special Collections Department's recently developed curatorial guidelines notes that "[e]xhibits are not meant to be exhaustive," yet a diversity statement notes that "where possible curators will seek to create exhibits that highlight the full spectrum of human experience, and not limit content to the narratives of a single group. When that diversity is not possible, the curator(s) will include language explaining the limitations either of our collections or the topic that led them to select the particular group of items."[12] For the Elaine exhibit, the introductory text acknowledged the limitations of our holdings and noted that:

> [t]o counter these biased narratives, the exhibit includes accounts from black journalists and activists of the era, along with recent historical studies that can aid in the contextualization of the event. Those who may have family records of the Massacre are encouraged to reach out to an archival repository—whether the University of Arkansas Special Collections or elsewhere—to add these stories to the record.

The exhibit text invited viewers to consider how their family history might intersect with—and complement—the narrative presented in the exhibit. By encouraging visitor donations, an exhibit may serve not only as an educational and outreach tool but also potentially a collection development opportunity—a way for us to fill in collecting gaps and offer valuable additional perspectives.

Our exhibit to commemorate the Massacre took a relatively typical Special Collections/archives approach toward a topic, in that it was based on academic historical research and driven by our collection holdings. Descriptive context in the form of exhibit labels accompanied primary and secondary source documents, arranged thematically. Other cultural heritage institutions around the state took different approaches, reaching additional audiences, and introducing new perspectives. In a local collaboration that allowed us to share our exhibit more widely, a selection of items from Special Collections' exhibit were displayed as a pop-up exhibit at a symposium on

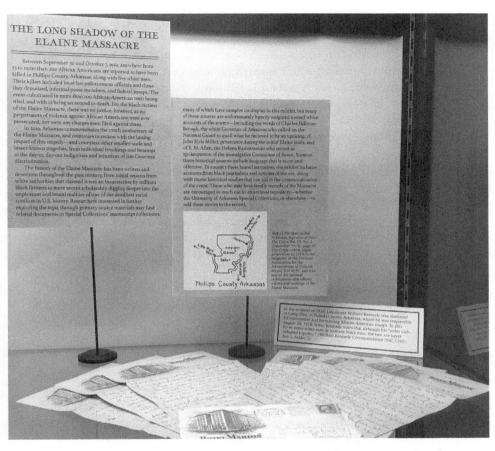

FIGURE 6.1. Introductory section of "The Long Shadow of the Elaine Massacre" exhibit on display at the University of Arkansas Special Collections, June 2019. Photo by Katrina Windon.

the Massacre hosted at the David and Barbara Pryor Center for Arkansas Oral and Visual History in Fayetteville. This symposium, which featured both researchers and community members, including relatives of some of the Massacre's victims, brought the exhibit materials into a broader community conversation and context. The website for the Elaine Massacre Memorial, located in Helena–West Helena, offered a near-comprehensive listing of statewide events and exhibits.[13]

The University of Arkansas Little Rock's Center for Arkansas History and Culture developed a digital exhibit featuring essays by noted scholars of the Massacre.[14] With its focus on African American heritage, the Mosaic

Templars Cultural Center hosted "Hateful Things," a traveling exhibit created by the Jim Crow Museum that chronicles racially stereotypical objects and imagery of African Americans throughout history and the present. The Center hosted the exhibit with the explicit intent that it was part of their efforts to commemorate the Massacre, even though the exhibit was in no way specific to Elaine or even to Arkansas. This programming approach can be particularly useful for contextualizing an event within a broader historical context; the Elaine Massacre is part of a broader, insidious tradition of lynching, racial violence, propaganda, and labor suppression, and examples of those themes in history can be found far beyond Arkansas' borders. Center Director, Christina Shutt, noted, "We chose to host this exhibit because we want to help people understand how these types of depictions create a culture of fear and hatred that has led to tragedies like the Elaine Massacre."[15]

Letting Go

For an archivist, attuned by training to issues of context and provenance, there is something uncomfortable about the very nature of an exhibit, which draws archival records out of their contexts to create a new narrative. Ideally, however, an exhibit sparks engagement, builds broader awareness, and reaches new constituencies, people who would not otherwise have encountered records or the stories those records tell. The victims of the Elaine Massacre—those killed and those prosecuted unjustly—were the driving force of Special Collections' exhibit, and their anonymous stories are both tragic and inspiring. That anonymity, however—and the fact that even the count of victims is unknown—makes telling their stories even more challenging. The Elaine Massacre's victims were not all union members; those killed included members across the spectrum of Phillips County's African American populace, as well as visitors, like the Johnston Brothers, two of whom were a doctor and a dentist—prosperous members of the middle class who presented a perceived threat to white dominance in other ways. Posse member H. F. Smiddy testified that posse members "shot and killed men, women, and children without regard to whether they were guilty or innocent of any connection with the killing of anybody, or whether members of the union or not."[16]

A document from the Negro Business League advertising the PFHUA noted, "[t]his Union wants to know why it is that the laborers cannot control their just earnings which they work for," and cites Biblical scripture in building to the question, "Why should we be cut off from fair play?"[17] A key part of giving fair play to the Elaine Massacre is acknowledging the organizing efforts, agency, and legacy of those Phillips County laborers, who saw their union die out, its leader, Hill, flee to Kansas, and its legacy continued by organizations like the Southern Tenant Farmers Union years later. Just as the Colored Farmers' Alliance had come before them, an ongoing struggle for fair play and equal justice unfolded.

How successful were we in meeting our exhibit goals? These included: educating students and the community about the violent suppression of African Americans and various labor organizing efforts in Arkansas, and the ongoing impact of that history in the present; encouraging viewers to consider how their family history might add to the historical record; sharing the work of contemporary scholars and community activists; and inspiring new avenues of research and inquiry into the Massacre and labor rights. Success—and impact—are difficult to determine. At the time of the exhibit, Special Collections did not have formal assessment procedures in place for its exhibit program, although developing such procedures is a future goal for the Department. When Special Collections staff introduced the exhibit to visiting classes and asked students what they knew of the Massacre, usually at least one student had some prior knowledge, although many did not. Those who grew up in Arkansas, taught from *An Arkansas History for Young People*, a commonly used textbook for seventh- and eighth-grade Arkansas History courses, would likely have read a few pages about the event if nothing else; out-of-state students—nearly half the student body—may never have heard of the event at all. Discussion of the exhibit was integrated into several instruction sessions held by Special Collections instructors, which allowed some students to have a more interactive experience than the average viewer. Direct viewer engagement and programming is something I wish we had been able to do more of, and that could help broaden the reach—and more challenge the viewers—of any similar exhibits we mount in the future. A physical exhibit, like a performance, or ephemeral art, has by nature a limited, time-bound impact in its original and fullest state, although documentation may remain. In this case, the documentary afterlife includes an entry in the Libraries' exhibit database, a copy of the exhibit text, and, perhaps most usefully, an item list that may be used or re-used by other Department members in reference or instruction. The University of Arkansas History Department offers two courses specific to U.S. labor history and integrates labor history into numerous other courses. The potential for collaborative teaching extends to other units such as the Department of Agricultural Economics and Agribusiness and the School of Business, as well, who may find in historic records of labor movements lessons highly relevant to current labor issues. Historians, activists, and family members have done, and continue to do, the work to bring to light the truth of the Elaine Massacre, and of other instances of racial violence, labor suppression, and intolerance in our communities. Our exhibit and outreach was a small step in highlighting the through line between the historical record and the ongoing truth and reconciliation work of the present; some of those researchers and advocates may themselves donate their records to an archive and continue the story.

Notes

1. "Orders of Washington, D. C. The Great Torch of Liberty Examination Certificate," 1919. Charles Hillman Brough Papers (MS B79), Box 18, Folder 3. University of Arkansas Special Collections Department.

2. Photograph of Cotton fields in Phillips County, Arkansas, undated. Samuel C. Dellinger Papers (MC 204), Series 2, Subseries 8, Box 27, Folder 6. Special Collections, University of Arkansas Libraries, Fayetteville.

3. John Elvis Miller. 1976. Interview with Walter L. Brown, Bruce Parham, and Samuel A. Sizer, March 18. Transcript. John Elvis Miller Oral History Interview (MC 279), Box 1, Folder 1. Special Collections, University of Arkansas Libraries, Fayetteville.

4. Jesse Laurence Charlton Photographs (MC 545), Box 1, Group 2, Items 21 and 23. Special Collections, University of Arkansas Libraries, Fayetteville.

5. Labor historian Eric Arnesson explores the latter in his "Up from Exclusion: Black and White Workers, Race, and the State of Labor History" *Reviews in American History* 26.1 (March 1998), 146–167.

6. Bureau of Labor Statistics. "Union Members—2018." News release, January 18, 2019. https://www.bls.gov/news.release/pdf/union2.pdf.

7. John Elvis Miller. 1976. Interview with Walter L. Brown, Bruce Parham, and Samuel A. Sizer, March 18. Transcript. John Elvis Miller Oral History Interview (MC 279), Box 1, Folder 1. Special Collections, University of Arkansas Libraries, Fayetteville.

8. See, for example, Grif Stockley's *Blood in Their Eyes: The Elaine Race Massacres of 1919* (Fayetteville: University of Arkansas Press, 2001); Guy Lancaster, ed., *The Elaine Massacre and Arkansas: A Century of Atrocity and Resistance, 1819–1919* (Little Rock, AR: Butler Center Books, 2018); and Robert Whitaker's *On the Laps of Gods: The Red Summer of 1919 and the Struggle for Justice that Remade a Nation* (New York: Three Rivers Press, 2009).

9. Theodore Kornweibel Jr. *"Seeing Red": Federal Campaigns against Black Militancy, 1919–1925* (Bloomington: Indiana University Press, 1998).

10. *Congressional Record* 58 (November 19, 1919): 8818–8821.

11. U. S. Congress, House, *Commemorating the 100th anniversary of the Elaine massacre,* HR 150, 116th Congress, introduced in House on February 26, 2019. https://www.congress.gov/bill/116th-congress/house-resolution/150/text?r=69&s=1.

12. University of Arkansas Libraries Special Collections Department. "Special Collections Exhibits: Curatorial Guidelines." 2018.

13. "Resources." Elaine Massacre Memorial. 2019. https://www.elainemassacre memorial.org/resources.

14. "Elaine Race Massacre: Red Summer in Arkansas." Digital exhibit. University of Arkansas Little Rock Center for Arkansas History and Culture. 2019. https://ualrexhibits .org/elaine/.

15. Mosaic Templars Cultural Center. "Mosaic Templars Cultural Center will open "Hateful Things" exhibit Sept. 19. Blog post. 26 Aug. 2019. https://www.mosaictemplars center.com/blog/mosaic-templars-cultural-center-will-open-hateful-things-exhibit -sept-19.

16. *Frank Moore et al. v. State of Arkansas*, 254 U.S. 630. 1920. 113.

17. Negro Business League. "Join the Progressive Farmers and Household Union of America." circa 1919. Charles Hillman Brough Papers (MS B56), Box 18, Folder 13. Special Collections, University of Arkansas Libraries, Fayetteville.

CHAPTER 7

Corrective Collecting and Democratizing Documentation

Preserving, Interpreting, and Promoting Regional Workers' History at the Labor Archives of Washington

CONOR M. CASEY

> The collection of records, papers, and memoirs, as well as oral history, is biased towards the important and powerful people of the society, tending to ignore the impotent and obscure: we learn most about the rich, not the poor; the successful, not the failures; the old, not the young; the politically active, not the politically alienated; men, not women; white, not black; free people rather than prisoners; civilians rather than soldiers; officers rather than enlisted men.

> history is a living weapon in yr hand
> & you have imagined it, it is thus that you
> 'find out for yourself'
> history is the dream of what can be, it is
> the relation between things in a continuum
> of imagination
> —Diane Di Prima "Revolutionary Letter #75: Rant"

Introduction: Collecting and Preserving Regional Labor History

The Labor Archives of Washington (LAW) is community-centered and specializes in documenting the history of unions and working people in the Pacific Northwest.[1] A collaboration between the Harry Bridges Center for Labor Studies and the Libraries Special Collections at the University of Washington, Seattle, and founded in 2010, the LAW's collections, exhibits, and programs are heavily tied into its regional stakeholder communities.

A community of stakeholders founded the LAW to address a crisis in curation, preservation, and access. During the 2008 economic recession, departing Special Collections technical services staff were not replaced. Curation and processing of hundreds of labor-related collections in various states of preservation remained physically or intellectually unprocessed and inaccessible. To remedy the situation, scores of individuals and dozens of labor organizations, including the International Longshore and Warehouse Union (ILWU) and the Washington State Labor Council (WSLC), donated money to the Harry Bridges Center's campaign to establish the LAW. With input from an advisory committee, in 2010, the University of Washington Libraries hired a labor archivist to direct the LAW.[2]

The LAW looks to create relationships with community organizations and scholars from racial, ethnic, occupational, and other communities to ask for input about which collections to curate, promote, and prioritize for processing. The LAW also solicits and draws from community knowledge in the description and contextualization of collections. Creating such partnerships is an ongoing process and requires an institutional commitment before and after the donation of collections. This multivariate model draws much from community organizing, public history, and archival administration.

The LAW's programs strive to leverage the power of representation within regional historical interpretations as a strategy for creating more relevant and impactful programming to those audiences who comprise the bulk of the working class today. In interpretive work, the LAW seeks out the history of the same communities or emphasizes the similarity between immigrant workers' positionality, precarious workers, and others to trace common thematic threads within the narratives of regional labor history. This approach can emphasize continuity and implicitly or explicitly contrast the experiences of similar groups over time. In this chapter, how corrective collecting, democratizing documentation, and the politics of representation influence the LAW's work becomes apparent.[3]

Collaboration Work Works

The LAW's most important collaborative network is its Advisory Committee, composed of historians, academics, union leaders, librarians, and library administrators. Committee members help with fundraising and acquisition. Their efforts helped to secure hundreds of thousands of dollars. The chair or representative from the Harry Bridges Center advises the Labor Archives staff. The LAW staff report to a dean within the University of Washington Libraries. In 2015, the LAW obtained funding from the Washington legislature, which enabled an expansion of staff and services.[4] These origins, the structure, and funding influence every aspect of archives administration, including collecting and processing prerogatives, outreach and instruction initiatives, and programming.[5]

Collections reflect the strengths unions with a historic membership of mostly European American male workers in manufacturing, extractive, and transportation industries had in the region. While building upon those strengths, the Archives has purposefully expanded its efforts to reflect the diversity of working-class history in the Pacific Northwest. Hence, to construct a more representative regional history, a proactive and inclusive documentation strategy is needed. This approach now determines priorities for collecting, processing, and descriptive practices. The aim is to address representation gaps in occupational communities, racial and ethnic groups, women, LGBTQ+ workers, and other historically marginalized communities. Included in this focus are nonunion workers, the topic of work itself, social justice and civil rights, and under-documented communities such as women workers, women-led organizations, immigrants, workers of color, and LGBTQ+ workers in an intersectional and class-based view of labor history.

The LAW also administers a regional archival records survey of labor and related organizations in the Pacific Northwest to understand the preservation and management needs of donor organizations, trends in records creation, and risks to collections and to identify historical records of enduring value for donation. The LAW staff designed the survey to foster relationship-building between the staff and officers of an organization and the archives. A complimentary survey of archives, museums, libraries, and historical museums has surfaced labor-related collections throughout the region, most outside of "labor" repositories. This survey was conceived of in the tradition of regional records surveys going back to the New Deal and informed a growing sense of urgency in the wake of *Janus v. AFSCME* in 2018. This Supreme Court ruling, which found that workers public-sector unions need not pay dues, made the finances of many regional unions uncertain. Thus, one aspect of this survey is to assess the likelihood and imminence of office moves, mergers, and closed union locals in the aftermath of the ruling. That way, vital records might be preserved, not disposed of.

Corrective Collecting and
Democratizing Documentation

Central to the LAW's curatorial and outreach ethos is the idea that what gets collected, made accessible, and promoted matters. *Corrective collecting* and *democratizing documentation* are shorthand for intellectual frameworks that place stakeholder communities' stories and the geographic region at the center of core archival activities, interpretation, outreach, public programming, and exhibitions and exhibition design. This approach democratizes the documentation of regional and topical collections, making them more reflective of the full spectrum of workers in the region.

Corrective collecting is strongly related to an archives' collecting scope—in the LAW's case, the Pacific Northwest's labor history—and has strong ties to geographic and/or subject areas. This approach assesses place-based or topical collections and identifies gaps that may exist, particularly about historically marginalized communities whose stories are omitted from the collections due to bias, mistrust of external academic institutions, lack of resources to collect and maintain records, and lack of physical primary source materials. Thus, at the heart of the LAW's efforts is relationship building and the fostering of community. Often, archival programs, exhibitions, and documentation projects can be one-sided, led internally by the organization, and can take a transactional form. This often re-creates a colonial relationship with donor communities in which their histories are treated as a cultural asset, valid only when entered in an academic context and divorced from that community and context. In this model, the relationship ends once a repository curates a collection, except when donors make new donations or wish to access their collections. In contrast, the goal of the LAW's community-focused strategy is to create overlapping collecting, outreach, education, and access initiatives to build ongoing collaborations that will benefit all parties: the archives, the community of creators, and the community of researchers.

A central goal and a necessary aspect of this approach is creating sustained, programmatic relationships with community partners. Corrective collecting has much in common with the appraisal of collections. However, instead of assessing individual collections and objects in hand for such criteria as rarity and anticipated research value, a curator reviews their existing collections holistically as part of a broader documentation strategy. Soliciting community stakeholders' opinions is essential to identify omissions in the corpus of the overall archives. This approach rejects the proposition that archival neutrality is possible, and—as the name suggests, it aims to self-consciously "correct" omissions in the archival created by the biases or the assumed neutrality of the past.

This process democratizes documentation strategy by proactively seeking input from creator communities and stakeholders. The process involves a survey of existing collections and the knowledge of past scholarship that has employed them. Secondary sources are reviewed in a topical/geographic area to determine what is already written. As previously mentioned, there is an emphasis on consulting scholars and the community of creators to help find essential collections still in the community. Another way to find gaps in collections is by negative results to researcher reference inquiries. By working with researchers to formulate research questions and locate materials, curators learn what is missing from collections, reflect on why, and then engage in corrective collecting.

This strategy looks to create relationships with community organizations and scholars from racial, ethnic, occupational, and other communities to ask for input about which collections to curate, promote, and prioritize for processing. The LAW also solicits and draws from community knowledge in the description and contextualization of collections. Creating such partnerships is an ongoing process and requires an institutional commitment before and after the donation of collections. This multivariate model draws much from community organizing, public history, and archival administration.

Hence, corrective collecting. Social power and implicit bias influence the writing and framing of history and the creation of the archives that enable that history. This approach has determined priorities for curating, processing, and describing collections. The aim is to address collection gaps regarding occupational communities, racial and ethnic groups, women workers, LGBTQ+ workers, and other historically marginalized communities. This is done to emphasize the contributions that history in general and mainstream labor history too often relegate to sidebar narratives, if they are included at all. Corrective collecting intentionally remedies omissions, addresses representation gaps, heightens the visibility of neglected stories, and enables the writing of more inclusive regional and topical histories.

Another consideration in designing exhibits, outreach programs, collection, and publicity is the politics of representation. By emphasizing the stories of women workers, workers of color, intersectional organizing, and civil rights unionism, the LAW looks to help the region's workers "see themselves" in the collections. The U.S. labor movement has been dwindling in numbers over the past generation. However, recently, Robert Forrant and Mary Anne Trasciatti note in the introduction to this book, support for unions among younger workers is growing. The LAW seeks to frame these narratives to include considerations of race, ethnicity, immigrant communities, and inter-sectional organizing as part of a strategy to make collections and program-ming relevant to audiences beyond dyed-in-the-wool labor unionists and labor historians. The labor movement and the U.S. workforce have changed much in the past forty years, with more organized labor belonging to public sector and service sector unions. The membership of these unions tends to have a higher density of workers of color, first-generation immigrants, and women—and certainly, more leaders drawn from these groups—than is reflected in perennial mainstream labor narratives.

Scope of Collections: A Work in Progress

At present, the Archives maintains more than 300 collections document-ing the local, national, and international dimensions of the labor movement. The majority of records cover the twentieth century. The primary geographic scope is the Pacific Northwest: Washington, Oregon, Alaska, and western Canada. Smaller collections relating to other U.S. states, the Philippines, Australia, and countries in Central and South America are also present. Labor-related holdings encompass logging, woodworking, mining, maritime work, and fishing. Collections about public-sector workers such as teachers, custodians, nurses, and state employees are growing. The archives house photographs, cartoons, banners, posters, prints, handbills, picket signs, fine art prints, and buttons.

Materials cover the Industrial Workers of the World, the Inlandboatmen's Union of the Pacific, the Cannery Workers and Farm Laborers Union, the United Farm Workers of Washington State, the United Food and Commercial Workers, the American Federation of Teachers, Washington Federation of State Employees, and nurses' unions. Personal papers documenting the lives of individual workers, labor leaders, attorneys, arbitrators, and labor-rights supporters are a collection strength. Some holdings focus on women work-ers and activists in "nontraditional" employment in their advocacy for equal rights and equal pay, and in female-led AFL-CIO constituency organizations such as the Coalition of Labor Union Women and Washington Women in Trades. The LAW collects materials from groups that have supported labor and civil rights, including African American workers. Other records relate to civil rights labor organizing as embodied in the Alaska Cannery Workers Association. Members of the Northwest Labor Employment and Law Office, these organizations pursued civil rights legal cases against employers and unions that discriminated in employment and access to membership and apprenticeships.[6]

Some of the region's most impactful organizing initiatives centered on nonunion workers, unions in coalition with community groups, and union members leading strikes and organizing efforts not endorsed by their leaders. Asking community members and advisory board members about events important to them, reviewing the historiography on these topical areas, and continually referring to an equity, inclusion, and diversity framework in collection development, the LAW identified events, organizations, and individuals not present in existing collections to be fast-tracked for collection, processing, description, and digitization.

Documentation projects have also employed corrective collecting to include the stories of rank-and-file workers and workers of color. For example, in 2015, the SeaTac-Seattle Minimum Wage Project focused on creating a web archive of over 60 oral histories, websites, and ephemera relating to organizing efforts by airport workers, comprised mainly of immigrants and people of color. In 2016, the LAW collected and described records from the United Farm Workers of Washington State, the Rosalinda Guillen papers, CASA Latina, Familias Unidas por la Justicia, and the Washington State Fair Trade Coalition oral history project as part of an initiative to curate collections relating to the Latinx community. In 2020, during the COVID-19 pandemic, the LAW launched the Working in the Time of COVID-19 Documentation Project to collect the stories of workers and document community responses to the pandemic—especially among essential workers. One aspect of the project will be oral histories with workers in health care, transit, retail, grocery, education, and gig-based occupations. Another part will preserve websites and social media long term, and another will proactively contact donor organizations for collections that can be curated when the pandemic subsides.

Recently added records sought to address omissions in the collections from Washington Women in the Trades and other tradeswomen activists documenting a protracted discrimination fight at Seattle City Light.[7] AFL-CIO constituency organizations such as the Seattle chapters of the Asian Pacific Labor Alliance and the A. Philip Randolph Institute, representing Asian American and Pacific Islander and black trade unionists, respectively, were curated to address collection gaps.

Since 2013, the LAW has partnered with community organizations on oral history projects. These include the Seattle Labor Chorus, the Puget Sound Advocates for Retirement Action, the ILWU's Pacific Coast Pensioners Association, and SEIU 1199 NW Healthcare to ensure their stories became part of the preserved record. Activities to enhance description and access have emphasized legacy collections from women, women-led organizations, and workers of color. Descriptive projects opened access to restricted boxes of the Tyree Scott papers. Scott's collection included organizational records of the United Construction Workers Association (UCWA), Northwest Labor and Employment and Law Office (LELO), and the personal papers of the African American tradeswomen activist, electrician, and cofounder of the UCWA and LELO, Beverly Sims. The LAW staff created a separate Sims collection, increasing visibility, and access.

The LAW created a distinct collection from the papers of Rosa Eyer. Earlier processing had subsumed Eyer's papers into those of her husband, though she donated both collections. To remedy this instance of archival coverture, the LAW made her papers more visible and consistent with the creator-based method by which archivists name collections. After intensive work, every labor collection has an online finding aid.[8] Intellectual accessibility is another area of consideration. Bilingual finding aids were prepared for collections with significant materials in Spanish, including for farmworker activists Rosalinda Guillén and Joseph Moore. The LAW has created bilingual finding aids for dayworker center CASA Latina's records and farmworker union Familias Unidas por la Justicia's records. Oral histories with primarily Spanish-speaking Latinx migratory workers, originally performed in Spanish as part of the Washington Fair Trade Coalitions, have been transcribed into Spanish and translated into English. Similarly, the LAW translated an online exhibit on Carlos Bulosan into Tagalog, the Philippines' national language.[9]

Outreach

Connecting with stakeholder communities on and off campus is a central goal of the LAW's outreach efforts. Outreach centers the stories of working people and their organizations—especially those of historically marginalized communities—and promotes awareness and use of collections. This approach requires a steadfast commitment by the archives to re-center the stories of workers and labor history into perennial narratives of regional history in its interpretive work, which often omit or downplay the stories of working people or cast them as "bit parts" in larger narratives. Here, too, the connections to regional historical narratives are clear; over time, this has created more worker-centered local history narratives. In a region dominated by corporations like Amazon, Microsoft, and Boeing, public history narratives often focus on business and technology. Collecting and telling the stories of workers as historic agents who transformed the area by their labor and activism is crucial to a fuller understanding of the Pacific Northwest's history and culture.[10]

Collaborative Programs and Events

The LAW understands the importance of planning programs within a broader context to draw more visitors to history-related events, build relationships with communities, and get feedback and input on outreach activities. While stand-alone efforts generate interest and visitors, scheduling in conjunction with conferences and commemorations and in close coordination with community partners almost always yields a larger audience and more impactful engagement with its collections. Coordinating with community stakeholders can also help those communities in terms of complementing their events and programs. When promoting events or programs, the LAW often seeks out community members to form a planning committee and ask for input about the needs and desires of the intended audiences. The goal of this collaborative approach to program design is to make programming relevant, correct, and more inclusive. In designing programs and events, the LAW looks to constrain its staff's role in talking about collections and inviting collections donors, scholars, and community members to be prominent speakers at events. Another consideration of inclusive programming is accessibility: the LAW often plans its programs to occur during nonworking hours, offsite in community venues, and when non-academic stakeholders are most available. At times, the LAW has even arranged to transport remote stakeholder communities to its events, as in the case of the farmworker history event, when a caravan of vans full of farmworker families made its way from Northern Washington to Seattle for an event relating their history.

This collaborative model has resulted in a more diverse audience for onsite exhibits, brought traveling exhibitions to community venues, and promoted online exhibits to an expanded public. In creating a larger enabling context for programs and exhibits, the LAW consciously links its collections to various audiences that might not otherwise visit an exhibit on a university campus. It is essential that the communities documented in collections can visit exhibits and have a hand in interpreting their histories as well. This approach creates new partners for the vital work of interpretation and draws on community knowledge and input to create projects valued by community stakeholders as well as the repository. Some key collaborations include the LAW staff's work as part of the planning committee of the Washington State Labor Council's annual monthlong celebration of worker culture and history, MayWorks.[11]

In 2015, the Archives launched an annual event to advocate for collecting, preserving, and donating labor history–related materials. In 2015, this event announced the launch of a documentation project focusing on the SeaTac and Seattle Minimum Wage campaigns.[12] The LAW undertook a responsive

FIGURE 7.1. Preserving Solidarity Forever. The Labor Archives' annual events communicate the desire to address known collection gaps and invite the labor, community, and other stakeholders onto campus to learn more about the LAW. Credit: Labor Archives of Washington.

collecting program to collect the stories of workers in a new era of labor organizing in a nationally significant organizing campaign that resulted in a qualified victory. The project included recent immigrant communities and the history of union locals not previously documented in collections; it also reflected the inventive coalition-building between nonprofits, unions, politicians, community activists, and small business owners. The project enhanced documentation relating to new organizing strategies within the regional labor movement. The buy-in of the stakeholder organizations garnered at the event resulted in the creation of rich web archives and oral history projects.

The second annual event was a strategic collaboration with another community of workers that lacked significant representation in the LAW's collections: migrant farmworkers whose members primarily come from Latinx and indigenous communities in México and Central America. The event itself focused on farmworker history and highlighted the collections of Rosalinda Guillén and Joseph Moore. They and a committee of workers co-organized with the United Farm Workers to win the first contract for Washington farmworkers. Featured speakers from more recent campaigns, Familias Unidas por la Justicia, discussed the organizing that resulted in the second-ever farmworker contract in Washington. Several farmworker-related collections were donated as a result.

At times, the LAW has taken an organizing role in creating a favorable environment for its programs and make related events more impactful for a network of related stakeholder organizations. In 2017–2018, the LAW organized a "Solidarity Centennial Committee" to coordinate a yearlong, statewide series of events commemorating the anniversaries of the 1919 Seattle General Strike, the 1919 Centralia Tragedy and the 1999 World Trade Organization (WTO) protests.[13] The committee organized readings, a musical performance employing primary sources, book launches, a labor history bus tour, two film screenings, and several other events to interpret these important stories. By promoting its onsite exhibit as part of an umbrella series of events, the LAW increased attendance at the onsite exhibit and brought a traveling version to the events themselves. Across 2019, this exhibit traveled to events, conferences, and conventions as far as Washington, D.C., and Maine. In 2020, the LAW's annual event celebrated the launch of its Working in the Time of COVID-19 Oral History project, focusing on the impacts of the pandemic on frontline workers and detailing the early results of the oral history project.

Media Outreach

To reach audiences of new potential users, the LAW has relied heavily on a robust outreach program that includes harnessing the power of new and social media as well as traditional media. Popular public history education took place via traditional and new media, while at the same time promoting exhibits, programs, collecting, and fundraising.

Programmatic commitments are an essential part of a social media strategy aimed at attracting new users and retaining existing users. Since its start, the LAW employed Facebook and Twitter, and in 2016 the LAW staff developed a more formal social media outreach strategy via Facebook, Twitter, and Instagram. Weekly posts feature items from collections, foregrounding women and people of color and commemorating significant events in regional labor history. This programmatic approach has significantly increased active engagement. The same community-centered and representation-informed approach informs the LAW's publicity strategy. When possible, the LAW staff speak about the contents of collections and the need to address representation gaps but have community voices and scholars interpret and recount that history.

For example, recurring radio segments describe how to use primary and secondary sources in storytelling, with the idea to inspire listeners to research those topics themselves. Shows featured researchers who had used collections, event participants, and members of the communities discussed. In looking to foreground the voices of historically marginalized communities, the approach mirrored the LAW's overall corrective collecting and collaborative outreach strategies, guided by the politics of representation. As part of this segment's design, the LAW sought out collection donors, community members familiar with the history, or scholars and invited them to "share the spotlight" by commenting on the collections and sharing their stories. The LAW employs this model to decenter the role of the repository and staff in describing the histories of communities it seeks to serve, emphasizing its role as records stewards, not the stories themselves. This is a strong consideration for collections documenting communities of color, as the LAW permanent staff, to date, have been of European American ancestry.

Local television is another channel for promoting the LAW's activities and collections. Since 2015, the Seattle Channel, a local public affairs station, has broadcast the LAW's annual events. Episodes stream online after that. Similarly, the LAW's collections were featured as part of a series on University of Washington's television news magazine, which aired on local television and streamed online. The segment foregrounded the stories of researchers and collection donors. Topics included the history of Filipinx-American cannery worker activism, the history of Latinx voter suppression in Washington, women in "non-traditional" maritime occupations, the SeaTac Seattle Minimum wage campaign, and the commemoration of the Everett Massacre. One episode featured the work of muralist Pablo O'Higgins and a researcher who had uncovered O'Higgins' links to Chicano student activism at the University of Washington.

Exhibit Programming

The LAW's exhibition program aims to highlight the way repository collections contribute to the cultural and intellectual life of the University of Washington and the community, enhance scholarship, and promote historical understanding. The exhibit program aims to elevate the stories of working people and their organizations, especially those from historically marginalized communities. It also connects labor and labor-related topics to significant events in regional history. The LAW's exhibits foreground worker-centered narratives as essential to a full understanding of the Pacific Northwest's history and culture. This is critical, because the dominant local history narratives focus on business, technology, and social elites as the significant historical agents in the region. Most funders and donors of cultural institutions in the Seattle area tend to have gained their resources from successful technology and industry roles or are foundations primarily funded by those sectors. These sources have conscious and unconscious impacts on the framing of local history. Far too often this marginalizes the experiences of workers and their organizations. Instead, the Archives encompasses all working people, whether union members or not, to reflect the full diversity of the Pacific Northwest's history.

A 2011 exhibit complemented a symposium the University hosted on Cesar Chavez. It centered on the role of U.W. student activists in the Farmworkers' Movement. It became clear in the exhibit design process that U.W. Special Collections and the LAW contained pronounced gaps in information about farmworkers or Latinx populations, so much so that the LAW borrowed materials from community members. Once that documentation gap was known, the LAW prioritized the acquisition of new records, partnerships with community groups, and the topical focus of programming relating to Latinx and farmworker communities.[14]

The LAW collaborated on a 2012 exhibit with other Library units using the Occupy Movement framework to showcase a continuum of regional activism to coincide with a campus conference on the topic.[15] That same year, the LAW created an exhibit on labor and civil rights printmaker Richard Correll's work. An onsite version ran for two years, while a surrogate version was part of a festival in Seattle Center. The LAW displayed the exhibit at the 2013 Northwest Folklife Festival and a traveling version of the exhibit at numerous labor conventions and conferences. An online version of the exhibit appeared in

FIGURE 7.2. Traveling Exhibit Installation. Traveling exhibits are part of the LAW's strategy for heightening collection visibility and extending the life of short-term onsite exhibits indefinitely. Such efforts expand the geographic reach for exhibits, allowing for them to circulate more widely within stakeholder communities. Photograph credit: Conor Casey.

2017.[16] The LAW produced its first online exhibit in 2013, using its Industrial Workers of the World Photograph Collection. This was critically important in heightening collection visibility to the labor movement and those not part of the University of Washington community. University-based exhibits tend to be restrictive in terms of access and availability. Open only during regular business hours, public access to exhibition spaces and collections is limited. The LAW digitized its entire Industrial Workers of the World photograph collection for this exhibit.[17]

As noted, emphasizing the role of workers of color and immigrants is still an essential part of the LAW's exhibit curation strategy. So, too, is the goal of making the connections to the labor movement and a working-class identity of figures often renowned for other accomplishments. Such was the case for "Author, Poet, and Worker: The World of Carlos Bulosan," in 2014. The exhibit centered on Bulosan's life and work as a Filipinx American writer and a chronicler of the Filipinx American experience from the 1930s through the early 1950s. It examined Bulosan's overlapping identities as an artist, farmworker, labor organizer, and culture worker to underscore his relationship to a broader community of Filipinx American labor activism. The scope included his large circle of friends, including radical activists and authors, and members of the cannery workers local ILWU, Region 37. This interpretive framework allowed the LAW to examine the labor activism of Filipinx workers as a key component of community history and as part of the more extensive history of the region's Asian Americans. The exhibit, part of a collaboration with the Carlos Bulosan Centennial Committee, a citywide series of events celebrating his life, linked to a U.W. conference. An online version of the exhibit appeared in 2015.[18]

The LAW curated onsite displays for the Washington State Labor Council on its history and initiated a collaborative exhibit program with the South Seattle College Labor Education and Research Center (LERC) to highlight the LAW collections in LERC's exhibit space. This offered an opportunity to bring the collections to a broader group of people since LERC provides direct trainings to labor unions and its exhibit space adjoins several apprenticeship programs. Past exhibits in this program include a history of the Society of Professional Engineering Employees in Aerospace's strike against Boeing in 2000; the history of apprenticeship programs; and a display that emphasized progressive, intersectional regional labor history.[19]

The LAW's "'An Injury to One is an Injury to All': The Legacy of the 1916 Everett Massacre and the Industrial Workers of the World in the Pacific Northwest" exhibit marked the centennial of the 1916 Everett Massacre.[20] The exhibit employed surrogates of photographs and documents, ensuring that the originals were preserved and secure. As with the Richard Correll exhibit, this enabled the LAW to bring the traveling exhibit to external community venues. It highlighted the history of the IWW in the Pacific Northwest and the events surrounding the Massacre. Portions of the exhibit appeared at the 2016 Pacific Northwest Labor History Association Conference; at an Everett Massacre Commemoration Centennial Boat Tour; and at conferences, labor council conventions, class sessions, and labor history mural dedications.[21]

The LAW curated a pop-up exhibit on "Women at Work: Highlights from Labor Archives of Washington Collections on Women in the Trades" as part of a local history event in 2017. A traveling version of "Women at Work" appeared at various labor history conferences and community events. In 2018, the exhibit was a central part of the LAW's fourth annual event focused on women in the trades. In 2019, the LAW curated the onsite and traveling exhibit, "Solidarity Centennial: The Legacy of the Seattle General Strike Era and the Centralia Tragedy of 1919," commemorating the Seattle General Strike. The exhibits used primary sources from the collections of the Labor

Archives and University of Washington's Special Collections to tell the story. Here, again, the LAW approach broadened the strike narrative, which too often centered only on participating union members. By so doing, it ignored the broad community support needed to accomplish a successful strike. That support included female or child members of union households who were neither engaged in wage labor or members of unions but who nonetheless contributed to the strike's success.

While communities of color often got turned away from American Federation of Labor unions in this era, they nonetheless experienced or took part in the general strike. One example here is the Seattle-based Japanese American Labor Association, which played a key role in the strike. By including this story, the interpretive framework elevated new voices as agents in the event. While the exhibit maintained the perspective of the Seattle Labor Council and its 110 local union affiliates as a central narrative, it presented the labor community as heterogeneous. It examined the spectrum of political opinions within the ranks of organized labor during that era. The exhibit placed the strike within the context of Seattle's transformation from regional backwater to world port. The LAW displayed the traveling exhibit at various community venues and conferences throughout 2019. An online version of the exhibit and an exhibit catalog will launch in early 2020.[22]

Conclusions and Reflections

Building upon collection strengths, the LAW expanded its core collections to emphasize the diversity of working-class history in the Pacific Northwest. This inclusive vision encompasses all workers, the topic of work itself, social justice, and civil rights, and it centers historically marginalized communities—especially workers of color—in a consciously intersectional and class-based framework. This has influenced archival activities that include an interpretive aspect such as collection description, outreach, public programming, and exhibition design. Historians are well aware of the roles bias and social power play in the writing of history. A sometimes neglected aspect of this discourse is the role of power and social norms in influencing the curation and processing of archival collections from which these histories are drawn. As we contemplate constructing more inclusive and diverse histories and push back against so-called archival neutrality, curators must proactively *construct* archives, not as passive receivers of records but as active collaborators with communities of creators, scholars, and potential users. As well, the LAW's work is heavily tied into the production of regional history narratives and is dependent upon collaboration with that region's community of stakeholders for almost every aspect of its activities, firmly situating it within the project of the historical production of narratives relating to the Pacific Northwest.

Notes

1. Diane Di Prima. 1969. *Revolutionary letters: [poems].* (London: Long Hair Books, 1969).

2. The Harry Bridges Center for Labor Studies, founded in 1992, memorializes and honors longtime International Longshore and Warehouse president Alfred Renton 'Harry' Bridges. Hundreds of ILWU members, local unions, and other labor organizations and supporters collectively donated millions of dollars to create an endowed Harry Bridges Chair for Labor Studies, with the Bridges Center supporting the chairholder's activities. The Center supports students and faculty in the study of labor and has strong connections in the labor community. The Center's faculty chair rotates every two to four years. Staffed by an associate director and a coordinator, it is located jointly in the departments of Political Science and History at the UW Seattle, working with students and faculty in departments and schools across all three UW campuses.

3. See Bill Adair, Benjamin Filene, and Laura Koloski, eds. *Letting Go? Sharing Historical Authority in a User Generated World* (London: Routledge, 2011), esp. Steve Zeitlin, "Where Are the Best Stories?" "Where Is My Story," "Curation in a New Media Age," and Deborah -Schwartz and Bill Adair, "Community as Curator: A Case Study at the Brooklyn Historical Society"; Michael Frisch, *A Shared Authority: Essays on the Craft and Meaning of Oral and Public History* (Albany: State University of New York Press, 1990), esp. ch. 4, "Oral History and the Presentation of Class Consciousness: The *New York Times* v. The Buffalo Unemployed,"; and, Cinnamon Catlin-Legutko's TedX Talk on issues associated with what she terms "decolonizing collections." Director of the Illinois State Museum, she previously directed the Abbe Museum in Bar Harbor, Maine. A leader in the museum field on the subject of diversity and inclusion, she worked to correct the ways museums in Maine depict native peoples. Her thinking can be applied to how archives collect and make available material related to labor and working-class history. https://amara.org/en/videos/aagIp19Jlklh/info/we-must-decolonize-our-museums-cinnamon-catlin-legutko-tedxdirigo/.

4. The fund-raising campaign raised over $765,000 to date. Conor M. Casey, "Community Connections: Inreach and Outreach as Archival Advocacy Activities: A Case Study of the Labor Archives of Washington, University of Washington Libraries Special Collections," Seattle Area Archivists, *Sound Archivist*, Fall 2016 Volume 3, No. 2, 8–12.

5. Casey, "Putting History to Work: The Labor Archives of Washington as a Model for Forging Stronger Connections between Labor and the Academy," *Labor*, 14 (2), 2017: 9–11; Casey, "Putting History to Work: The Labor Archives of Washington, University of Washington Libraries Special Collections," *Pacific Northwest Quarterly*

Volume 108, Number 1, Winter 2016/2017; James Gregory, "Advancing the Ivory-Collar/Blue-Collar Partnership," *Labor* 11 (3), 2014: 13–14.

6. A full listing of the LAW's collections is at http://guides.lib.uw.edu/research/laborarchives. Finding aids are now available on the regional database Archives West and in worldwide catalogs such as ArchiveGrid and WorldCat. To view the LAW's digital primary sources, photographs, and oral histories, among other resources, visit http://content.lib.washington.edu/portals/law.

7. Seattle City Light is a public utility power company serving the Seattle area.

8. Here, I distinguish between collection inventories, which list the contents of the collections at varying levels of description and finding aids, a broad term for the many formats of guides to collections that may or may not include inventories. Finding aid formats vary widely depending on the repository, processor, processing date, collection formats, processing funds, and expected research value of the collection. Deepening access to collections is vital to promote research in our collections, particularly from new audiences of users and scholars.

9. Staff will soon conduct and transcribe oral histories of farmworker activists in Spanish and then convert them to English. Some projects have centered on digitizing thousands of documents, photographs, and oral histories for a Labor Archives Digital Portal. Topics include the Seattle General Strike, the Industrial Workers of the World in the Pacific Northwest, Filipinx and Asian American Cannery Workers, the World Trade Organization protests, the Maritime Labor History of the Pacific Northwest, and the SeaTac/Seattle Minimum Wage History Project.

10. The LAW makes presentations to highlight the value of its collections, show people how to use them, and explain why donors should convey collections for preservation. Overviews for classes at the U.W. and other area colleges instruct students how to use collections. Staff attends conferences to share the value of the LAW's collections and the lessons learned from being stewards of a very active community archives program. The LAW often presents at local union and state labor council meetings and labor cultural events.

11. As of 2019, MayWorks in Washington State seemed to be on hiatus; the Solidarity Centennial substituted for MayWorks during that year.

12. Casey, "Preserving Solidarity Forever: The Minimum Wage History Project April 11," *Sound Archivist*, Seattle Area Archivists, Winter 2015.

13. The General Strike, a five-day general work stoppage in February by more than 65,000 workers, electrified the country. Thousands of workers in several unions touched off the strike to gain higher wages after two years of World War I wage controls, and employer and government recalcitrance to bargain sparked a larger regional sympathy strike led by the Seattle Labor Council. In Centralia, on November 11, 1919, a gun battle erupted during an Armistice Day parade of American Legionnaires, leaving four dead and resulting in the lynching of Wesley Everett, a member of the Industrial Workers of the World (IWW).

14. Casey and Mudrock, curators, "University of Washington Activists and the Farmworkers' Movement." April-June 2011. University of Washington Libraries Spe-

cial Collections. The LAW also takes care while trying to address these not to conflate these categories. For example, assuming all farmworkers identify as Latinx, or that all Latinx workers were farmworkers would be problematic.

15. Albano, Casey, Hartnett, Mudrock, and Pearson, curators, "Taking It to the Street: Protests, Strikes, and Activism in Washington State." April 2012. University of Washington Libraries Allen Library North Lobby.

16. Casey, curator, "Images of Labor and Social Justice."

17. Casey, ed., and Senteara Orwig, "Industrial Workers of the World Photograph Collection," August 2012. http://guides.lib.uw.edu/research/IWWPhotos.

18. Casey and Hedden curators, "Author, Poet, Worker: The World of Carlos Bulosan," University of Washington Libraries Special Collections, November 2014—March 2015.

19. Townsend, curator. "Past Forward: Snapshots from Social Justice Unionism." Labor Education and Research Center, South Seattle College, 2017; Townsend, "Past Forward: Labor Archives latest exhibit on display at the LERC!" University of Washington Libraries Special Collections. *Pacific Northwest Features* blog.

20. Three hundred IWW members faced off with the Everett sheriff and armed deputies at the Everett City dock. In the aftermath, at least five Wobblies lay dead, and two citizen deputies had been killed by "friendly fire" from their fellow deputies. Police arrested 74 IWW members.

21. Casey and Rodgers, curators. "An Injury to One Is an Injury to All: The Legacy of the 1916 Everett Massacre and the Industrial Workers of the World in the Pacific Northwest," University of Washington Libraries Allen Library, December 2016-January 2017.

22. Casey, Rodgers, and Robinson, curators, "Solidarity Centennial: The Legacy of the Seattle General Strike Era and the Centralia Tragedy of 1919," University of Washington Libraries Special Collections, February-June 2019. The exhibit was geared toward broader access in another way. It was the first time the LAW employed the Smithsonian's *Guidelines for Accessible Exhibition Design* (2013) to ensure it would be accessible to people of various physical and cognitive abilities.

PART II

Writing the History

The essays in Part II of this collection offer critical insights into the possibilities and limitations of public labor history initiatives. Not all of the essays are place-based in the strict sense of focusing on a still-standing structure of either formally or informally recognized historical significance. Labor's stories do not fit neatly within triumphalist national narratives of unity and consensus, progress and prosperity. In the U.S., where powerful interests go to great lengths to downplay the importance of class and deny the existence of class struggle, it is not unusual for requests for formal designation of labor sites to meet with resistance, often in the form of inaction. The first two essays in this section offer reflections on the potential of formal historic recognition to elevate the profile of a site and confer legitimacy on the people, organizations, and events with which it is associated. They consider how a more visible labor presence on the national landscape could help shift the narrative paradigm about working people in the U.S. and contribute to a more nuanced and expansive narrative that includes conflict as well as consensus, regress as well as progress.

Many National Parks and numerous designated historical sites are places where complex and unsettling history occurred. By recounting stories of the oppressed and the victimized, such places are commemoration sites that make it possible to engage in social justice education, civil discourse, and human rights advocacy.[1] Are such stories being told? The answer is yes, and no. Erik Loomis makes the point in his discussion of whether and how the National Park system considers labor history. "In recent years NPS historical interpretation has gone far to integrate histories from below, a stark departure from the officially sanctioned history in many European nations," he writes, "where imperial history remains dominant in public discourse and social movements receive little attention in signage, tours, or other hallmarks of public history." Nonetheless, labor history remains a rarely told story. Upon examining numerous NPS and other sites with significant labor stories, Loomis concludes that "Overall, our national commemoration and preservation of labor history sites is abysmal." For this to improve, Park Service historical workers, historical archeologists, and preservationists must move beyond too narrow efforts at excavation and protection, engaging instead in interpretive conversations with audiences. We hope this volume moves such work forward.[2]

In her essay on the Southern Tenant Farmers Museum, Rachel Donaldson begins with the claim that historical sites related to the labor movement confer legitimacy on class struggle as an inherent part of the American story. The designation of working-class history sites relating to the labor movement, she observes, "identifies places of struggle and radicalism as important sites in the national collective past, and therefore teaches public audiences that these forms of oppositional history have been intrinsic aspects of the American experience." Donaldson explores how this process operates in a regional context where labor organizing has proved especially difficult. In an earlier article, Donaldson pointed out that factories, mills, and other industrial plants "are almost universally recognized as sites of labor."[3] Additional structures that might not readily come to mind as labor sites worthy of preservation and/or interpretation include ethnic meeting halls or social clubs, houses, bakeries, diners, shuttered hospitals, closed schools, and agricultural spaces. Expanding the locus of storytelling increases the likelihood that sites will encompass more than the traditional narrative of who worked and where. Critical here is space interpretation. For as historian and urban planner Donna Graves explains, historic preservation focuses on identifying a historic site, the documentation of that place, and its registration as a landmark. She argues that there is a fourth task, that of historical interpretation.[4] Donaldson takes this point up in some detail herein.

The third essay calls our attention to the challenges of interpreting an industrial past for workers in the twenty-first-century service economy. Kristin O'Brassill-Kulfan observes in her study of Paterson, New Jersey, that twenty-first-century residents of that city do not readily find connection with its industrial past. The first planned industrial city in the U.S., Paterson has a rich history of labor organizing and worker militancy, especially among its immigrant populations. Since the mid-twentieth century, however, Paterson and its residents have been ravaged by deindustrialization. Not surprisingly, historical sites that celebrate the city's industrial past fall flat. Stories of immigrant silk workers and their past struggles in the mills must be made present and relevant for current residents of Paterson and the surrounding communities. One way to bridge this gap is by engaging bodies as well as minds. O'Brassill-Kulfan considers how Paterson's labor sites bridge past and present by interpreting body memory, defined by philosopher Edward S. Casey as the process by which we remember "in and by and through the body." In Paterson, a mobile application for a walking tour of the Mill Mile includes detailed descriptions of sights and sounds to convey a sense of what it was like to work in a crowded, noisy factory. Another way to activate body memory is to bring people into spaces that position them as historical actors. Visitors to the Botto House in nearby Haledon can stand on the very balcony where rousing orators, such as Elizabeth Gurley Flynn, Hubert Harrison, and William "Big Bill" Haywood, addressed thousands of speakers on the lawn during the Paterson Silk Strike of 1913. Part of the story that one gets from a place-based encounter with labor history, then, is inscribed on one's own body.[5]

The final pair of essays invite us to consider place as something we make, rather than a static location. According to the Project for Public Spaces, "placemaking inspires people to collectively reimagine and reinvent public spaces."[6] The essays by Rob Linné and Rebekah Bryer and Tom MacMillan are case studies of this process. Each considers how acts of political intervention have transformed ostensibly neutral sites—streets, parks, government office buildings—into places that resonate with labor history. Mindful of the constraints placed on professionally curated exhibits at museums and historic sites by their dependence on public and private sources of revenue, Linné directs our attention instead to graffiti and street murals in cities and towns around Texas, a state in which official narratives consistently downplay the contributions and struggles of Latinx workers. He convincingly argues that these "outdoor museums informally curated for the masses throughout Latinx neighborhoods represent the state's most impressive memorial to labor, working-class culture, and the immigrant experience." Alternatively, in their essay on the Maine Labor Mural, Rebekah Bryer and Tom MacMillan present an example of an effort to unmake a place. Their study considers official efforts to expunge history and politics from the Department of Labor offices in Augusta. They examine how removing artist Judy Taylor's 11-panel mural from that space sparked a national debate regarding "the relevancy and role of the labor movement in the nation's history." Bryer and MacMillan conclude that threats to public history installations and art may do more to "ignite broad-based passion" than controversy over wages, collective bargaining agreements, and work stoppages.

Notes

1. Julia Rose, *Interpreting Difficult History at Museums and Historic Sites* (Lanham, MD: Rowan and Littlefield, 2016), 21.

2. Denise Meringolo, *Museums, Monuments and National Parks: Toward a New Genealogy of Public History* (Amherst: University of Massachusetts Press, 2012), 167.

3. Rachel Donaldson, "Placing and Preserving Labor History," *The Public Historian* 39, No. 1, 2017, 61–83, 67.

4. Donna Graves, "The Necessity of Interpretation," in *Bending the Future: 50 Ideas for the Next 50 Years of Historic Preservation in the United States*, Max Page and Marla R. Miller, eds. (Amherst: University of Massachusetts Press, 2016), 94–95.

5. Margaret Kohn, *Radical Space: Building the House of the People* (Ithaca: Cornell University Press, 2003), 3–4.

6. Project for Public Spaces, "What Is Placemaking?" https://www.pps.org/article/what-is-placemaking.

CHAPTER 8

Labor History and the National Park Service

How the Government Does and Does Not Remember Our Working Past

ERIK LOOMIS

Introduction

The National Park Service (NPS), founded in 1916, is one of the world's only state-based agencies charged with officially promoting national history. Although mandated initially to protect the nation's most pristine natural areas, it has taken on a mission of telling historical stories over the century of its existence. The stories the federal government has decided are worth telling reflect the shifting interests of historians. In recent years NPS historical interpretation has gone far to integrate histories from below, a stark departure from the officially sanctioned history in many European nations, where imperial history remains dominant in public discourse and social movements receive little attention in signage, tours, or other hallmarks of public history. Yet, labor history remains a rarely told story in our national parks. While the NPS has done a wonderful job integrating traditionally oppressed groups into its histories, workers largely remain absent. Where workers do exist, the narrative often deemphasizes economic conflict in favor of focusing on other parts of American identity that tell stories of innovation and cooperation instead of class struggle. This piece explores the contours of this issue and suggests what labor historians can do to help move this process forward, noting the large number of critical labor history sites that remain completely unprotected and would make excellent additions to our national park system.

What We Memorialize

The first historical sites protected by the federal government were significant Civil War battlefields, such as Gettysburg and Antietam, originally housed in the Department of Defense and transferred to the Park Service in 1933. For much of the Park Service's history, battlefields and a few historic homes were the center of its historical holdings. It told a story of top-down history that represented the post-Reconstruction sectional reconciliation that erased slavery from the Civil War and then consensus-based political history of the postwar period. However, with the rise of the New Social History in the late 1960s that has blossomed into a thousand flowers by the early twenty-first century—ranging from environmental history to the history of sexuality and very much including labor history—pressure came from citizens for the government to tell the stories of oppressed Americans. As early as the 1960s, the NPS began creating new sites to tell stories of Native histories, such as the Nez Perce National Historical Park, established in 1965. By the time of the Clinton administration, the pressure to remember sites of racial oppression became overwhelming and, frankly, offered a way for the government to demonstrate interest in the nation's racist history without addressing structural racism in the present. Bill Clinton signed legislation to memorialize Japanese internment, genocidal attacks on Native Americans, and key sites of the civil rights movement in the National Park Service. These were all significant additions to the Park Service and to our public memory.

George W. Bush's administration was completely uninterested in this process, and the only historic site it commemorated in its eight years was the Flight 93 crash site in Pennsylvania. The Obama administration built on Clinton's legacy, largely through the National Monument designation established in the 1916 Antiquities Act. Obama's creation of national park sites in both Birmingham and Anniston, Alabama, to remember critical moments in the civil rights movement and the first site of remembrance of Reconstruction in South Carolina were crucial additions to the park system, as was the home of the National Woman's Party in Washington, D.C. and the Stonewall Tavern in Manhattan. Obama also added sites with relevance to labor history. These include Fort Monroe, the site where the first enslaved people were brought from Africa in 1619 and where fugitives fled to the encampment of General Benjamin Butler, who classified them as contraband during the Civil War; the site of the Pullman strike in 1894; and the United Farm Workers complex in California, created to honor Cesar Chavez. The Park Service now has a webpage dedicated to the labor history it tells, though it is quite brief and insufficient to provide much help to visitors.[1]

National Parks and Labor History

As a whole, the NPS has simply not taken labor history very seriously. Class conflict and the heroic stories of working-class struggle do not have the same caché in public history as the victorious struggles or tragic losses of other American social movements. Several recent additions to the parks commemorate early capitalism's history, yet labor history remains a peripheral part of those stories. Paterson Great Falls National Historical Park, created in 2009, is an example. Paterson was a major site of American industrialization. That is why the Great Falls became a likely site for NPS protection and interpretation. Its role in early industrial development and its connection with Alexander Hamilton is the Park's central narrative. There is certainly nothing wrong with this framework, as those stories are critical in the history of American capitalism.

However, the Park also misses easy opportunities to talk about workers. Paterson is the location of two critical strikes in American labor history. Most famous is the 1913 silk workers' strike led by the Industrial Workers of the World (IWW). Thanks to the technological advancement that allowed new mills to move past the initial water-based power sites of the initial Industrial Revolution, the site of the big mills that were the focus of IWW organizing in 1913 are not part of the national park site. The American Labor Museum in the city does provide that public history, even if a lack of funding means limited hours. However, with a relatively broad mandate to interpret the site as park managers see fit, there is little reason for the NPS not to discuss this critical event of American history. Even if one sees the 1913 strike as outside the purview of the Park's core mission however, there is also the 1835 strike involving over 2,000 textile workers, many of them children, a critical moment in early labor organizing more closely related to the Park's focus on early capitalism. Historical signs on its self-guided walking tour remain silent on this strike as well. Perhaps a more developed visitor center will include more labor history in the future. However, as a nation, to focus on commemorating foundational sites of industrial capitalism without discussing the role of workers in producing that wealth and resisting the exploitation that adjoined it is a serious lapse in our public history that labor historians must take seriously. Chances to talk about workers and their fights for dignity are missed throughout the national parks in ways similar to Paterson.

Even the new parks with more labor focus were not created to commemorate union struggles per se. Take, for example, the Cesar Chavez National Monument in California. The Chavez site was created primarily so the Park Service would have a site to tell stories of Latino history, which is also a critically underrepresented subject in the agency. Of course, this is great, but it's worth noting that the labor union history of the United Farm Workers has something of a secondary emphasis in the justification of the site. As it opens to the public, we can expect it to tell the story of the exploitation of farmworkers, the grape strike and boycott, and the role of Chavez as a heroic figure. However, given the investment in the site by the Chavez family and other surviving members of the UFW hierarchy, a critical look at the UFW's legacy—including its failures in the 1970s—in the exhibits and interpretation remains perhaps something for the future. The site itself is a major addition for the interpretation of labor history in the Park Service, but its reason for being and the vested interest in telling heroic stories of a complicated figure almost inherently ensure its limitations.

Pullman National Historical Park is another promising Obama-commissioned site. Its creation is complicated. Perhaps the most important reason it is now a national park is that President Obama wanted a Park Service site in Chicago. Historical NPS sites are often evaluated in terms of their political support as much as their historical relevance; thus the First State National Monument, which exists because Joe Biden wanted Delaware to have a national park site. Yet Pullman's qualifications are impeccable. The company's critical role in the development of the black community in Chicago, the remnant buildings on the site, as well as the Brotherhood of Sleeping Car Porters and the rise of A. Philip Randolph as the nation's foremost civil rights activist in the 1930s and 1940s, make it an excellent choice. If this was just the place where the 1894 Pullman Strike occurred, it would likely not be an NPS site today. However, between its labor history and its African-American legacy, plus the company housing that is still occupied today, it is a lovely addition to the Park Service that brings labor history into the parks in a critically important way. And yet, as services open at Pullman, interpreters again have choices to make. The physical condition of the remaining Pullman factory buildings is pretty sorry, and given the low funding for the NPS—not to mention that it is sacrificed any time the government has one of its increasingly common shutdowns—it will be some years before a fully fleshed-out park with tours and a good visitor center comes online.

A good Pullman visitor experience must focus on the variety of experiences encapsulated there. The development of the black community is critical, as is the history of railroads. But this must be the work experiences of both Black and white workers, including the 1894 Pullman Strike, and the story of how the American Railway Union and Eugene Debs came out in support of striking Pullman workers and how the Grover Cleveland administration, with former railroad attorney Richard Olney encouraging, sent in the

U.S. military to crush the strike with murderous violence. There are already concerns that the Park will choose to focus more on stories that bring us together—especially around transportation and railroads—than stories that demonstrate how Americans have torn themselves apart: the nearly medieval fiefdom George Pullman created in his company town, the strike that launched government repression by which we defined the Gilded Age, and the racism faced by the African American workers who labored as Pullman porters and lived in the local community. The choices any national park makes in the history it chooses to emphasize and how it frames that history are contested, and labor historians need to be at the front lines demanding that the dramatic stories of work, poverty, and oppression be at the forefront of the new site.

I do not mean to pick on the Park Service. When it can, the NPS does a good job with labor history. The mill town of Lowell is a fun place to visit for labor historians. NPS incorporated labor history as a central narrative in the creation of the Keweenaw National Historical Park in 1992. This includes the town of Calumet, Michigan, where a stampede on Christmas Eve in 1913 killed several workers' children, a tragedy that Woody Guthrie commemorated in his legendary labor song, "1913 Massacre." The inclusion of the Lower East Side Tenement Museum in New York into the NPS provides amazing tours that focus on the sweatshop conditions of workers, although while affiliated with the Park Service this museum is primarily run privately.[2] Finally, the development of the Rosie the Riveter World War II Home Front National Historical Park in Richmond, California, is another positive step.

The NPS still faces hard challenges. It is a woefully underfunded agency, even when Democrats control all levers of government as they did early in the Obama administration. A major problem for decades, the 2011 Organization of American Historians and National Park Service report, *Imperiled Promise: The State of History in the National Park Service*, explored many issues related to the presentation of history at our park sites, but strongly stated that the biggest problem was the chronic underfunding of the NPS.[3] Under Republican governance, seeking to shrink social and cultural agencies, undermine environmental protection, lower taxes for the nation's wealthiest people, and expand the military, the funding of the NPS was even more dire. Donald Trump's 2017 budget sought to cut NPS spending drastically, to $2.55 billion, part of an eleven percent cut in Department of Interior funding, making not only interpretation but physical infrastructure, security, and the hiring of park rangers even more tenuous.[4]

The NPS has enough popular support to reverse some of these proposals, but it also faces a multibillion-dollar backlog for maintenance projects alone, not to mention the need for law enforcement officers to keep the parks safe. Under Democratic presidents, the number of sites the NPS is ordered to interpret increases. However, there is too little funding to do an even adequate job in many places. It is telling that the Paterson Great Falls site lacks a full-fledged visitor center ten years after its creation. No part of the Coltsville National Historical Site in Hartford, Connecticut—created in 2014 to interpret the story of Samuel Colt and the legacy of his firearms factory—is available for visitors and likely will not be for years. This is a tragically underfunded agency pulling historical interpretation together on a shoestring.

The Politics of Interpretation

The Park Service also faces political pressure in its interpretation, as does any government agency tasked with telling stories about our collective history. The milquetoast historical interpretation at the Smithsonian Museum of American History since the Enola Gay controversy of the 1990s is a visceral symbol of the pitfalls of using historiographically relevant interpretation to take an honest look at the nation's past. The conservative firestorm over telling a balanced story about the nation's use of atomic warfare against Japan in 1945 ruined interpreters' careers and made the museum fearful of telling any controversial stories. Staffers for right-wing legislators can walk into that museum, report back to their congressman that an exhibit talks too much about race or gender or does not portray American history in a heroic light, and angry calls from powerful people will be made to Smithsonian administrators. Despite good interpretation in the newer Museum of the American Indian and the African American History Museum, the exhibits in the Museum of American History are little more than celebrations of American political, military, and entrepreneurial greatness, with some attention paid to stories of national crimes, such as Japanese internment, that today are used for ways to bring us together. I envy no historian working there.

While the National Park Service has not faced a similar controversy, the pall of the Enola Gay exhibit hangs over every piece of national historical interpretation. On top of all of this is the fact that the top NPS positions are political appointees, and when there is a conservative president, an NPS head demanding conservative-friendly historical interpretation is going to result. Thus, labor historians have to organize and demand that the stories we tell are part and parcel of this national narrative.[5]

The NPS also has no authority over the sites that it is mandated to interpret. These are choices made by Congress or the President, depending on the route the park takes for recognition. Even the crown jewel of labor history in the Park Service—Lowell—was created in 1978 more as an economic development project for the city that gathered the support of powerful Massachusetts politicians—particularly Tip O'Neill and Lowell's native son Paul Tsongas—than because it was the most deserving site available. The economic development project did have some success, bringing 437,000 visitors to Lowell every year by 1983. The old mills and the canals provided the necessary historical artifacts, but it was a political process through and through. The Park's real purpose in Lowell is to serve as a community gathering space, from holding summer concerts to interpreting the stories of recent immigrants that have made Lowell one of the nation's most diverse small cities. Upkeep of the old buildings, in particular, ensuring that the looms in one building that allow visitors to experience something of the life of the Mill Girls, is expensive, visitor numbers are low. Any future park designations around labor history have to deal with the realities of low budgets and limited visitation.[6]

All true. That said, the recent strides for sites that represent civil rights, women's rights, gay rights, and even labor history suggest that pushing for national park status for key labor history sites is worth the while of labor historians, who need to provide critical expertise on the significance of these places to push this project forward. Overall, our national commemoration and preservation of labor history sites is abysmal. Homestead is a mall with a small monument. Blair Mountain, the site of the nation's largest domestic insurrection since the Civil War when armed miners went to war against the coal companies and the law enforcement who served as their private army, may be destroyed through mountaintop removal.[7] The building the IWW offices occupied in Centralia, Washington, still stands, but the 1919 Centralia Massacre site lacks any official commemoration.[8] The site of the 1892 Frisco Mill explosion during the battle between the Western Federation of Miners and the Pinkertons outside of Coeur d'Alene, Idaho, has a state-funded marker, but the mill ruins are crumbling with the elements. In Flint, most of the General Motors plant where the 1937 sit-down strike took place is torn down, commemorated only by a small historical marker. The site of the Everett Massacre is not possible for someone to visit today. While it is possible to visit the West Virginia train tracks where the Great Railroad Strike of 1877 started, there is little there to help visitors understand the magnitude of what happened.

This is hardly to say that labor historians and community members are not working hard to protect the sites they love. They are. The site of Homestead may be a shopping mall, but the Battle of Homestead Foundation does a great job working on remembering the significance of the site and Pittsburgh's robust labor history writ large, including sponsoring speakers (myself included, in 2015) and working to place historical markers around the region. If you are paying attention in Homestead, you can see markers not only about the 1892 strike but about the 1933 Frances Perkins speech at the town's post office after U.S. Steel refused to let her speak elsewhere. There are great groups of people doing much to commemorate the Triangle Shirtwaist Factory fire and the Lawrence Bread and Roses strike. These are all obvious candidates for federal protection through the creation of national park sites directly telling the story of the workers' struggle. There are many other sites as well that would serve as great additions to the Park Service and where historians and local communities can make a compelling case for inclusion. Perhaps nowhere is more deserving than the Ludlow Massacre site in Colorado. The area surrounding it is either public land or private land that the government could cheaply acquire, which is necessary to national park site creation. There are tremendous historical stories to be told there, even outside of the 1914 Colorado coal wars—the history of immigration, of coal, and of the development of welfare capitalism after the massacre. Creating a park would serve as an economic development project for communities from Pueblo south to Trinidad desperately in need of tourist money.

There is significant community investment in Ludlow from both locals and from the historical community. The late labor historian James Green did much to publicize Ludlow's history and memory. So has Betsy Jameson at the University of Calgary, and so do local historians, such as Fawn Amber Montoya at Colorado State University–Pueblo, who has served as a local leader on remembering Ludlow for years. Local historians have succeeded in making Ludlow a National Historic Landmark, the required step before a park designation.[9] Keeping this project alive is a herculean effort. United Mine Workers of America District 4 president Bob Butero has put the burden on his own shoulders. Butero was born in a coal camp, started work as a coal miner at the age of 16, and became a safety inspector for the UMWA before rising as a union official. He has taken it upon himself to lead the effort to preserve Ludlow.[10]

Ludlow demonstrates both the potential and limitations of what a small group of people in a community can do by themselves. In recent years, the community raised money for a new memorial after its defacing a decade ago. There are interpretive signs around the fence that now protects that memorial. The Southern Colorado Coal Miners Museum in Trinidad is a great local museum with a number of artifacts. The miners' memorial outside the museum brings home the sadness of coal's casualties. The Park Service has helped in limited ways. NPS officials have shown some interest in creating a National Heritage Corridor for southern Colorado that would include Ludlow and other sites: the Sand Creek Massacre, where the Colorado militia massacred Cheyenne and Arapaho people in 1864; Bent's Fort, the early nineteenth-century fur trade fort; and Fort Amache, a Japanese internment camp. The NPS has provided a grant to help preserve the cellar where the women and children died, the core of the monument. Butero has a vision of a permanent museum with tents that replicate miners' strike dwellings, with one including a cellar to commemorate the Ludlow deaths. This would make a great visitor experience.

Barring state support to create a historical site with meaningful interpretation, this is probably achieved only through NPS status. Unfortunately, the state of Colorado has shown relatively little interest and that includes indifference from Governor John Hickenlooper. It's also worth noting that even Ludlow remains controversial in public memory; in meetings leading up to the centennial celebration, the Colorado National Guard and its historian were highly defensive over the Guard's actions at Ludlow. Butero himself is more optimistic. He believes that creating this interpretative site would cost perhaps $250,000–300,000 and believes that seed money from the UMWA might kickstart it. Given that much of that union is now sadly not much more than a pension fund for a dying industry, I do not know if Butero's expectation is realistic. I do know that we should demand the government step in and tell these stories in the National Park Service.[11]

Part of the problem we face in creating labor history sites within the National Park Service is that there is no sanitized history of class conflict as has unfortunately developed with memories of the civil rights movement. With the new civil rights parks, for example, local white conservative Republican politicians in Alabama and South Carolina have jumped on board because it becomes an easy way for them to claim ties to the African American communities through embracing the past, even as they then vote for racist legislation in the present. The depoliticization of the classic civil rights narrative is central to this, which we see every Martin Luther King Day with right-wing politicians claiming King's mantle. To say the least, we have no such reconciliation with labor history. Perhaps this is a rather extreme example, but the West Virginia Mine Wars Museum in Matewan, discussed in chapter two of this collection, faces notorious Massey Energy CEO Don Blankenship casually wandering in and aggressively questioning volunteers by talking about its pro-union slant, or at least he has when he hasn't been in prison for murdering twenty-nine miners at the Upper Big Branch Mine through his flaunting of mine safety laws.[12] The current rightwing attacks on unions are a fight to the death; there is no place for agreement on telling stories about past labor history when corporations and politicians are giving unions no quarter in the present. Moreover, public discussions of labor history a century old can still lead to great tensions in communities, as Robert Weyeneth's work on memory and the lack of commemoration around the Centralia Massacre demonstrates.[13]

Historians, History Sites, and Where To?

As a collective, perhaps labor historians have not invested as much time into the details of protecting these sites as other historians. One point many experts have made to me in this research is that for the government to prioritize labor history in the national parks, it is critical for labor historians to get involved. That starts with getting critical sites listed as a National Historic Landmark. I had a conversation with Dwight Pitcaithley, the former NPS Chief Historian who now teaches public history at New Mexico State University. He noted that the 2000 National Park Foundation's *National Landmarks: America's Treasures* included only seventeen labor history sites, far fewer than nearly every other subcategory of history.[14] When I called him, he was working on a project to list sites of New Mexico's famed art community under National Historic Landmark status. If we are serious about protecting these sites, historians have to commit to fighting to preserve them as National Landmarks. Pitcaithley strongly encouraged labor historians to lobby the Park Service for a new Labor History Theme Study and make a case that the historiography has changed enough that we need to review our labor history sites. He strongly suggested we work with the National Landmark specialists in the NPS and get the Organization of American Historians behind the project. He knows there was not money in the Park Service under the Trump administration for an expansion of the parks, but he believes that eventually there will be again and that labor historians need to be prepared for that opportunity when it arises.[15]

What everyone I spoke to emphasized was the critical role labor historians must play in preserving our labor history sites. Many of us do this already. Part of the problem though, is that labor historians are also busy fighting for worker justice in the present. Our interest in labor history is highly motivated by our outrage with injustices today. We only have so much energy. Yet, we live in a period with a unique opportunity to start this process. Despite the nation's extremely divided politics, there is a greater public interest in remembering past stories that highlight the grimmer side of American history than ever before. Public interest in writers such as Ta-Nehisi Coates, acclaim and great sales for the book on Attica by Heather Thompson, and the recent

National Park sites preserving sites of injustice are all signs of this interest. At the same time, conservatives seek to expunge any meaningful discussion of civil rights from our textbooks and to play down class conflict in favor of a history of national glory.[16] Fighting to preserve our sites of labor history, with the ultimate goal of inclusion within the National Park Service, is not an easy task and is an addition to the work and struggles we take on every day, but it is also worthy work that will provide ourselves and our descendants a more honest examination of our nation's history.

Notes

1. https://www.nps.gov/subjects/labor/index.htm.

2. Rachel Donaldson, "Placing and Preserving Labor History," *The Public Historian* 39, No. 1 (February 2017): 61–83.

3. Anne Mitchell Whisnant, Marla R. Miller, Gary B. Nash, and David Thelen, *Imperiled Promise: The State of History in the National Park Service* (Organization of American Historians: Bloomington, IN, 2018). See also Anne Mitchell Whisnant, Marla R. Miller, Gary B. Nash, and David Thelen, "The State of History in the National Park Service: A Conversation and Reflections," *The George Wright Forum* 29, No. 2 (2012): 246–63.

4. The United States Department of the Interior, *Budget Justifications and Performance Information Fiscal Year 2018: National Park Service*, https://www.nps.gov/aboutus/upload/FY-2018-NPS-Greenbook.pdf.

5. Edward T. Linenthal and Tom Englehardt, eds., *History Wars: The Enola Gay and Other Battles for the American Past* (New York: Henry Holt, 1996).

6. Author interview with Jack Herlihy, April 5, 2017. For information on the creation of Lowell National Historical Park, see Cathy Stanton, *The Lowell Experiment: Public History in a Postindustrial City* (Amherst: University of Massachusetts Press, 2006).

7. Heather Pringle, "Coal Firms to Strip-Mine Historic Battlefield?" *National Geographic*, June 4, 2010, https://www.nationalgeographic.com/news/2010/6/100520-science-environment-blair-mountain-coal-massey-energy-nation/; Ron Soodalter, "In the Battle for Blair Mountain, Coal Is Threatening to Bury Labor History," *The Progressive*, January 31, 2018, https://progressive.org/magazine/the-battle-over-blair-mountain-famous-labor-site/.

8. Robert R. Weyeneth, "History, He Wrote: Murder, Politics, and the Challenges of Public History in a Community with a Secret," *The Public Historian* 16, No. 2 (March 1994): 51–73.

9. James Green and Elizabeth Jameson, "Marking Labor History on the National Landscape: The Restored Ludlow Memorial and Its Significance," *International Labor and Working-Class History* 76 (Fall 2009): 6–25, provides an excellent discussion of how historians have worked within their field to spearhead the fight to remember and preserve the Ludlow Massacre site.

10. Author interview with Fawn-Amber Montoya, January 9, 2017; Author interview with Bob Butero, January 25, 2017.

11. Author interview with Butero, January 25, 2017.

12. Author interview with Katey Lauer, March 1, 2017.

13. Weyeneth, "History, He Wrote."

14. S. Allan Chambers, Jr., *National Landmarks, American Treasures: The National Park Foundation's Complete Guide to National Historic Landmarks* (Hoboken, NJ: Wiley Press, 2000).

15. Author interview with Dwight Pitcaithley, March 6, 2017.

16. Ta-Nehisi Coates, *We Were Eight Years in Power: An American Tragedy* (New York: One World, 2017); Ta-Nehisi Coates, *Between the World and Me* (New York: Spiegel & Grau, 2015); Heather Thompson, *Blood in the Water: The Attica Prison Uprising of 1971 and Its Legacy* (New York: Pantheon Books, 2016).

CHAPTER 9

The Southern Tenant Farmers Museum and the Difficult History of Agricultural Organizing

RACHEL DONALDSON

Introduction

In the timeline of labor organizing among farmers and agricultural workers in the United States, there are two main peaks: the Populist Movement of the 1880s through the 1890s and the rise of the United Farm Workers (UFW) in the mid-1960s. While these two movements captured national attention, this does not mean that agricultural organizing was in a state of abeyance during the sixty years in between. In the decades following the populists' People's Party's collapse, poor farmers and agricultural laborers joined forces with various political organizations and formed their own collective associations to continue the fight to improve their working and living conditions. From the late nineteenth century into the twenty-first century, efforts to organize groups of agricultural workers at times transcended ethnic, racial, and even regional boundaries. Furthermore, these organizing campaigns often challenged dominant norms of political, social, and cultural conservatism in rural areas.

Southern Tenant Farmers' Union

During the 1930s, the Southern Tenant Farmers' Union (STFU) exemplified these traits, and the ways in which it did so form the interpretive core of the Southern Tenant Farmers Museum (STFM) in Tyronza, Arkansas. On the one hand, the union reveals the regionalism of agricultural organizing, for it focused on the particularity of the sharecropping system of the South. On the other hand, many of the tribulations that sharecroppers endured—such as evictions, starvation earnings, debt—were shared by other agricultural workers around the country, thus illustrating the interconnected patchwork of agricultural strife in the United States. Through photographic, audio, and film materials, the STFM educates public audiences on this legacy, turning this site into a visible reminder of oppositional history in a rural cultural landscape. Using the STFM as a case study, I explore how historic preservationists and public historians have used the tools of landmark designation to commemorate a difficult site of labor history and how public historians have interpreted this history for general audiences. By analyzing the interpretation provided in the STFM—assessing what is included and excluded from the historical record being presented—I provide insight into the unique challenges of interpreting oppositional history, particularly in rural communities, and how public historians have attempted to navigate these challenges.

In many respects, the STFM shares similarities with another more well-known historical site of agricultural labor: the Cesar E. Chavez National Monument at the United Farm Workers' (UFW) headquarters, Nuestra Señora Reina de la Paz, in Keene, California. The monument is the centerpiece of a network of sites relating to the UFW. These sites were not the first historic properties of agricultural labor to be federally recognized as significant, as several sites relating to agricultural work patterns, education, and technological advancement have achieved National Historic Landmark status and been listed on the National Register of Historic Places.[1] While these preservation efforts are significant for protecting historical places of agricultural work and life and educating the general public about them, what is particularly significant about the UFW sites is that they are devoted to interpreting the history not just of agricultural labor, but of agricultural labor *organizing*—a history that is steeped in oppression and violence that labor activists endured in their efforts to improve the living and working conditions of farm workers. As such, while these sites celebrate Cesar Chavez and other important figures in the farm workers' movement, as Erik Loomis observes in his essay, they are also sites that open the door to interpreting a painful history of labor struggle, and one that is of a relatively recent past.

Official designation and commemoration of sites of difficult history of the labor movement is important in several respects. For one, it helps to secure the standing of these places in the public understanding of what is historically important.[2] Furthermore, the designation of sites of working-class history, particularly those relating to the labor movement, identifies places of struggle and radicalism as important sites in the national collective past and therefore teaches public audiences that these forms of oppositional history have been intrinsic aspects of the American experience.[3]

The STFM is situated at the center of the current effort in historic preservation to identify and commemorate places of difficult history. The museum site comprises three structures: the H. L. Mitchell Building, the Clay East Lion Gas Station, and the Bank of Tyronza, which were listed on the National Register of Historic Places in 2010 as key contributing factors to the Tyronza Commercial Historic District.[4] The primary historical significance of one of these structures—the Mitchell Building—is that it served as the original headquarters of the STFU. As such, the STFM reveals the challenges that a commemorated site of the history of labor and labor organizing faces and illustrates why such sites ought to be protected and preserved.

While historic designation is an essential step in generating public awareness of agricultural labor organizing, which can translate into efforts to protect these sites, it is also critical for preservationists to work with public historians to interpret these sites for general audiences. As historian and urban planner Donna Graves explains, historic preservation focuses on three main actions: identification of a historic site, the documentation of that place, and registration as a landmark. Graves calls for a fourth to be added to that list: historical interpretation. After all, a site cannot convey its historical significance; rather, it must be interpreted through signage, educational programs, tours, and other forms of historical narration. Interpreting sites of labor and working-class history, for example, broadens popular understandings of the labor movement, specifically by expanding the geographical boundaries beyond urban industrial centers to encompass rural areas and reflecting the diversity of labor activism to include economically dispossessed, politically disenfranchised, and socially marginalized peoples of various social and cultural backgrounds. Furthermore, interpretation, Graves argues, allows preservationists to move beyond merely "conserving the physical remains of past eras—with robust storytelling historic sites become sources of information, platforms for education, and vehicles for crossing barriers of time and personal experience." Interpretation also enables preservationists to explore the multiple layers of meaning within a place by accessing different perspectives on why a site is important that, in turn, "can provide a route to the holy grail of 'relevance' that many preservation organizations seek" if they are willing to work with local communities in interpreting a site.[5] For small sites in less well-known locations, this kind of connection with a local community is critical and can have profound implications on how a site is interpreted for the public.

Sharecropping and Tenant Farming in the South

The issues that spurred agrarian labor organizing in the South during the twentieth century stemmed from patterns of agricultural work that developed after the end of chattel slavery. In this region, the systems of sharecropping and farm tenancy came to dominate agricultural production, especially among African Americans during the years between Reconstruction and the rise of farm mechanization, just before the Second World War. Under sharecropping, individual families signed contracts with planter-landlords to take charge of a plot of land, rather than working as wage laborers across the plantation as a whole (which many formerly enslaved people refused to do). Theoretically, sharecroppers were entitled to a third of their yearly crop when planters furnished all necessary tools, seed, animals, and fertilizer; they could retain half of the crop if they supplied those necessities themselves.[6] For those whose supplies were entirely furnished by the landowner or local merchant, as was often the case, a mandatory lien was placed on the crop for repayment.[7] This created a system of debt peonage in which the debt that tenants owed to the landlord or merchant carried on through the following year such that they were never able to settle their debts and leave the land if they so desired. While this hurt all sharecroppers, the inability to escape the system—being tied to the landowner—was especially bitter for those who had recently gained freedom from enslavement.[8]

Like kudzu, the system of sharecropping spread across the South such that by 1900, farmers who did not own land, including black and white tenant farmers and sharecroppers, operated almost half of all farms in the region. Cotton continued to dominate the South because it was a nonperishable product that always had a market, even as prices fell. As such, landowners refused to allow tenants to diversify their crops. Diversification would require taking a risk and investing in new products and equipment, which meant spending money without a guarantee of return; hence, landowners continued to prefer to hoe the same row they had for decades.[9] While economic conditions were never good for cotton-growing sharecroppers and tenant farmers, their situation became unbearable during the Depression.

The problems in the cotton fields constituted one piece of an elaborate puzzle of agricultural strife in the United States during the Depression. To help alleviate the problems that farmers faced, Congress passed the Agricultural Adjustment Act (AAA) on May 12, 1933. New Deal officials designed the Act to decrease surpluses and thus increase prices for cotton, tobacco, hogs, corn, rice, dairy, and wheat—an action for which farmers had pushed since the 1920s. The Act's primary goal was to raise prices for farmers' goods and thus increase their purchasing power. One way to do so was by paying farmers not to plant or to plow up a percentage of their crop to decrease supply. By the time the AAA was passed, much of the cotton crop had already been planted, which led southern farmers to "plow under" a portion of their fields. As a result, the Act led to the reduction of cotton acreage by 25 percent in 1933 and by 40 percent in 1934–35.[10] However, even though sharecroppers and tenant farmers were the ones plowing up the fields that they had worked for years, in many instances landowners refused to pay them, keeping the government funds for themselves.[11]

Since they were not landowners, the government denied sharecroppers and tenant farmers direct relief. The relief that the government allocated to landowners led to the tenants' eventual displacement due to a decrease in acreage under cultivation and mechanization. Without the need for tenant farmers and sharecroppers to grow as much as possible to complete with falling prices, and with tractors increasingly doing work that humans and mules had done, landowners started evicting tenants from their homes, oftentimes dumping their belongings on the side of a road when the sharecroppers had no means of transportation. Sometimes, they would rehire them as day laborers, but only during harvest season—a move that also made the workers ineligible for governmental assistance.[12] The AAA, in effect, ended up hurting the people who actually needed financial relief the most.

In response to these hardships, some sharecroppers and tenant farmers decided to fight back. During the summer of 1934, eleven white and seven black men met in a schoolhouse near Tyronza, Arkansas, and decided to form a union of non–land-holding workers. They were a motley crew of socialist sympathizers, former members of the Colored Farmers Alliance, and even former Klansmen, all of whom were from tenant families that had, until that point, lived and worked on a 5,000-acre plantation owned by Hiram Norcross.[13] According to their account, Norcross had evicted twenty-three families (out of 248 that worked and lived on his land) to avoid having to loan them money so that they could survive through the planting season. They had an idea to start an interracial union but were wary; memories were still fresh of the 1919 Elaine Massacre, which occurred in the Mississippi Delta of Arkansas, approximately 100 miles south of Tyronza.[14] The extreme white-on-black violence at Elaine made it clear that attempts at organizing sharecroppers and tenant farmers would have to be integrated for any chance of success in the region.[15] With help from local socialists, notably H. L.

Mitchell, they drafted a constitution for the STFU and secured a charter for the fledgling organization. The office for the STFU became a back room of Mitchell's dry-cleaning and laundry business in Tyronza.

One of the union's first actions was to get legal recourse for the tenants evicted from the Norcross property. The union even engaged in direct action techniques when nine members staged a picket outside of the AAA headquarters in May 1935 and brought the problem to Secretary of Agriculture Henry Wallace, but to no avail. They also faced local losses when the Supreme Court ruled in favor of Norcross, thus spurring other large landowners to evict tenants with impunity.[16] Despite their indefatigable efforts, the union could not stem the tide of mass evictions that swelled across the South. Even in the face of these setbacks, the union quickly spread across seven states and garnered thirty thousand members; from 1934–1938 membership in the union rose to 35,000, with the highest percentage of members located in Arkansas.[17]

Not only does the STFU illustrate a nonindustrial dimension of the American labor movement, but also it demonstrates the potent strains of political radicalism in early-twentieth-century labor organizing. While syndicalist IWW organizers worked with migrant workers in the bonanza farms of the upper Midwest and California during the first two decades of the century, and Communists helped organize sharecroppers in Alabama during the early 1930s, socialism prevailed among the STFU leadership.[18] H. L. Mitchell and Clay East were both Socialist Party members; Mitchell, along with fellow activist Alvin Nunally established the state's first chapter of the Socialist Party, which was also one of the earliest in the South.[19] The political activities (and proclivities) of Mitchell and East were renowned in Tyronza to the extent that local residents referred to the corner where Mitchell's dry cleaning store and East's gas station were located as "red square."[20] While local conservative pressure eventually forced Mitchell to relocate the STFU headquarters to Memphis, it is important that the "radicalism" that the STFU leaders espoused emerged from, and was in response to, *local* conditions; leaders and members were all local residents. This is significant for two reasons: the union's interracial stance illustrates a rebuttal to the entrenched segregation of the region, and the leaders' socialist views challenged the region's marked political conservatism.

Preservation and Interpretation

At its core, the STFU was a diffuse organization; historians often refer to it as a "movement," shaped by cultural conditions and historical circumstances particular to the different places in which it took root.[21] The decentralized

nature of the union renders the sites relating to the STFU historically significant for both national and local history—a fact that is also highlighted
in the preservation of the Mitchell-East Building, for the property is designated as a contributing factor in the Tyronza Commercial Historic District.
Simultaneously, the only properties recognized as nationally significant in
the district nomination form are the Mitchell Building and the Clay East
Lion Gas Station for their association with the STFU. For both historical and
historic preservation purposes, it is important to highlight this site's national
significance because it ties the events that occurred there to the larger labor
movement. The organization of sharecroppers and tenant farmers was not
just a regional aberration; rather, it was part of a larger pattern of radical
efforts to organize agricultural workers during the first half of the twentieth
century, which adds a national dimension to the story.

Labor historians have explored the history and significance of the STFU in
numerous scholarly studies that detail the extent of the union's significance,
its cultural characteristics, its strengths and shortcomings regarding gender
and racial inclusivity, and its influence on the larger labor movement. While
these studies, largely published in academic journals or as monographs with
academic presses, are important for understanding the historical significance
and nuance of the STFU, it is critical that this history is publicly interpreted
for historians to impart the message that labor history is an important component of national history to a general audience. As Roy Rosenzweig and
David Thelen have argued, the majority of American adults engage with
history the most at historic sites and trust the interpretations provided at
these sites more so than other sources.[22] Therefore, the best way of reaching
and educating a public audience is in preserved spaces of past. Local, state,
and national designation helps to secure the standing of places of labor in the
public understanding of what is historically important. For too long, historic
preservation in the United States had been about protecting and preserving
places connected to famous citizens or that are notable for their architectural
grandeur. But, this is beginning to change. As Tuan has argued, a place's
significance does not necessarily lie in its "visual prominence;" many places
that are important for individuals and groups can easily go unnoticed by
those unacquainted with their history.[23] Therefore, it is especially imperative
for preservationists to identify and commemorate sites significant to labor's
past to encourage the public to recognize that these too are important to
American history—sites as ordinary and unremarkable as a dry cleaning
store and a gas station.

While the effort to designate the physical places of labor history as historical resources has done much to encourage the presence of these structures

in the built environment, many sites of labor history lack physical structures to tell their stories. Historians James Green and Elizabeth Jameson have recognized this fact, observing, "Few structures with architectural integrity remain on the national landscape to remind the public of the contributions of workers and unions."[24] This is often the case in the agricultural sector, where many former plantations, fields, orchards, and the like have either fallen victim to development or are too far off the beaten path to attract visitors. Therefore, wherever the structures of this history remain extant, they ought to be protected and interpreted to ensure that this history remains a tangible aspect of the cultural landscape. Interpretation is key because audiences need to know *why* a site is historically significant, not just *that* it is so. Interpretation also has the potential to engage more people in the act of preserving and maintaining a site; through interpretation, the voices and stories of those connected to these histories can be brought to the fore. This is all because, as Graves explains, it's largely the stories of the places that lead communities to seek to preserve them; if a site is not telling those stories then it is merely an "empty shell."[25] This combination of preservation and interpretation is exemplified at the Southern Tenant Farmers Museum.

The founding of the museum was not without controversy. Unlike industrial areas, the community of Tyronza is small; the town's population as of the 2010 census was 762. Furthermore, many community members remember the controversial nature of the STFU, and those memories have shaped their attitudes regarding the museum. Those whose families did not support the union itself did not support the museum; some families still do not support it.[26] However, while some local opinion is hostile to the history and memory of the STFU, it was also local interest that precipitated the formation of the museum. Some town residents knew of the site, but it took the filming of the PBS documentary about labor organizing during the New Deal and the government's failure to include agricultural workers, *Mean Things Happening*, to galvanize efforts to do something with it. After seeing the PBS truck in front of the site, local historian John Austin launched the effort to preserve the structures. Under the direction of Dr. Ruth Hawkins, a history professor at Arkansas State University, the buildings became a site for concentrated graduate student research. This research formed the basis of the museum's permanent exhibits, which focus on the early formation of the STFU as well as the history of the region and cotton farming more generally. The museum officially opened its doors in October 2006. Currently, the Heritage Sites Office of Arkansas State University manages the STFM, and it is part of a network of regionally and nationally significant sites in the Arkansas Delta that serves as "living laboratories" for students enrolled in the Heritage Studies PhD program.[27]

The museum entrance is in the old Tyronza bank building; the tour begins with an exhibit space dedicated to the history of Tyronza and it is the only aspect of the museum's exhibit space that changes. While the original bank teller desk is still standing, the adjacent building—the main part of the museum—has been gutted such that there are no internal features indicating its former life as a dry cleaners and laundry facility. The first of the permanent exhibit spaces informs viewers of the region's history, beginning with the Madras Earthquake and the creation of the Arkansas "sunken lands" region. The walls leading down a narrow corridor into the main museum are lined with nineteenth-century sketches pertaining to cotton production under slavery.[28] After photographic materials documenting the rise and fall of logging in the region, the interpretation moves into the early twentieth century and the rise of cotton production specifically in this region. Almost immediately, it depicts the problems of labor exploitation in the sharecropping system and efforts to fight it with materials such as reproductions of newspaper accounts of the Elaine Massacre. This lays the groundwork for the center of the museum's focus on the exploitation of sharecropping and the STFU's early efforts to combat these. The period of significance for both the historic designation of the site and the museum's interpretation is the period of time just prior to, during, and immediately after the site served as the STFU headquarters.

According to Linda Hinton, the former STFM Director, the museum's interpretation centers on two key aspects of the STFU's history: the interracial character of the union from its inception and its inextricable ties to the radical politics of the Socialist Party. Although historians debate the extent of the union's interracial character, it was founded as the first integrated agricultural union in the country in a staunchly segregated region. Therefore, the museum relies on photographic material, much of which comes from the Southern Tenant Farmers' Union Records at the University of North Carolina, Chapel Hill, to illustrate the union's emphasis on issues of class unity rather than racial difference. Images of white, black, male, and female leaders in the union are incorporated throughout the exhibit and interpreted through informational exhibit tags. In addition to the dominance of visual images in the museum's interpretation, sound is also incorporated. Visitors can listen to oral histories recounting the union's origins that Mitchell and other early members recorded in Memphis during the 50th anniversary of its founding.[29] The museum also features an antique radio through which audiences can hear songs written and performed by the STFU songwriter John Handcox and view "King Cotton's Slaves," a 1936 *March of Time* film that dramatizes the cruelties of sharecropping and the formation of the STFU. Although the historical narratives presented in the museum largely end with the Second World War, the exhibit materials do connect the STFU to subsequent agricultural organizing through materials linking the union to the United Farm Workers. While these connections could be expanded on, they point in the direction of connecting the story of the STFU to the larger history of agricultural organizing in the United States.

As an educational facility, the museum offers programs that vary depending on the age of the visiting group. Young children are taught about how cotton was grown, while older groups are introduced to the hard history of the exploitative nature of sharecropping/tenant farming. The nuances of the tour interpretations do not stop with age divisions. Lead STFM interpreter Cathy Hunt alters her tours based on the cues that audience members give her. Some visitors grew up as sharecroppers and are interested in only the story of sharecropping itself. Therefore, for those more interested in farming, she focuses on that story; for audiences more interested in the radical history of the STFU, as one tour group consisting of members of the Memphis chapter of the Young Democratic Socialists of America was, she shifts focus to the story of the union and the events that led to its formation. While the general tours tend to gloss over the details of the violence and brutality of key events like the Elaine Massacre, Hunt provided more detailed information to a local Junior High group that was studying racial violence during the summer of 1919.[30] Indeed, all museums, especially small ones, must maintain an audience base, and tailoring a tour specifically to viewers' interests is one way to ensure positive responses.

One complication in creating an interpretation that can change according to audiences' interests (and lack of interests), however, is that it dampens the museum's ability to lead audiences into the "discomfort zone." This is a term that Carl Weinberg coined to describe living history programs that use audience immersion to educate about painful histories, but it can also apply more broadly to the current effort among museums to engage directly in interpreting difficult topics and designing the interpretive experience in such ways that force audiences to confront these issues. Creating a discomfort zone as part of a museum experience not only provides a more complex and inclusive historical interpretation, but it also causes visitors to think about the relevance of the past in contemporary society.[31] For the STFM, the entire content is, in one way or another, painful, and audiences need to be exposed to that history in order to understand what caused local residents to form

FIGURE 9.1. Interactive audio display of the songs and historical significance of Southern Tenant Farmer Union organizer and musician John Handcox. Photo by Rachel Donaldson.

the STFU. They need to learn *why* local sharecroppers and tenant farmers' exploitation pushed them to organize and how especially dangerous that action was, given the recent memory of the Elaine Massacre. Without ensuring that all audiences learn of these historical details—details that in and of themselves create a discomfort zone—some audiences leave without being fully exposed to this complicated history.

Interpreting hard histories within local communities of the not-so-distant past can be particularly difficult because many residents remember their families' feelings about that past. Indeed, this is a problem that the STFM has had to grapple with from the outset. The museum's mission is to promote "knowledge and understanding of tenant farming and agricultural labor movements in the Mississippi River Delta, in an effort to preserve the history and promote the legacy of sharecropping, tenant farming and the farm labor movement."[32] Although the museum mission statement encompasses regional sharecropping as a whole and does not specifically reference the STFU, much of the interpretation *is* on the Union's rise during the time that it was headquartered at this site with one particularly glaring historical omission.

The event that catalyzed the formation of the STFU was the sharecropper evictions from the Norcross property. While this narrative is presented in detail in the National Register nomination form, it is notably absent in the museum. The tour and exhibit materials do discuss sharecropper evictions in the wake of the AAA and detail the circumstances of the Norcross eviction in particular, but the Norcross name is not mentioned in the exhibit materials and panel texts or in the docent-led tour. In fact, Hiram Norcross, who shoulders the historical blame for the widespread evictions, is described as a cousin from outside the community who took over the property after the death of the family patriarch, although the outsider-as-perpetrator narrative is not emphasized in the historical nomination of the site. As Cathy Hunt explained, the Norcross family is still very present in the community, and several members did not support the establishment of the museum, which is why the interpretation will not cite them by name unless prompted by visitors (like myself).[33] Local opposition did affect the design of the museum's historical narratives as a whole because it is not just the Norcross name that is absent; all local landowners' names are omitted from the museum's narrative.[34] On the one hand, this kind of historical omission can compromise the historical narratives presented at the site by leaving out key facts like the names of historical actors. The evictions did not just befall sharecroppers; landowners like Norcross executed them. On the other hand, these decisions regarding interpretive design illustrate the difficulty of interpreting painful history in a community that has varying degrees of open hostility to the existence of an interpreted historic site.

Similar to the close relationship Loomis describes between the National Park Service and the relatives of Cesar Chavez in the Cesar Chavez National Memorial, the Southern Tenant Farmers' Museum is inextricably tied to the descendants of those whose stories are at the center of the Southern Tenant Farmers' Union narrative. The museum is a part of the small community of Tyronza and thus has to respond to community concerns and views in their historical interpretations—even in order to simply avoid the perception of offense. We can see this tension with what the mural that adorns the side of the museum does and does not feature.

FIGURE 9.2. External mural depicting sharecropping on the Southern Tenant Farmers Museum building. Photo by Rachel Donaldson.

As Rob Linné (chapter eleven) and coauthors Rebekah Bryer and Tom MacMillan (chapter twelve) argue in their essays, public murals can be enormously effective in calling attention to underrepresented narratives and for stoking political controversy. Unlike the examples they cite, the STFM mural is about as politically innocuous as it can be while still illustrating sharecropping. Rather than provide a visual representation of sharecropping families evicted with all their belongings on the side of the road, or of sharecroppers striking in protest of their exploitation, it is just a long image of a cotton field with some figures standing in the foreground; only one of them—a woman with her face turned from the viewer—is engaged in the grueling act of picking cotton by hand.[35] This is just one example of how the STFM deals with the balancing act with which many small museums of local history struggle.

Another notable aspect of the museum is how it engages a core tenet of public history: the necessity of connecting the past to the present. It is in this regard that the political aspects of the museum fade almost completely from view. Overall, the museum's interpretation is firmly rooted in the past without commentary on the current plight of agricultural workers in the region. Like the historical interpretations of industrial sites in Paterson, NJ, which, as Kristin O'Brassill-Kulfan (chapter ten) explains, fail to adequately engage in contemporary problems that the city's working-class residents face, the STFM's silence regarding the contemporary plight of farm workers in and around the Mississippi Delta represents a missed opportunity. Whether this is by design or happenstance is unclear. The museum has begun to address the contemporary problem of regional underemployment, not by designing new exhibits exploring this problem but rather by reaching out to the local community through specialized programming. Tapping into their identity as a museum rooted in agricultural history, the STFM has initiated a series of adult education programs through the county extension services on sustainable living through workshops on gardening, soil testing, canning, and animal husbandry (rabbits and chickens). According to Linda Hinton, the museum offers these programs because they tie into the mission of the site.[36] While these may not seem directly in keeping with the museum's mission of preserving the historical legacy of sharecropping and the farm labor movement, one of the demands that organizing sharecroppers had in the 1930s was the right to plant gardens on the land that they rented. Therefore, to learn about how to start of garden of one's own is much more of a connection to this past than might appear on the surface.

The Southern Tenant Farmers Museum illustrates what can happen when historic preservationists, public historians, and academic historians work together to preserve and interpret an important chapter in the history of labor and labor organizing in the United States. While the STFU was a union that emerged in response to the peculiarities of local conditions, it speaks to the larger narrative of the exploitation of agricultural workers in the United States. It is therefore, an important component in the history of the national labor movement—a connection that is well documented in the historical designation of Mitchell-East Building. Although the nature of farm work in rural Arkansas that spurred the formation of the STFU differed remarkably from those of rural California that catalyzed the UFW, both unions are intrinsic components of the national narrative farm labor organizing efforts; their stories mirror the narratives of success and failure that mark the history of the labor movement in the United States.

We need small sites like the STFM as much as we need large sites like the Cesar Chavez National Memorial because they all teach audiences the struggles of these groups—the oppositional history of activists who fought to change local, regional, and national conditions for marginalized workers—whose histories are often left out of textbooks. We need their presence in the built environment to serve as physical reminders of a difficult past—and we need them to show that the struggles of farm workers have not ended.

Notes

1. The National Historic Landmarks Program of the Department of the Interior has identified sites significant for shaping patterns of labor (Frederick A. and Sophia Bagg Bonanza Farm, NHL 2005); sites associated with particular ethnic and racial groups engaged in agricultural work (Nicodemus Township, NHL 1976); places associated with important changes in production and labor processes, as well as sites of notable agrarian educational programs (Porter Farm, NHL 1964); and even sites associated with leading figures that improved social, cultural, and educational opportunities for farmers and agricultural workers, such as Oliver Hudson Kelley, the founder of the National Grange (Oliver H. Kelley Homestead, NHL 1964), and Booker T. Washington, founder of Tuskegee Institute (NHL 1965).

2. Yi-Fu Tuan, *Space and Place: The Perspective of Experience* (University of Minnesota Press, reprint), 162.

3. Max Page, *Why Preservation Matters* (New Haven: Yale University Press, 2016), 130; Julia Rose, *Interpreting Difficult History at Museums and Historic Sites* (Lanham, MD: Rowman & Littlefield, 2016), 28.

4. National Register of Historic Places, Tyronza Commercial Historic District, Tyronza, Poinsett County, Arkansas, National Register # PO0078, p. 36. The Mitchell Building and the East Gas Station are recognized for their local significance, for they are contributing members to this local historic district, but they are also noted for their national significance in their association with the history of the Southern Tenant Farmers' Union.

5. Donna Graves, "The Necessity of Interpretation," in *Bending the Future: 50 Ideas for the Next 50 Years of Historic Preservation in the United States*, Max Page and Marla R. Miller, eds. (Amherst: University of Massachusetts Press, 2016), 94–95.

6. Eric Foner, *Reconstruction: America's Unfinished Revolution* (New York: HarperCollins, 1988), 173–174.

7. R. Douglas Hurt, *American Agriculture: A Brief History* (West Lafayette, IN: Purdue University Press, 2002), 169. In the aftermath of the economic upheavals of the 1870s and 1880, many formerly independent white farmers also fell into farm tenancy.

8. David Eugene Conrad, *The Forgotten Farmers: The Story of Sharecroppers in the New Deal* (Urbana: University of Illinois Press, 1965), 6. Pete Daniel, *Breaking the*

Land: The Transformation of Cotton, Tobacco, and Rice Cultures Since 1880 (Urbana: University of Illinois Press, 1986).

9. Hurt, *Problems of Plenty: The American Farmer in the Twentieth Century* (Chicago: Ivan R. Dee, 2003), 7.

10. Erik Gellman and Jarod Roll, "Owen Whitfield and the Gospel of the Working Class in New Deal America, 1936–1946," *Journal of Southern History*, Vol. 72, No. 2 (May, 2006): 308.

11. Agricultural Adjustment Act of 1933 Pub. L. No. 73–10, 48 Stat. 31 (Originally cited as ch. 25, 48 Stat. 31), 32–35, 38, The National Center for Agricultural Law Research and Information University of Arkansas, http://nationalaglawcenter.org/wp-content/uploads/assets/farmbills/1933.pdf. Each state that participated in the program was given a quota of how much cotton acreage must be plowed up, based on a 30 percent reduction of the production figures from 1931. In Arkansas, this meant that 1,002,300 of the 3,341,000 acres of cotton had to be destroyed (Keith J. Volanto, "The AAA Cotton Plow-Up Campaign in Arkansas," *Arkansas Historical Quarterly*, Vol. 59, No. 4 (Winter, 2000): 392, 404).

12. Volanto, "The AAA Cotton Plow-Up Campaign in Arkansas," 390.

13. M. Langley Biegert, "Legacy of Resistance: Uncovering the History of Collective Action by Black Agricultural Workers in Central East Arkansas from the 1860s to the 1930s," *Journal of Social History*, Vol. 32, No. 1 (Autumn, 1998): 73–75.

14. To fight the exploitation inherent in sharecropping, black sharecroppers formed the Progressive Farmers and Laborers Household Union of America to demand a more equitable share of the profits for the cotton they produced. During a meeting the night of September 30, a group of local whites fired into a church where the sharecroppers were meeting. One of the perpetrators was killed in the return fire, which sparked heavy retaliation by local whites and law enforcement. For days, white mobs, law enforcement, and soldiers killed an estimated 200 black men, women, and children (some estimates are higher) in Phillips County, Arkansas (Jason Manthorne, "The View from the Cotton: Reconsidering the Southern Tenant Farmers' Union," *Agricultural History*, Vol. 84, No. 1 (2010): 22).

15. Members of this organization pushed for a written, legal contract with plantation owners to ensure a fair profit for their labor and to increase wages for cotton pickers. Despite these seemingly modest demands, sharecropping families received death threats directly from plantation owners should it be discovered that they had joined this organization (Biegert, "Legacy of Resistance," 85–86, 88).

16. National Register of Historic Places, Tyronza Commercial Historic District, 10.

17. Anthony Dunbar, *Against the Grain: Southern Radicals and Prophets, 1929–1959* (Charlottesville: University of Virginia Press, 1981), 88–89, 95; Hurt, *Problems of Plenty*, 73–75; Biegert, "Legacy of Resistance," 88.

18. Syndicalism is the view that workers' unions should control the means of production rather than private interests or the state.

19. Some sources spell his name as Alvin Nunnally. In 1932 the Tyronza chapter

hosted the Arkansas Socialist Party Convention that featured presidential candidate Norman Thomas as a speaker.

20. National Register of Historic Places, Tyronza Commercial Historic District, 8–10.

21. Biegert, "Legacy of Resistance," 88; Elizabeth Anne Payne and Louise Boyle, "'The Lady Was a Sharecropper: Myrtle Lawrence and the Southern Tenant Farmers' Union," *Southern Cultures*, Vol. 4, No. 2 (Summer 1998), 10–13; Manthorne, "The View from Cotton," 23; Gellman and Roll, "Owen Whitfield and the Gospel of the Working Class in New Deal America," 316 (Gellman and Roll specifically refer to the STFU as a "movement" after it became affiliated with UCAPAWA in 1937).

22. Roy Rosenzweig and David Thelen, *The Presence of the Past: Popular Uses of History in American Life* (New York: Columbia University Press, 2000).

23. Tuan, *Space and Place*, 162.

24. James Green and Elizabeth Jameson, "Marking Labor History on the National Landscape: The Restored Ludlow Memorial and its Significance," *International Labor and Working-Class History*, no. 76 (Fall 2009): 11.

25. Graves, "The Necessity of Interpretation," 94–95.

26. Cathy Hunt, interview by author, oral interview, Southern Tenant Farmers Museum, November 16, 2018; Linda Hinton, interview by author, phone interview, Charleston, SC, July 1, 2018.

27. Cathy Hunt, interview by author, November 16, 2018; "A-State Heritage Sites," Arkansas State University, http://arkansasheritagesites.astate.edu/.

28. This is an interesting choice of content because during the antebellum period, the region was still swampland adjacent to the Mississippi River such that there was no cotton planting at this time. After the Civil War, timber companies first moved into the region, clearing the old growth trees, which made the already swampy area even more flood prone. Cotton farming did not begin until the early twentieth century.

29. Linda Hinton, interview by author, July 1, 2018.

30. Cathy Hunt, interview by author, November 16, 2018. In the tour that I took with Hunt, for instance, she spent a good deal of time detailing the events of the Elaine Massacre. The museum itself had only a couple pictures and newspaper clippings dedicated to the event, but the tour provided much more historical detail about the massacre and its aftermath.

31. Carl R. Weinberg, "The Discomfort Zone: Reenacting Slavery at Conner Prairie," *OAH Magazine of History*, Vol. 23, No. 2 (Apr., 2009); Cherstin M. Lyon, Elizabeth M. Nix, Rebecca K. Shrum, *Introduction to Public History: Interpreting the Past, Engaging Audiences* (Lanham, MD: Rowman & Littlefield, 2017), 124.

32. Southern Tenant Farmers Museum website, http://stfm.astate.edu/.

33. Cathy Hunt, interview by author, November 16, 2018.

34. Linda Hinton, interview by author, July 1, 2018.

35. There are some figures in the far back of the mural who also appear to be picking cotton but they essentially blend into the background.

36. Linda Hinton, interview by author, July 1, 2018.

CHAPTER 10

Labor Sweated Here

Commemorating Workers and Their Activism in Paterson, New Jersey

KRISTIN O'BRASSILL-KULFAN

> "To say labor sweated or had
> sweated here / a flame, / spent."
> —"Sunday in the Park," Paterson,
> William Carlos Williams (1946)

Introduction

Paterson is a city alive with its past and present. From the Great Falls Historic District to Little Lima on the west side and Little Ramallah on the south side, it teems and bustles, its sidewalks overflowing with workers, workseekers, and their histories. The remnants of the city's once-humming mills reside in the Great Falls Historic District, one of the "cradle[s] of American industry." Offering visitors some natural wonder, some preserved factory buildings, and local history with no small amount of grit, Paterson, New Jersey is not, as one commentator noted at the start of the city's efforts to preserve its historic essence in the early 1980s, the "Colonial Williamsburg of industrial development."[1] The city's path from manufacturing hub to depressed postindustrial landscape to hopeful historical landmark destination has been circuitous and remains uncertain. However, Paterson contains a remarkably compelling cityscape outlined by brick, stone, water, and the nearly perceptible sounds of centuries-old loom shuttles flying.

Heritage tourism sells the idea that nearly every city has significant offerings to make to visitors eager to learn more about the art, architecture, and culture of historic towns, cities, and landscapes. However, historical interpretation often requires a fair amount of suspension of disbelief on the ground in modern cities that contain contradictions and harsh realities, leaving visitors to peer over an invisible gulf between the view in front of them and that conjured by the text on a street-side marker. Place-based epistemology and interpretation offer opportunities for deep exploration of how the past shapes the present. Paterson is home to intense industrial and labor histories that have acted as a guiding force in the city's social and cultural history. However, since the mid-twentieth century, deindustrialization has left many of its communities with little capital or confidence. Paterson's public historians and other cultural sector workers address this cognitive dissonance directly by foregrounding the city's labor history, emphasizing workers' experiences and decisions, from the eighteenth century to the present, and both directly and indirectly, considering the impact the city's relationship with capitalism has had on its residents. By drawing on the historical resources of the landscape, the archives that document it, and the shared knowledge of historical actors and those who share their stories, a powerful place-based history of labor can transform the way residents and visitors interact with this city.

Paterson originated as the first planned industrial city in the nation. Not long after the new nation's birth, the rushing river and dramatic waterfalls that moved through the Passaic River Gorge drew industrialists' attention. Alexander Hamilton, as Secretary of the Treasury, cofounded the Society for Establishing Useful Manufactures (SUM), a joint public-private initiative to promote industrial growth in the fledgling United States.[2] When the Society bought the land that would become Paterson, about 700 acres surrounding the falls, in 1792, the city was named after SUM charter member New Jersey Governor William Paterson. The city faced initial financial and technical challenges with its efforts to create a booming manufacturing center. From the start, Paterson workers paved their own way, starting one of the first factory walkouts in United States history at a cotton mill in 1828, a strike led primarily by women and children.[3] A Paterson resident, Matthew Maguire, compounded the city's labor reputation by organizing the first Labor Day Parade in the United States, held in New York City on September 5, 1882.[4]

Silk Strike

The city began to specialize in silk production from the mid-nineteenth century, earning the moniker "Silk City." By the 1910s, Paterson's mills were producing the lion's share of the nation's silk with the labor of more than 20,000 workers—women, men, and children. The city is best known for the agitation of these workers in a 1913 strike, where the bulk of the millworkers

FIGURE 10.1. Crowds at the Botto House for a meeting during the 1913 silk strike. Credit: American Labor Museum/Botto House National Landmark.

in the city, some estimates suggest as many as 24,000 workers, walked off the job to protest low wages, doubling of loom duties, long work days, danger-ous working conditions, and threats of unemployment. The city had seen its fair share of worker-led resistance in the previous decades. In just twenty years leading up to the turn of the century, Paterson's workers led nearly 150 strikes. But the 1913 action was remarkable for its size, length, publicity, and iconography, drawing the support of some of the nation's most prominent labor organizers and activists, including William "Big Bill" Haywood and Elizabeth Gurley Flynn. The renowned author Upton Sinclair even lent his voice to the cause, addressing crowds of thousands of strikers, their families, and sympathetic neighbors.[5]

Paterson's workers arguably inaugurated the public history of the city's labor history when they began to commemorate the silk strike before it had even ended. Months into the strike, workers and their families were run-ning out of funds and out of food. Having garnered widespread news cover-age, sympathetic intellectuals and artists in New York City, primarily from Greenwich Village, saw an opportunity to raise awareness and funds for the strikers with a performance. Strikers themselves performed the "Pageant of the Paterson Strike" in Madison Square Garden, selling out the entire venue on June 7 and 8 of 1913. A well-known wealthy patron of the arts, Mabel Dodge, was instrumental in bringing the strikers to the stage, while John Reed, journalist and eventual author of *Ten Days that Shook the World*, assisted in drafting the script. The pageant crew re-created Paterson's city streets and mill doors in painted backdrops while the workers performed standing on the picket line in front of their workplaces, on stage in front of thousands.[6] They asserted the importance of telling working people's stories, reminding spectators and the strikers themselves that "workers have memories. . . . They had many memories and much knowledge—that waiting throng of many thousand workers . . . when at last the doors were opened . . . the memories and knowledge found a voice."[7]

Although the pageant did not raise enough money to offset the growing needs of the strikers (they returned to the mills about six weeks later with many of their demands unmet), it solidified the significance of the Paterson strike in public memory as one of the most significant and longest nonviolent strikes in American history. The pageant revealed the prescience of strikers and their sympathizers in their understanding of the significance of the action. It set the tone for the public memory of the strike over subsequent decades. The image on the cover of the pageant's program—a mill worker emerging from and towering above the mills—has become an iconic symbol of early-twentieth-century labor activism, in a style still used by activists today.[8]

Place Matters

As Dolores Hayden argued in *The Power of Place* in 1995, stories about places can often link into conversations about broader issues such as immigration, local politics, and work patterns. This history is manifest in the urban landscape, which "stimulates visual memory," rendering it an invaluable "resource for public history."[9] While in recent years, public historians have begun to recognize how important such sites are, there are still some key gaps in the interpretation of urban history, especially the experiences of workers. Labor and public historian Rachel Donaldson made this argument in her 2017 article "Placing and Preserving Labor History." While "sites of work have long been identified as historically significant," she wrote, "all too often the workers have been excluded from these narratives."[10] There are inklings of efforts to change this trend at many sites, though, including at Monticello, the National Museum of Industrial History, and the California State Railroad Museum, which have begun to channel their interpretation through the lens of workers' experiences even, or perhaps especially, where doing so undercuts dominant narratives about American capitalism.

Labor historians have done their part to excavate workers' lives, but in public history, it remains a subject woefully under-addressed at historic sites and museums. One way forward may be through attempting to interpret what Hayden, echoing philosopher Edward S. Casey, refers to as "body memory." Casey defines body memory as "memory that is intrinsic to the body" and the process by which "we remember in and by and through the body."[11] Moving beyond engagement with space and history in intellectual spheres, body memory is deeply personal, visceral, and subjective, "modified," as Hayden notes, "by the postures of gender, race, and class." Distinct from place memory, which "encapsulates the human ability to connect with both the built and natural environments that are entwined in the cultural landscape," body memory explores the "shared experience of dwellings, public spaces, and workplaces, and the paths traveled between home and work" through physical presence and even impressionist re-creating of corporeal conditions. In Paterson's case, this would be through interpreting the "experience of physical labor," which could allow us to understand better what it meant to work "in a crowded sweatshop" or factory.[12]

This sort of interpretation has drawn high praise for sites like the Lower East Side Tenement Museum and some Southern plantation tours, which refer directly to the physical conditions in which visitors stand, and historical actors lived and worked. Many of Paterson's historic sites and agencies aim to use body memory as they interpret workers' schedules, home lives, and the physical demands of their jobs. A public history-oriented mobile application for the Mill Mile (a walking tour resulting from a partnership between Paterson Great Falls National Historical Park and the Hamilton Partnership for Paterson) draws on the senses to document their experiences. In an excerpt of an oral history with Senator Frank Lautenberg, a Paterson native featured in the app, he candidly describes the "noise," "how dark it was" in the mills, and how dangerous the byproducts of the silk manufacturing process could be.[13] Such reminders balance the impression given by the built environment of the city, where, as Pulitzer Prize–winning architecture critic Paul Goldberger has noted in his assessment of Paterson's preservation efforts: "it is almost easy to romanticize these buildings and to forget that they were, for all their architectural splendor, far from wonderful places to work."[14]

The National Park Service, among the entities most recently compelled to take up the mantle of interpreting Paterson's history, contributes to the representation of the history of the workers who filled the mills, operated the silk looms, and resisted oppressive labor practices in the city's industrial center. In

2009, President Barack Obama authorized the creation of Paterson Great Falls National Historical Park. It was officially established as the 397th national park in the nation in late 2011, just before the famous strike's centennial.[15] The park comprises primarily the "Mill Mile," generally visited via a walking tour through the historic sites of the city. The tour, the brainchild of NPS staff and the Hamilton Partnership for Paterson, is a well-branded overview of the most notable corners of the Great Falls Historic District, including the mills and the raceways from which they drew their power. Important stops include the Rosen Mill, a major silk ribbon factory, and the Rogers Locomotive Works, now the home of the Paterson Museum. Two locomotives sit in front of the museum, while inside, the building holds historical looms and other machinery used to dye, wind, warp, and weave silk and other textile products. Exhibition panels offer visitors insight into the silk mill workers' demographics, conditions within the plants, and the technical processes by which Paterson mills contributed to the textile industry. The gem of the park is Great Falls Lawn View, a vista overlooking the gorge and the falls, with the hydroelectric plant built by the SUM that harnesses the power of the falls for electricity balancing the natural beauty of the view with a reminder of the city's industrial heritage.[16]

Botto House National Landmark

Nearby, at the American Labor Museum (ALM)/Botto House National Landmark, located just outside of Paterson in the suburb of Haledon, workers hold an even more prominent place in the interpretation of the city's history. Haledon's socialist mayor, William Brueckmann, sympathized with the millworkers, allowing the suburb to serve as an annex to Paterson's union halls, where organizers and strikers could strategize after their activities got them driven out of Paterson proper.[17]

The Botto House property, with a large yard, garden, and multifamily Victorian home built in 1908, now houses a private nonprofit house museum with well-preserved turn-of-the-century artifacts, many belonging to the original inhabitants themselves or their neighbors and nearby contemporaries. The home's owners, Pietro and Maria Botto, and their four grown daughters were all skilled laborers in the silk mills, earning enough to purchase the tract of land on which they built their house, with apartments upstairs that they rented to local workers. From this home, the Bottos shared their hospitality with mill workers, regularly hosting strikers and activists. On tours of the museum, guides detail the causes of the strike and the Bottos' involvement, focusing particularly on the experiences of immigrants like themselves who worked in the mills. From the Botto House balcony, the museum's tour guides note, speakers addressed crowds in nearly a dozen languages, while attendees cycled through the audience to stand in the front to hear their language spoken before returning to the back of the crowd in order to allow the next group of speakers and listeners to repeat the process.

The ALM's mission is to advance "public understanding of the history of work, workers and the labor movement throughout the world, with special attention to the ethnicity and immigrant experience of American workers."[18] It has achieved this since it opened in 1983, in part by functioning as something of an activist organization, devoting half of the property to displaying international histories of workers and cultivating relationships with local teachers, young students, and labor-oriented groups. These efforts by the ALM predate the recent pleas of Deborah Ryan and Franklin Vagnone in the *Anarchist's Guide to Historic House Museums* for sites to ensure their relevance through working with their surrounding community and inviting neighborhood activity into the museum.[19] Rather than placing red velvet rope between artifacts and visitors, the ALM invites guests to stand on the same balcony where striking silk workers, national leaders of the Industrial Workers of the World, and labor activists stood to address weekly assemblies of more than twenty thousand people during the 1913 strike.

The museum sees itself as sharing a mission and function with the site's original role as a rallying place for strikers by acting as a partner to present-day activists. They achieve this mission through purposeful interpretation of and exhibit curation at the Botto House site and in their public engagement. The ALM is an extension of local labor organizations, where local shops send their union apprentices to learn about labor history. In promotional materials, the museum boasts, "In 1913, thousands of striking silk workers found a safe haven at the Botto House. Today, we continue that tradition by hosting union meetings."[20] The museum also maintains a free lending library specializing in labor history topics. Local union officials comprise a majority of the museum's Board of Trustees and members of the local chapter of the International Brotherhood of Electrical Workers help with repairs around the site, while other union members assist in fund-raising.

These relationships bolster the sense of community among workers in the city, as the museum holds a place of high regard in commemorative activities such as Workers' Memorial Day and on the May Day and Labor Day holidays, hosting events that gain prominence by being held at a National Historic Landmark property. This designation, which not only facilitates preservation of the site, is also significant as a recognition by the Department of Interior of the importance of labor history sites like the Botto House for their rela-

FIGURE 10.2. Botto House today. Photo courtesy Dmadeo.

tionship to labor *organizing*, as Rachel Donaldson notes in chapter nine of this volume. The museum's involvement in local commemorative activities helps staff stay abreast of current labor issues and contemporary workers' concerns and keep the site's interpretation relevant as the demographics of the area shift. Events like these also generate visitorship throughout the year, and museum staff report that the guests they bring in, particularly those in the under-thirty-five crowd, tend to be the most diverse of the site's visitors.

The Botto House focuses on the experience of middle-class Italian Americans. The Paterson Museum, the NPS, and the members of the Hamilton Partnership, recognize the robust populations of these and other immigrants to the city. Paterson's mills had, in the nineteenth and early twentieth century, "attracted workers from France, Italy, Poland, Syria" and beyond.[21]

While the Botto House interprets one Italian American family's story, it generalizes about their labor and also that of other immigrants in the early-twentieth-century mills. This creates a fluid transition between exhibit narratives and the tours given by staff to visitors, some of whom are part of the newer immigrant groups that now define the city, including Peruvian and Syrian immigrants. On the grounds of the ALM, museum staff, volunteers, and visitors maintain an "Old World Garden" or "Immigrant Garden," as they refer to it. In planting the same herbs and vegetables as the Bottos did, local students, many of whom are themselves immigrants or the children of recent arrivals, preserve the "body memory" of the property. In Paterson, immigration is central to the public history of labor history.

Because it was the home of skilled laborers with numerous incomes, the Botto House is an example of a fairly well-appointed working-class residence. The Bottos earned enough to own a reasonably large property and procure some creature comforts for their home. In the portion of the museum tracing their lives, the middle-class luxuries on display, like a phonograph and violin, showcase their status. To drive home the point, then, about what prompted agitation and frequent strikes in Paterson, the exhibit space in the museum carefully outlines the struggles of the city's lowest-paid millworkers. The poverty and dire working conditions that animated Paterson's labor movement are presented in the museum's permanent exhibition in the 1913 Strike Gallery, though the Botto House also hosts rotating exhibits dealing with themes related to labor, immigration, and social activism. Through tour guide commentary and careful programming, visitors, especially local schoolchildren, are invited to compare their own and their neighbors' living conditions with those of the city's former residents. In 2018, an estimated 29 percent of Patersonians lived at or below the federal poverty line, nearly triple the statewide average.[22] In archival collections housed within the museum, the work of photojournalists documents, in the style of Jacob Riis, the lives of many millworkers living in dilapidated housing with limited access to heat and hot water.

As Paterson endeavors to expand its interpretation of the city's labor history, there is a real opportunity to re-create one of these residences, perhaps similar to the preserved apartments in the Tenement Museum, to highlight the body memory of Paterson's workers. The ALM interprets its own history as a National Historic Landmark through the lens of its connection to the rest of the city, both in the spatial history sense, offering bus and walking tours that visit numerous sites of labor history in the area, as well as through alliances with other county cultural and historical organizations. Public history agencies in Paterson are highly collaborative, creating robust opportunities for interpretation across institutional boundaries. One of the best examples of such a partnership is that of the ALM/Botto House and Belle Vista/Lambert Castle Museum. The latter is an 1892 Medieval Revival mansion turned museum, which houses the Passaic County Historical Society. Originally built for English immigrant Catholina Lambert, owner of the large and successful Dexter silk mill in the city, the opulence of the castle is presented as a foil to the living conditions and struggles of the workers Lambert's mill employed. In regular excursions between the ALM/Botto House and the Castle, billed as the "Mill Worker & Mill Owner" tours, the sites invite visitors to "discover how the other half lived."[23] This purposeful interpretation of place-based labor history not only elucidates an insufficiently discussed piece of workers' legacy but also promotes a contemporary understanding of the historical precedents for the economic divides that have underpinned labor relations in the United States for centuries.

Each May, Paterson's historic sites collaborate to offer another popular bus tour, billed as the "Experience Paterson" tour, inviting participants to explore the city's labor and immigrant history through visits to its museums and historic sites. The tour takes visitors from the Botto House to Lambert Castle to Great Falls National Historical Park and the Paterson Museum, passing by the remnants of the mills where the Bottos and other silk mill employees worked. This tour drew special attention during the 2013 Centennial of the Paterson Silk Strike, when it was offered alongside hundreds of other commemorative events throughout the year, highlighting the city's history of labor activism, immigration, and artistic and cultural production.

Despite a citywide emphasis on commemorating Paterson's industrial past, especially the contributions made by workers to the early-twentieth-century labor movement, there are gaps in the city's representation of its labor history.

While most of the interpretation in Paterson and its historic sites take a measured approach to addressing the industrial and social development of the city and its history of labor agitation, some recent efforts to draw tourists to the city err on the side of celebration. Promotional materials for the national park and the Mill Mile walking tour, for example, include the following explanation of Hamilton's contributions to the city: "True to Hamilton's vision, manufacturing and innovation spread rapidly throughout Paterson and the country, and people of any class, creed, or color soon found the ability to climb higher than they had imagined. In Paterson, Hamilton created what we have come to call the American Dream."[24] Indeed, as Erik Loomis notes in chapter eight of this volume regarding labor history, National Park Service interpretation tends to favor a focus on the history of industry and capitalism as opposed to those who worked at the sites they preserve.

For all of the city's efforts to connect Paterson's current residents with its past, many residents find that this celebratory focus on the city's manufacturing heyday falls flat. Paterson is a postindustrial city exploiting an industrial past. There are clear connections between the experiences of the Peruvian and Turkish immigrants of the twenty-first century and the Italian and Syrian immigrants of the late nineteenth century in Paterson. But too often, the stories of labor in the heyday of the Silk City end up emphasizing differences as opposed to similarities of experience, as the focus on bygone industries reminds many current residents of the rising rates of unemployment, the prevalence of service sector jobs among Paterson's current residents, and the frequent expatriation the city now faces.[25]

As one Patersonian recently reflected, "The upper-level residents—let me put it that way—they're blushing over this thing, . . . But, who are they doing it for? That money could be better spent revitalizing some of this mess here. It's just going to be another pretty picture for a postcard." Much of the efforts to preserve the city's history have been questioned along these lines, while Paterson remains plagued by poverty and a reputation as a haven for illicit drug trade and violence. A survey of city residents around the time the National Park opened revealed that "65 percent of residents say they're afraid to venture" into the historic district "at night." Journalists, too, have bemoaned a "lipstick on a pig" type strategy to commemorate the city's history; in 2017, an article in *The Nation* argued that, "while it may be good marketing," these efforts ignore "both the lessons of Paterson's past and what the city's residents really need. In that sense, Paterson remains, as Hamilton intended it, a microcosm of the country at large. Lacking the resources for genuine renewal, its people are asked to celebrate a history of which they have been, at almost every turn, the victims."[26]

This assessment, echoed by the working people and recent immigrants who form the majority of the city's committed residents, captures the impact of deindustrialization and twenty-first-century capitalism. However, many Patersonians from these communities also express "deep connections to and sincere love" for the city and excitement about sharing "Paterson's history with others as a way to elevate outsiders' perceptions of the town," as recent community listening sessions conducted by the New Jersey Historical Commission reveal. The city's contemporary challenges drive some residents' interest in historic preservation and interpretation, which they see as an opportunity to change the perception of Paterson "as a rough place." The preservation of "interesting . . . historic buildings" and architectural "craftsmanship," they argue, underscores their view of the city as a home to "a city of intelligent people that have education . . . not just gangs and drugs and what you see in the news."[27]

Paterson, New Jersey, and Lowell, Massachusetts, were the first two planned industrial cities in the United States. They both flourished during manufacturing booms and declined as economic production shifted elsewhere, and the local workforce moved to service sector jobs. Each of these now postindustrial cities has followed a similar path toward preservation and revitalization, as historians and city officials collaborated to commemorate and capitalize upon these cities' cultural heritage. Lowell was ahead of the game. The city's historic industrial district got transformed into a National Historical Park in 1978, so we know far more about the impact that this designation had on residents and workers there. As Cathy Stanton has documented in her 2006 book *The Lowell Experiment: Public History in a Postindustrial City*, the critical interpretation of the labor, immigrant, and gender history of the city created a roadmap for similar productive public history partnerships, which public historians and officials in Paterson have clearly tried to emulate.[28]

Conclusion

Paterson has only just embarked on the journey of "culture-led redevelopment" that has defined Lowell's economy for the past few decades. It is still unclear whether Paterson's minimally nascent redevelopment efforts will end up following a similar path of sequestration between the "heritage realm" and the much larger population of workers in the new postindustrial economy.[29] While many historic buildings across the city, including many of the mills as well as millworker housing, are extant, very few are formally preserved. There are organizations actively working to change that, however, such as the Hamilton Partnership for Paterson, which asserts that "historic preservation in Paterson is not about visiting stately mansions with rooms protected by velvet ropes. Preservation's primary purpose is not to re-create life as it used to be in Paterson," but rather, "improving the quality of life for people today and in the future."[30] These improvements have not yet fully manifested. At present, the relationship between the city and its public history sites and agencies is tenuous. For example, most visitors to Great Falls National Historical Park do not stop in Paterson to eat or shop, offering little of the heritage tourism boost to the local economy that many had hoped for. This may not appear to be much of a loss for those displeased with the capitalization of historic districts, but it may endanger the larger preservation efforts across the city, which have tended to be most successful where economic incorporation has defined the redevelopment efforts.[31]

The ALM's efforts to connect Paterson's labor history with its contemporary labor landscape and with twenty-first-century workers should act as a model for the city's heritage planning. While Lowell has been economically successful, it has not yet incorporated the city's changing demographics into its public history efforts in a tangible way.[32] Paterson's heritage and cultural agencies, especially those affiliated with the local government, could learn from this lesson by taking up ALM's mantle of interpreting labor and immigration history, making clear twenty-first-century linkages that speak to twenty-first-century urban dwellers and museumgoers. The real challenges that Paterson faces in the present can improve the interpretation of the city's past by exploring the impact of unequal distribution of political and economic power on workers and other vulnerable populations, past and present.

While each city likely has its own story to tell in this regard, there are universals in the shared experiences of labor history that may help to ensure that the city invests in preserving its heritage in ways that matter to its residents. These goals raise the question, though, of what the successful interpretation and preservation of labor history should look like. Is it revenue generation, such as has resulted from the transformation of Lowell? Is it the physical preservation of individual historic structures comprising the overall built environment of a city? Is it the educational impact that historic sites like the ALM have pursued in their training of local teachers and hosting of school groups on field trips? These practical concerns are significant to the public history and heritage tourism advocates working in Paterson. So, too, in Paterson and beyond, should be the possibility of building a sort of public history of labor history in which "the [workers'] memories and knowledge [find] a voice."[33] Without the effort to excavate their stories, we cannot hear the strikers' chants bouncing off of brick walls; we cannot fully understand the legacy of workers who fought on these streets to change the course of labor history.

Notes

1. Paul Goldberger, "Metropolitan Baedeker; Historic Paterson Renewing Its Past," *New York Times*, July 17, 1981.

2. "Prospectus of the Society for Establishing Useful Manufactures, [August 1791]," Founders Online, National Archives, last modified June 13, 2018, http://founders .archives.gov/documents/Hamilton/01–09–02–0114. [Original source: The Papers of Alexander Hamilton, Vol. 9, August 1791-December 1791, ed. Harold C. Syrett (New York: Columbia University Press, 1965), 144–153.

3. Garret Keizer, "Labor's Schoolhouse: Lessons from the Paterson Silk Strike of 1913," *Harper's Magazine*, July 2017.

4. Grace-Ellen McCrann, "Matthew Maguire, Father of Labor Day?" New Jersey Historical Society, https://jerseyhistory.org/matthew-maguire-father-of-labor-day/.

5. Steve Golin, *The Fragile Bridge: Paterson Silk Strike, 1913* (Philadelphia: Temple University Press, 1988).

6. Golin, *Fragile Bridge*; Martin Green, *New York 1913: The Armory Show and the Paterson Strike Pageant* (New York: Charles Scribner's Sons, 1988).

7. "Pageant of the Paterson Strike: Madison Square Garden, Saturday, June 7, 8.30 P.M." (New York: Success Press, 1913), 7.

8. Golin, *Fragile Bridge*; Green, *New York 1913*.

9. Dolores Hayden, *The Power of Place: Urban Landscapes as Public History* (Cambridge, MA: MIT Press, 1995), 47.

10. Rachel Donaldson, "Placing and Preserving Labor History," *Public Historian* 39, No. 1, February 2017, 1.

11. Edward S. Casey, *Remembering: A Phenomenological Study* (Bloomington: Indiana University Press, 1987), 147.

12. Hayden, *Power of Place* 46–47.

13. "Mill Mile," Hamilton Partnership for Paterson, Apple App Store (2017).

14. Goldberger, "Metropolitan Baedeker; Historic Paterson Renewing its Past," *New York Times*, July 17, 1981.

15. "America's Great Outdoors: Salazar, City Officials Sign Agreement to Establish Paterson Great Falls National Historical Park," U.S. Department of the Interior, November 7, 2011, https://www.doi.gov/news/pressreleases/AMERICAS-GREAT-OUTDOORS-Salazar-City-Officials-Sign-Agreement-to-Establish-Paterson-Great-Falls-National-Historical-Park.

16. "Mill Mile," Hamilton Partnership for Paterson.

17. George William Shea, *Spoiled Silk: The Red Mayor and the Great Paterson Textile Strike* (New York: Fordham University Press, 2001).

18. "Who We Are," American Labor Museum, https://www.labormuseum.net/.

19. Franklin D. Vagnone and Deborah E. Ryan, *Anarchist's Guide to Historic House Museums* (Walnut Creek, CA: Left Coast Press, 2016).

20. "The Trustees and Staff of The American Labor Museum/Botto House National Landmark congratulate the New Jersey Work Environment Council and the outstanding honorees for 2014," American Labor Museum, 2014.

21. "Mill Mile," Hamilton Partnership for Paterson.

22. "Paterson city, New Jersey," U.S. Census Bureau, 2018.

23. "Lambert Castle," National Park Service, https://www.nps.gov/pagr/learn/history culture/lambert-castle.htm, last updated May 17, 2018; "Discovery Passaic County: Mill Worker & Mill Owner," *DiscoveryPassaicCounty.org*, https://www.discover passaiccounty.org/DocumentCenter/View/195/Mill-Worker-and-Mill-Owner-PDF?bidId=.

24. "Mill Mile," Hamilton Partnership for Paterson.

25. Niall Conway, "The value of the historic urban landscape in postindustrial city of Paterson, New Jersey," Master's thesis, Rutgers University, 2018.

26. Richard Kreitner, "Forget the Musical—Alexander Hamilton's Real Legacy Is the Poverty-Stricken City He Founded," *The Nation*, February 21, 2017.

27. "Understanding Communities Study: Audience Research, Hispanic and Latino Residents of New Jersey," RK&A (for the New Jersey Historical Commission), April 2019,

https://www.state.nj.us/state/historical/assets/pdf/2019-RKA-NJHC-Understanding Communities-AudienceResearch.pdf.

28. Cathy Stanton, *The Lowell Experiment: Public History in a Postindustrial City* (Amherst: University of Massachusetts Press, 2006).

29. Ibid., 3, 32.

30. "Preservation & Development," Hamilton Partnership for Paterson, https://www .hamiltonpartnership.org/preservation-development.

31. Conway, "The value of the historic urban landscape," 83.

32. Stanton, *Lowell Experiment*, 29.

33. "Pageant of the Paterson Strike," 7.

CHAPTER 11

Latinx Murals of Texas

Memorials to Immigrant Experiences, Working-Class History, and Solidarity

ROB LINNÉ

History Uncurated

Professionally designed and curated museums, memorials, and historical sites play a vital role in educating the public and enlivening civic discourse. However, not all stories are well represented, and the sharp edges of history get smoothed over in museums or public projects dependent on large-scale funding, both public and private. As my colleagues have documented in other chapters within this collection, the story of labor is constantly silenced by those who manage our institutions' funding streams. Eric Loomis discusses our National Park Service's reticence to include class conflict in the stories our parks tell. Rachel Donaldson reveals the power wealthy community families hold to censor, or at least minimize, "uncomfortable" local history related to the Southern Tenant Farmers Museum located in the Delta Region. And Rebekah Bryer and Tom MacMillan share a cautionary tale focused on a conservative state governor of Maine who claimed the power to remove a mural of Frances Perkins. Each of these case studies illustrates the tenuous position labor history, as well as labor arts and culture, must grapple with when funded, maintained, and approved by capital or government.

For history-from-the-bottom-up to be told free of such constraints, alternative sites of discourse must be included in the larger project of telling labor's story. "Un-curated" street memorials and participatory public art projects already play an essential role in memorializing and educating about radical histories, and these sites hold the power to push the more mainstream institutions to reflect and begin telling more accurate or balanced stories themselves—especially if we give them more attention. Latinx street muralism offers an exemplary model for local, participatory, emancipatory public humanities projects that give voice to the underserved and underrepresented while facilitating community pride and inspiring activism. These murals offer a counter-narrative revealing the shortcomings of our grand museums and historical sites.

Where Everything Is Bigger
(Except Labor Museums)

When the editors of this collection put out a call for essays on important labor memorials and museums across the country, my first thought was that it would be important that my home state of Texas be included. My second thought was: *is there a labor memorial or museum in Texas?*

Unfortunately, the number of labor memorials in the vast state is minimal, and for the most part, they consist of small roadside historical markers. An historical marker noting the site of the first Farmers Alliance chapter can be visited in Lampasas, and another in Edinburg honors the important 1966 Chicano Farmworkers Strike and March.[1] There is a small park in Texas City dedicated to the 581 victims of the 1947 port inferno, the deadliest industrial accident in U.S. history.[2] A somewhat hidden statue of Samuel Gompers (lacking context) confuses tourists in San Antonio, his place of death.[3] And, University of Texas at Austin students advocated for a statue of César Chavez that now stands at the West Mall. However, there are no museums or large-scale memorials focused on labor and working-class history in the state.[4]

Yes, Texas does have a rich labor history worthy of attention. Important rural movements, including the Farmers Alliance's founding in the Texas Hill Country and the interracial Southern Tenant Farmers Union, hold significant stories, both inspiring and cautionary. Philip Foner contends the Texas/Louisiana Timber Wars, the Great Piney Woods IWW battle, was one of the most fascinating and inspiring labor struggles in our nation's history.[5] There was even a Texas Cowboy Strike in 1883 that, although failed, would be fascinating to examine in the context of all of the cowboy mythologizing at Texas historical and tourist sites.[6]

Although these movements were ultimately defeated, some labor uprisings in Texas have had a more long-lasting impact. *La Marcha* of 1966, a farmworkers strike coupled with a 400-mile march in the summer heat to the state capital, galvanized the nascent Chicano Movement and eventually led to major improvements in working conditions for farmworkers as well as stronger legal labor protections for all Texans.[7] After the major 1917 strike in East Texas oil fields, successful early organizing of oil workers created a powerful block of the Congress of Industrial Workers (CIO) and unionized much of the refinery industry across the Gulf Coast for decades to come. This unionized industry has brought generations into the middle class, where other Southern industries have largely failed to do so. The long-term success of this workforce counters the common belief that organizing in the South is futile while offering an instructive model that has yet to be followed in the region.[8]

Howard Zinn argues that for history to be usable in helping envision new possibilities, we must uncover "those hidden episodes of the past when, even if in brief flashes, people showed their ability to resist, to join together, occasionally to win."[9] Indeed, some Southern activists and unionists believe we must look back in order to move forward. Progressive politics in the region have remained especially timid and apologetic in recent decades, in part because working-class people have been so successfully cut off from any history of resistance. As Chris Krom has observed, "Consciously or unconsciously, too many buy into the myth of a monolithically conservative and unchanging South, a mindset which in turn lowers our vision of what's possible in the region now as in the future."[10] Contemporary ideologues deftly control the civic conversation by the repetition of the trope "conservative Texas values" in a never-ending circular argument that insists the state is the way it is simply because it always has been. Putting a working-class history out in the open for all to see would lay bare the fallacy inherent in *Don't mess with Texas exceptionalism*.

One site that flips the ideological script while loudly, colorfully producing art and culture from a decidedly working-class perspective is the Texas *barrio*. Across the state, in large cities and small border towns, graffiti and street murals tell Texas history from the bottom-up. Vibrant murals remind us of the vicious labor struggles that are left out of school curricula, and powerful Latinx iconography counters the cultural erasure of an entire people.[11] I argue that the informal, outdoor museums collaboratively curated for the masses throughout Latinx neighborhoods represent the state's most impressive memorial to labor, working-class culture, and the immigrant experience.

Chicano Muralism in Texas

Chicano Muralism grew out of the Mexican-American Civil Rights and labor movements of the 1960s and 1970s. Muralists brought art out into the streets of working-class communities as part of a larger project to produce and popularize cultural representations created and curated by Chicano writers and artists. These works countered the negative representations (or invisibility) offered up by mainstream media and educational institutions and arts organizations. Chicano pride was proclaimed on the walls of grocery stores, community centers, and schools, along with messages of solidarity and self-determination. The creative bricolage of the form demanded attention: imagery from Mayan temples framed scenes from the Mexican Revolution, *Tejano* music concerts, lowrider gatherings, *El Movimiento* marches, alongside joyful, everyday slice-of-life images of farm life, soccer, and home-cooking. Local oral history traditions were honored with images of neighborhood legends, myths, and folk stories.[12]

The eclectic mix of the local and every day, with scenes from historical movement politics, connected the rhetorics of identity politics with working-class solidarity. By juxtaposing images of the barrio with great revolutionary heroes and labor leaders, the artists were encouraging the viewer to consider their material lives and pocketbook issues in the framework of a larger political past, present, and future. Keeping the history alive on the walls all around the neighborhood was meant to connect "moments of community solidarity and political action and as a consequence, enhance[s] the feelings of pride attached to them as well as the belief that social change is possible."[13]

Chicano Muralism in Texas echoes the earliest art produced in the state: from indigenous rock painting to the first frescos on the missions of San Antonio and El Paso. The historical line of influence runs through the revolutionary-era Mexican muralists known as *Los Tres Grandes*—Diego Rivera, José Orozco, and David Alfaros Siqueros, as well as lesser-known artists who painted Work Projects Administration (WPA) projects across the state. For example, in 1933, Antonio Garcia completed a large, colorful mural for San Diego (Texas) High School depicting the radical Bonus Army March in Washington D.C., the previous year. Xavier Gonzalez completed a WPA mural for the San Antonio Municipal Auditorium in 1933 that drew much attention but was ultimately removed and lost to time because of bold imagery such as an upraised fist and a palm with a bleeding wound.[14]

Chicano Muralism of the 1960s and 1970s, however, was purposely more grassroots in theme and production than the muralism of the 1930s and 1940s. The works avoided censorship by the dominant white capitalist culture as they were displayed not on grand buildings where WPA art was most likely found—central post offices or municipal auditoriums—but on the walls of neighborhood businesses or parish community halls. The works were typically not the production of a well-known individual artist but were created communally, often by a team that purposely included emerging artists and community youth. These neighborhood works often did not depend on large

FIGURES 11.1 AND 11.2. "Braceros: A Legacy of Triumph" mural by Raúl Valdez and community team. Photographs by Rob Linné.

grants from the federal government or wealthy patrons, so censorship was less of an issue. Grassroots efforts influenced the works in both form, material, and theme. Graffiti street art styles and motifs were incorporated as well as the use of spray paint. The imagery, often youthful and playful, incorporated the forms familiar in folk and outsider art.

Today a new generation takes up the paintbrush and spray can to add their marks to the historical record as told on neighborhood walls. For example, muralist Raul Valdez recently led crews of university students, community leaders, and children in the painting of a mural on the San Juan, Texas community pool house honoring the *Bracero* and the farmworker past of many families in the area.[15] Before painting, the university students conducted oral history projects and researched the *Bracero* legacy that enabled many of them to become university students.[16]

The current flowering of muralism across the Southwest and other urban centers with growing Latinx communities, has honored these traditions while experimenting more with the forms and materials advanced over recent decades by graffiti, outsider, and new media artists. Murals produced today are often more substantial, more diverse in styles, and aimed at a broader online audience vis-à-vis social media. Mural artists understand their audience will widen if people *Instagram* their work or share selfies with the work in the background. Many street artists are attempting to globalize their messaging via issues such as immigration, borders, and human rights.[17]

In the following sections, I offer an overview of some of the best neighborhoods to explore Chicano Muralism in Texas as well as some of the more interesting murals focused on Latinx labor struggles and triumphs. The list is not comprehensive, but I hope this guide will offer a good beginning for people (especially educators) looking to engage with Latinx working-class culture and history from the perspective of those whose stories are being told.

East Austin

Every few years, the Texas Board of Education committees on curriculum standards or textbook adoptions meet, and all hell breaks loose. The public meetings are raucous and usually devolve into histrionics and public prayer, meant more for a television audience than for the Lord. Committee positions are politicized and typically include powerful voting blocks of conservative ideologues with little or no expertise in history, curriculum studies, or pedagogy.[18] Attempts to make the standards and curriculum materials more inclusive of diverse voices or inclusive of any examination of the political economy beyond cheerleading for the free enterprise system are met with stiff opposition.

For example, recent attempts to include Cesar Chavez and Dolores Huerta in state standards have been voted down at various stages of the process. David Barton of *WallBuilders*, a fundamentalist religious organization dedicated to ensuring school curricula remain conservative and Christian-centered, argued that Chavez lacked stature, impact, and overall contributions. After her membership in Democratic Socialists of America was revealed, the committee voted to remove Dolores Huerta.[19]

Huerta and Chavez, as historical figures, intimidate culture warriors on several fronts: they are both Latinx labor leaders, and Huerta is a female and a known socialist. Despite recent efforts and legislation encouraging and/ or mandating multicultural and global perspectives in education, content analysis studies continue to conclude "that Latinos and Latin Americans are frequently omitted from the story of the United States and often get depicted in pejorative and stereotypical ways."[20] Open discussion of political economy is rare in U.S. curricula (or most any public forum for that matter), while the most effective force advocating for working-class economic interests— the labor movement—receives minimal attention at best. These curricular gaps are a symptom of the larger project of schooling as an effective site for reproducing the status quo and maintaining the hegemony of capital.[21]

Some pedagogical models do, however, offer educators ways of circumventing this hegemony. Those teaching models that focus on *culturally relevant curricula* and prioritize local *funds of knowledge* are among the most powerful, especially when honoring marginalized communities.[22] *Place-based learning* for example, offers educators a theoretically grounded philosophy of teaching that removes the textbook and official curriculum as the focus of learning while taking students out into the community for service and exploration. The act of centering the curriculum on students' home cultures and histories counters messages of inferiority often written into school materials created for, by, and about dominant groups.[23]

Chicano murals offer a tremendous opportunity for educators to develop place-based curriculum projects that build on student knowledge and increase student motivation by making the school day relevant to the everyday. Research has documented how the inclusion of Chicano murals in the education of Latinx students has profound effects on their teachers, who often may be cultural outsiders to the communities where they teach. Through interactive work with students and community out in the streets, teachers learn to see their students from a new perspective, and they experience "a model of how to challenge passive routines of teaching and passive acceptance of or resignation to, curriculum disconnected from their students' lives."[24]

The street artists of East Austin have organically curated an engaging, accessible outdoor museum that may serve as a counter-curriculum to the dominant educational discourse constructed across town in state education buildings. A tour of the compact neighborhood will reveal many exemplars of both long-standing, traditional murals, as well as newer pieces that pop up overnight (and sometimes disappear as quickly), revealing the more ephemeral nature of the street art scene.

For example, many visitors are flocking to a few new pieces that have made the rounds on social media. The image of a Latinx Wonder Woman, who shares iconography with the traditional Virgin of Guadalupe, illustrates the *sampling* of popular culture in street murals.[25] The piece incorporates stenciling and spray paint and includes a tattoo on this superhero that reads: "*Paz Justicia, Respeto*" (Peace, Justice, Respect). The Beto O'Rourke mural that brought many to East Austin during the 2018 elections depicted O'Rourke as a superhero called to duty by a Batman-like signal flashed across the clouds of Austin.[26] And in 2018, a large work with meta-commentary on both muralism and the nativist talk of walls in our political discourse appeared on the side of a large hostel in East Austin, proclaiming: "These Walls Bring Us Together."[27] Many murals, both historic and contemporary, enliven the city with traditional Latinx iconography and offer homegrown memorials to the working-class. I will discuss two as exemplars: The Hillside Theater Mural and the César Chavez Mural.

Hillside Theater Mural

The Hillside Theater Mural at the Cantu/Pan-American Recreation Center illustrates the grassroots communal ethos of the movement.[28] In 1978, artist Raul Valdez surveyed locals, asking how they would like to see their community represented in a public work of art. The resulting 4,000 square-foot work includes many historical references often found within the first wave of Chicano murals: Aztec warriors; Miguel Hidalgo of the Mexican War for Independence; hero of the Revolution Emiliano Zapata and Mexican freedom fighters (including women); protest images from the Chicano civil rights movement; and striking farmworkers marching under the banners of *Justicia* (justice) and *Huelga* (strike). Contemporary images of *barrio* life were given equal weight to the historic and the heroic. Colorful *baile folklórico* dancers and *mariachi* players serenade kids in the back of a pickup truck and a bright red lowrider car with a license plate proclaiming "*Aztlan*." At the very center, a powerful looking mestizo woman looks over the stage of the amphitheater, with a pair of upraised fists showing broken shackles.

Hundreds of neighbors and school children helped Valdez with the painting, while many more stopped by to watch the creation take shape. One octogenarian, given a paintbrush after watching the youth work, was able to contribute to the story. The mural brought the community together at this site, and the outdoor amphitheater quickly became the place to hear *Tejano* music. The historian for the Austin Parks and Recreation Department added that the space grew to mean much more to the community than a concert venue: "It became *lo nuestro*. . . . something that belongs to us."[29] The importance of the mural to the community was in evidence when the neighborhood pushed to have the fading work restored in 2011, over 30 years after it was first painted by the youth and elders of East Austin.

Cesár Chavez Mural

A more recent work, the massive César Chavez mural framing the used car lot at Long Motors on East César Chavez Boulevard, has also become a beloved landmark for the neighborhood.[30] Long rows of produce draw the eye into the piece and to the words across the horizon: *¡Si Se Puede!* A larger-than-life César Chavez stands to the side holding a basket brimming with fruit and vegetables. But produce is not the only harvest in his basket. Chavez's harvest basket also includes documents labeled "Contract," "Workers' Rights," and "Better Pay."

The juxtaposition of the car lot commercialism with the iconography of Chavez as labor saint might at first strike some as jarring, but the placement works beautifully and speaks to the egalitarian ethos of Chicano Muralism. Out on the car lot blacktop, under the hot Texas sun, there is no cultural gatekeeper, no textbook committee deciding who is worthy of a place in our history. Art is not reserved for a hushed museum downtown in Austin or the halls of the state capital. The people's stories are told on the walls of bakeries, tamale houses, and tire shops lining these pecan-shaded streets.

San Antonio *Chicanisma*

San Antonio uniquely offers layers upon layers marking the historical developments of Latinx wall art. The oldest traces of Western art in the region remain visible in the primitive frescoes painted on the walls of Catholic missions lining the San Antonio River. Several Southwestern-style tile murals created by local artisans in the WPA remain intact along the banks of the

River Walk, a massive WPA project that transformed the city and brings millions of visitors annually to the historic sites of the city center. Walls on the West Side of San Antonio exhibit many works exemplifying early Chicano Muralism, and contemporary murals have recently flowered across the city, bringing new media and themes to the form.

One outstanding theme of the mural scene in San Antonio is the strong representation of *Chicanisma* (Chicana feminism). San Antonio murals portray many images of Zapata and Villa with guns drawn, rugged *Tejano* musicians and cowboys, and boys working on their cars or playing soccer. And, some of the city's most popular murals now celebrate the beloved Spurs basketball players and their outspoken, radical-leaning coach Greg Popovich. However, San Antonio women are well represented in murals across the city as well. These powerful women rarely make appearances in school textbooks or museums across the state, but local artists are making sure they are seen.

Chicanisma in San Antonio street art begins with the ubiquitous Virgin of Guadalupe—a symbol of Mexican identity, Mestiza strength, female empowerment, and social justice. Her image graces many murals across the city but is most pronounced on the four-story Virgin of Guadalupe saint candle with eternal flame burning at the top.[31] The massive mural of San Antonio's other saint—Selena—by 19-year-old self-taught graffiti artist Christopher Montoya has become one of the most popular murals for young people to visit and *Instagram*.[32] And while the "San Antonio Wall of Fame" mural at Pico de Gallo restaurant in Market Square does include local political heroes, Julián and Joaquin Castro, their mother Rosie, organizer and one of the founders of *La Raza Unida* Party,[33] holds court at the center of the mural.[34]

Emma Tenayuca Mural

Women are the center of many Latinx works across the city, but perhaps one of the most important is painted on a laundromat's walls. The wraparound mural on South Presa Street honors the legacy of Emma Tenayuca.[35] *La Pasionara*, as Tenaycua came to be known, organized and led the first successful, large-scale Mexican-American uprising and made all future civil and labor rights struggles seem possible.[36] Tenayuca's early education included a high school extra-curricular reading club that explored the works of Thomas Paine, Charles Beard, Karl Marx, and the Industrial Workers of the World (IWW), as well as time spent listening to the soapbox speakers at San Antonio's Plaza del Zacate, many of whom were veterans of the Mexican Revolution, anarchists, and socialists. Early on, Tenayuca became a tireless organizer who helped organize cigar workers, charter chapters of the International Ladies' Garment Workers Union (ILGWU) in San Antonio, and fight the abuse of Mexican-American workers through the Workers Alliance.[37]

In 1938, over 10,000 pecan shellers, mostly Mexican-American women, followed Tenayuca out on strike for over three months. The strike was one of the largest in the country at the time, but the workers were subjected to mass arrests, violence, and tear gas. The strike was successful (until the owners retaliated by mechanizing much of the processing), and the intense national media attention galvanized the community and demonstrated the power in Mexican-American solidarity. The groundwork was laid for all Mexican-American movements in the U.S. that followed.[38]

Artist Theresa Ybáñez produced the mural honoring Tenayuca as part of her series titled *Mujeres de San Antonio* (Women of San Antonio). The work was communally painted with other artists, local students, and customers waiting for their clothes to dry inside the laundry. The images include pecan trees, pecan shellers at work, and striking workers with fists raised, proclaiming: "We are not a conquered people!"[39]

Just about all students in the region are carted at some point to the Alamo, to learn the mostly mythical legend as told by the docents there. I contend that this shrine to *La Pasionara* tells an equally compelling story and one more relevant to the material lives of the young people of Texas. Educators should make every effort to stop by the laundry on Presa street and see how their students react to this story of the woman whose passion allowed millions to dream of the possibilities for a Mexican-American movement.

El Paso's *Segundo Barrio*:
The Other Ellis Island

El Paso del Norte has always served as a natural crossing point for travelers between north and south, even before Spanish explorers made their way through. El Paso has continued to serve as an entry point for many into the U.S. and the city has welcomed them with assistance and shelter at settlement houses or tenements. As the starting point for thousands of families in the U.S., El Paso has proudly taken to the name "The Other Ellis Island," and has begun to seek ways to preserve this history and educate from the usable past easily accessible throughout this historic city.

The Rio Vista Farm on the city's outskirts was recently named a National Treasure by the National Trust for Historic Preservation. The historic compound of mission-style adobe buildings, surrounded by lush crops irrigated by the Rio Grande, was founded in 1915 as a "poor farm" for families and neglected children. From 1951 to 1964, the complex served as an entry point and processing center for thousands who came to work U.S. farms through the *Braceros* program. Although many *Braceros* were eventually repatriated, many U.S. citizens today trace their family lines back through Rio Vista. The farm, the last *Braceros* complex standing in the country, is in early stages of planning for preservation. Hopefully, nudged along with encouragement and activism, this important American gateway will become a memorial many will make pilgrimages to, just as others take their children or their classes to Ellis Island. Texas will have its first large-scale museum focused on labor history.[40]

El Paso's *Segundo Barrio* (second neighborhood), one of the most historical communities in the Southwest and the U.S., also serves as a living memorial to the immigrant experience and working-class history. The traditional, colorfully painted neighborhood is known for its many murals telling stories of the people living in the community or who passed by at important moments. The neighborhood has become a tourist destination of late, with visitors mostly focused on street art, and guides have been produced mapping out some of the highlights.[41] Many murals include Mexican Revolutionaries who spent time in the barrio planning and organizing. Other paintings highlight Chicano movement leaders and farmworker organizers.

Sacred Heart Mural

Sacred Heart Church has long offered services for new immigrants as well as longtime residents of *Segundo Barrio*. To counter gentrification and urban renewal plans, the church had artist Francisco Delgado paint a large mural on the gymnasium, illustrating the important history enveloped in shared values of the community.[42] A beloved parish priest shares a scene with Pancho Villa—who frequented the neighborhood—digging into a plate of the local fast food: Chico's Tacos. Farm workers can be seen protesting in the background, while the infamous alligators that used to entertain children in the pond in the middle of the *Plaza de Los Lagartos* (Plaza of the Alligators) saunter freely among them. Other heroes portrayed include Olives Villanueva Aoy who started an early bilingual school at the site and Mariano Azuela, resident and author of the first novel of the Mexican Revolution. The focus of the mural, however, is the Virgin of Guadalupe morphed yet again into another female symbol: The Statue of Liberty. This Lady Liberty's beacon is a flashlight, lighting the way of a young family crossing the river. In her other hand, she holds a blanket, ready to welcome the new Americans.

The lively mix of cultural references illustrates the new cultures constantly being created and creative in the border region. As muralist Jose Burciaga (1997) contends: "Mexicanos came to settle in *El Segundo*, not to assimilate but to transculturate and form a new culture."[43] The current renaissance of muralism across El Paso and Juárez clearly mirrors the ever-evolving culture of the border through experimentalism and hybrid approaches using new media. Some of the most creative artists of large-scale street art have made it a point to make their mark on both sister cities as a meta-commentary on border politics. For example, internationally known muralist El Mac has painted photo-realistic murals of local people fighting for justice on both sides of the border and encouraged visitors to cross the river as part of the experience.[44]

This purposefully transnational art movement reminds the viewer that the border is but a sociopolitical construct that cannot contain a living culture that so easily flows back and forth, like water through fencing, regardless of how high the physical walls get built. Drawing attention to the fluidity of culture and the shared experiences and extended families living in the borderlands, the artists ask us to challenge the contemporary rhetoric of the border wall. Rather than reinforcing "us/them," these murals proclaim "*solideridad*/solidarity" among people on both sides of the border while calling into question unexamined notions underlying nationalist discourse.

Sister Cities/ Ciudades Hermanas

Augment El Paso's series of digitally augmented murals across the city perhaps best exemplifies the ideals of "transculturation" and the ever-adapting creativity of the mural form.[45] Upon downloading an app, one can visit cutting edge street art around El Paso that will then come to life digitally on your device. For example, *Sister Cities/ Ciudades Hermanas* by the artist collective *Los Dos*, portrays El Paso and Juárez as almost identical twins wrapped together in clothing with a pattern suggesting border fencing.[46] When you look at the image through the Augment ap, an Aztec jaguar floats above their heads and comes to life. The jaguar image suggests power, stealth, and craftiness. As the entire mural animates, the sisters' hair morphs between black and blonde, perhaps asking the viewer to consider how different the rhetoric might be if we were examining another border, such as the U.S./ Canadian divide. Other images float in and out of perspective, constantly shifting meaning and leaving the viewer to contemplate the wide-open future of this most accessible and dynamic art form.

Living Memorials

Even the most beloved of Latinx street murals remain in a constant state of endangerment. Images may become weathered over time, crack and peel, or the space may be tagged over. Gentrification always threatens to replace local art with commercial signage or even the destruction of historical buildings. Neighborhoods change and new residents may not remember the excitement from the time of a mural's creation and reveal. New principals take jobs at schools and want to place their own mark on school walls and may decide it is time to replace the dated artwork. Murals come and go.

The fragility and impermanence of these public works will always be problematic, but the constant state of flux also offers advantages over more permanent memorials and museums. Because street art is constantly being challenged, revised, updated, or completely painted over and begun again, active engagement is required. Each new generation must add to the collection that the neighborhood collaboratively curates. This continual creative work keeps both memory and the memorial alive. Through this process, marginalized communities tell their own stories, memorialize working-class histories written out of the "great men" texts, and build the solidarity needed to take on the continuing fights for social and economic justice.

Notes

1. Texas Historical Commission, "State Historical Markers," Angelina (Peyton) Eberly—A Pioneering Spirit | THC.Texas.gov—Texas Historical Commission. http://www.thc.texas.gov/preserve/projects-and-programs/state-historical-markers.

2. Ugc (User Generated Content), "Texas City Memorial." *Atlas Obscura*, Atlas Obscura, Nov. 18, 2015, www.atlasobscura.com/places/texas-city-memorial.

3. "Samuel Gompers—Awful Statue, San Antonio, Texas." Roadside America—Guide to Uniquely Odd Tourist Attractions. https://www.roadsideamerica.com/story/47522.

4. "Inventory of American Labor Landmarks," Labor Heritage Foundation. December 27, 2011. https://www.laborheritage.org/inventory-of-american-labor-landmarks/.

5. Philip Foner, *History of the Labor Movement in the United States, Volume 4.* (New York: International Publishers, 1964).

6. Mark A. Lause, *The Great Cowboy Strike: Bullets, Ballots & Class Conflicts in the American West.* (London: Verso Books, 2017).

7. *Texas Standard*, 2018. https://www.texasstandard.org/stories/la-marcha-the-worker-strike-that-started-a-movement/.

8. T. Priest, and M. Boston, "Bucking the Odds: Organized Labor in Gulf Coast Oil Refining." *Journal of American History* 99, No. 1 (2012): 100–110. https://doi.org/10.1093/jahist/jas085.

9. Howard Zinn and Anthony Arnove. "Columbus, The Indians, and Human Progress." In *A People's History of the United States*, 11. New York: Harper, an imprint of HarperCollinsPublishers, 2017.

10. Chris Krom, "Our Progressive Legacy: The Southern Wobblies." *Facing South*, June 9, 2005, 1. https://www.facingsouth.org/2005/05/our-progressive-legacy-the -southern-wobblies.html.

11. I use Latinx as an inclusive way of referring to communities of today. Chicano and Mexican-American are used in relation to the particular time period or movement under discussion.

12. Carlos Francisco Jackson, *Chicana and Chicano Art: ProtestArte*. (Tucson: University of Arizona Press, 2009).

13. Margaret LaWare, "Encountering Visions of Aztlan: Arguments for Ethnic Pride, Community Activism and Cultural Revitalization in Chicano Murals," *Argumentation and Advocacy*, 34, No. 3 (1998): 140–153, 146.

14. Teresa Palomo, "CHICANO MURAL MOVEMENT." The Handbook of Texas Online| Texas State Historical Association (TSHA), June 12, 2010. https://tshaonline .org/handbook/online/articles/kjc03.

15. The Mexican Farm Labor Agreement between the U.S. and Mexico, initiated in 1942, encouraged workers from Mexico to sign contracts in the U.S. for seasonal farm work.

16. Utpamas blog, "Bracero and Farmworker Mural," Published June 25, 2012. https://utpamas.wordpress.com/author/utpamas/.

17. Paul Ratjel, "The Street Art of El Paso, Texas—in Pictures," *The Guardian*, December 28, 2018. https://www.theguardian.com/artanddesign/gallery/2018/dec/28/ the-street-art-of-el-paso-texas-in-pictures.

18. Stephanie Simon, "The Culture Wars' New Front: U.S. History Classes in Texas," *The Wall Street Journal*, July 15, 2009.

19. Dan Quinn. "David Barton's Problem with Hispanic Civil Rights Leaders," Texas Freedom Network, March 15, 2016. https://tfn.org/david-bartons-problem -with-hispanic-civil-rights-leaders/.

20. Barbara C. Cruz, "Don Juan and Rebels under Palm Trees," *Critique of Anthropology* 22, No. 3 (2002): 323–342, 336.

21. James W. Loewen, *Lies My Teacher Told Me: Everything Your American History Textbook Got Wrong*. (New York: The New Press, 2018); Douglas Foley, *Learning Capitalist Culture: Deep in the Heart of Tejas*. (Philadelphia: University of Pennsylvania Press, 2010).

22. Gloria Ladson-Billings, "Toward a Theory of Culturally Relevant Pedagogy—Gloria Ladson-Billings, 1995." https://journals.sagepub.com/doi/abs/10.3102 /00028312032003465; Melvin Delgado and Keva Barton, "Murals in Latino communities: Social indicators of community strengths," *Social Work* 43, No. 4 (1998): 346–356.

23. Matt Dubel and David Sobel, "Place-based teacher education," In *Place-Based Education in the Global Age*, (Oxfordshire, U.K.: Routledge, 2014).

24. Donahue, "Connecting Classrooms and Communities Through Chicano Mural Art," *Multicultural Perspectives* 13, No. 2 (2011): 70–78.

25. Located 419 Congress Ave, Austin.

26. Located on Waller St. between Cesar Chavez and E. 2nd. .

27. Located at 807 E. 4th St., Austin.

28. Located 2100 E. 3rd St. Austin.

29. Juan Castillo, "Bold and Colorful Once Again, Mural at East Austin Outdoor Theater Comes into Focus," *American-Statesman* Staff, September 27, 2018.

30. Located 1200 E. Cesár Chavez, Austin,

31. Located 1301 Guadalupe St., San Antonio.

32. Located 4913 S. Flores St., San Antonio.

33. La Raza Unida, established in South Texas in 1970 as a third-party alternative, spread across Texas and California.

34. Located 111 Leona St., San Antonio.

35. Located 1100 S. Presa St., San Antonio.

36. "Jan. 31, 1938: Emma Tenayuca Leads Pecan Sheller Strike," Zinn Education Project. https://www.zinnedproject.org/news/tdih/emma-tenayuca-leads-pecan-sheller -strike/.

37. "Emma Beatrice Tenayuca Civil Rights Activist, Labor Organizer and Educator," Chief Standing Bear | AmericansAll. https://americansall.org/legacy-story -individual/emma-tenayuca-0.

38. Ibid.

39. Theresa Ybañez, "Murals of Emma Tenayuca, Corazones de la Comunidad, and Rosita Fernández," *Frontiers* 24, 2 (2003) 237–243.

40. "Rio Vista Farm." National Trust for Historic Preservation. https://saving places.org/places/rio-vista#.XGBRt9F7nBI.

41. https://visitelpaso.com/places/segundo-barrio-murals.

42. Rafael Garcia, "Mural Tells Segundo Barrio Neighborhood's History, Priest Says," *El Paso Times*, November 29, 2017.

43. Miguel Juárez, José Antonio Burciaga, and Cynthia Weber, "Colors on Desert Walls: The Murals of El Paso," Foreword. In *Colors on Desert Walls: the Murals of El Paso*. (El Paso: Texas Western Pr., 1997), xvi.

44. Alex Duran, "El Paso X Cd. Juárez Border Murals by EL MAC," *FUSION MAGAZINE*, January 27, 2016.

45. "Augment El Paso." AR Murals. http://augmentelpaso.com/.

46. Freddy Martinez, "On the Streets of El Paso and Juarez, 'Sister Cities' Art Project Pays Tribute to Border Communities," *Remezcla*. http://remezcla.com/features/ culture/interview-los-dos/.

CHAPTER 12

Labor and Art

Interpreting the Maine Labor Mural Controversy

REBEKAH BRYER AND
THOMAS MACMILLAN

A lot of energy in this country is expended in an effort
to suppress, alter or censor history for the benefit of
power and maintaining a narrative that wants very
much to have people forget that they can win rights,
and economic and political benefits by organizing and
opposition. The removal of the labor mural was obviously
one such attempt—one that backfired because it brought
attention to history many people were ignorant of.
—Maine-based activist and artist Robert Shetterly, 2018

Introduction

In 2011, the abrupt removal of a previously little-known mural from the reception area of a government building in Augusta, Maine sparked a national controversy and conversation about the place of labor, politics, and public art in twenty-first-century American life. As Robert Shetterly points out, it was one of many attempts.[1] The work in question is eleven panels painted by muralist Judy Taylor depicting the history of labor in Maine. The mural, depicting Mainers of many races and genders throughout the state's history, was public art that celebrated working people in their successes and failures. It became a symbol in the national arguments over the relevancy and role of the labor movement in the nation's history.[2] The ultimate fallout from the dispute, which included the defeat of priority antiunion legislation for the incoming Republican officials, speaks to the uneasy positioning of the labor movement in current policy and public memory, where right-to-work is the norm for some. The mural now hangs in the lobby of the Maine State Museum and gives no clues to the controversy that surrounded it. The struggle over it demonstrates how representations of the past often make contentious meaning in the present, and how the legacies of the United States working-class broadly and the labor movement, in particular, continue to shift today.

This chapter traces the linkages between the Maine Labor Mural and its removal by then-Governor Paul LePage and to the fight over antiunion legislation in both Maine and around the United States. We argue that its opponents viewed the art as pro-worker rather than as a faithful or accurate interpretation of Maine's labor history by examining the two events in connection to each other. Once in power, those opposed to organized labor sought to demonstrate the administration's pro-business intention by removing the mural permanently. This understanding serves as a symbol of the larger fight between conscious workers and the LePage administration over various pieces of legislation, with the most important being the so-called "right-to-work" law. While the debate over the labor mural was ultimately deemed a distraction by LePage's Republican allies, its removal from the walls of the Department of Labor a little over two months into LePage's term made clear that his administration would be staunchly opposed to collective action by the state's working class.

Known for audacious comments before getting elected governor, throughout his time running for and serving in office LePage attacked Democrats, independents, public schools, people of color, socialists, organized labor, and other opponents with language not often used in public discourse. Early prominent attacks included promising to tell the Obama administration to "go to hell" and the NAACP to "kiss my butt," as well as mocking those concerned with chemicals in plastic by claiming that "the worst case is some women may have little beards."[3] While his comments opposing labor unions were within the conservative mainstream prior to getting elected, these earlier attacks invited increased scrutiny by the national media. Beyond setting the stage for the political machinations of right-to-work in Maine, LePage's actions to remove the mural, which beforehand was relatively unknown, drew national attention to the history and memory of Maine's labor movement. The conversation shifted concerning how the labor movement would be commemorated.

As this particular dispute happened in the recent past, much of this chapter concerns the public discourse about right-to-work laws and the Maine Labor Mural. Our focus is on the reporting surrounding the mural's removal and right-to-work through interviews with individuals connected to the conflict

FIGURE 12.1. The Maine Labor Mural, Judy Taylor, muralist. Maine State Museum photograph.

and legislation. By looking at this controversy and the political fight over right-to-work in tandem, the connections between public art, right-to-work, and the interpretations of both become more apparent and new questions get raised about the relationship between public art, politics, and organized labor. Most importantly, the controversy that surrounded the Maine Labor Mural was not only a fight about the representation of workers and employers in public art but also part of the much larger and longer conflict between organized labor and organized capital.

Setting the Stage: Maine Labor, the Mural's Beginnings and Right-to-Work

Maine has a long history of labor disputes. In 1636, lobstermen near what is now Cape Elizabeth conducted the first documented work stoppage in colonial North America.[4] Despite conflict between labor and capital virtually coinciding with permanent European settlement, fierce strikes by shoemakers in Lewiston-Auburn, trolley operators and longshoremen in Portland, and papermakers in Jay, Maine, the state has few public spaces that commemorate workers and their struggles. More rural than most other New England states,

Maine's decentralized working class struggled against but rarely bested capital throughout the nineteenth and twentieth centuries. However, during the peak of labor's power in the decades after World War II, the tide turned in favor of organized labor, at least in the dispute over "right-to-work" legislation.

Since the passage of the 1947 Taft-Hartley Act, its inaccurately named 'right-to-work' provision has been a political football across the United States. Rather than guaranteeing the right to a job, as the phrase suggests, right-to-work refers to allowing workers to opt-out of paying an administrative fee (often inaccurately called dues) to the union, which represents them on the job regardless of their membership in the organization. This fee, used to cover the so-called fair share of the cost expended on negotiating and enforcing a union contract, is often met with opposition by antiunion workers, employers, and their allies in government. Before 2011, opponents of unions made five attempts at grouping Maine with other primarily rural states that adopted 'Right to Work' legislation. The initial effort in 1948 failed in a statewide referendum. Opponents included unions and esteemed Republican Senator Margaret Chase Smith, who criticized the proposal as "not workable or sound."[5] Bipartisan forces defeated similar bills before the Legislature in 1961, 1963, 1979, and 1999. Throughout the latter half of the twentieth century, the majority of Mainers and their representatives repeatedly rejected "right-to-work" and other antiunion legislation. This pro-union legacy played a vital role in igniting support for the labor mural and its visual representation of the state's working-class in 2011 and beyond.

Unlike the "vernacular" Latinx street murals of Texas discussed in Rob Linné's chapter 11, the Maine Labor Mural has always been a piece of "official" public art.[6] In 2007, the Maine Arts Commission posted a call for proposals for artwork to decorate the reception area of the Maine Department of Labor offices in Augusta, funded in part by the U.S. Department of Labor.[7] The completed mural by Maine-based artist Judy Taylor depicts the state's labor history over time. Featured among its scenes are the struggle to end child labor, a 1937 strike of shoemakers in Lewiston-Auburn, and the 1987 International Paper strike in Jay.[8] The mural became a way to establish a very public and tangible link to the state's labor past as it moved into a modern building.[9] Taylor's design consisted of eleven seven-foot-high oil-on-board paintings totaling 35 feet in length. It featured groupings of people imposed on a background of photographic images. Deputy Commissioner of Labor Jane Gilbert stated that the mural would be "an accurate depiction of organized labor's role in the history of Maine," and that Taylor's vision "grasped what we were trying to do around the history of labor in Maine and was really able to reflect that best."[10] Robert Shetterly, an artist involved with the protests surrounding its removal, described it as "subdued—both in color and content. A gentle telling of labor history."[11] Taylor consulted closely with Charles Scontras, then a University of Maine professor and Research Associate with the Bureau of Labor Education, to select scenes and industries that were important to the state's labor history.[12]

The mural achieved its intended goal. Laura Fortman, then the state's Labor Commissioner, stated that it inspired her every time she walked into the building. In an unusual move for commemorative artifacts, it also depicted failures like the unsuccessful but historically significant strike in 1937.[13] In an opinion piece for the *Bangor Daily News* shortly after the mural was unveiled, Scontras described the primary theme of the mural: "Maine is a bit more than the stereotypical romantic images. . . . Maine was not Nirvana. The creative role of dissent, protest, conflict, and the demand for social justice in the workplaces of the state, form an integral part of our historical legacy."[14] To reiterate, the piece forms an argument where Maine's labor history exists in spaces of both triumph and loss. This is an unusual tactic for commemoration in general, but particularly for a piece of public art initially intended for a government building's reception area. It commemorates labor history while complicating notions about the state of labor in Maine. Organized labor's role is championed yet its struggles are not hidden.

Without controversy, the mural remained in the Department of Labor from its unveiling in 2008 until its removal in early 2011. That year marked a nationwide shift toward austerity and increased scapegoating of public sector workers and their labor unions. The financial crisis and late 2007 through 2009 economic recession soon turned the public art into a point of controversy. In the context of the financial crisis, right-to-work once more came before the Maine State Legislature. This time, public-sector unions received blame for the recession. The crisis led to calls for austerity and for legislation to curtail organized labor's already declining power. Despite the election of labor-endorsed Barack Obama and Democratic majorities in both the Senate and House, no meaningful labor legislation got approved by the 111th U.S. Congress. With little to show for its long-term support of the Democratic Party, the 2010 midterm elections demonstrated that organized labor was highly vulnerable to attack from its opponents on the right. In Maine and elsewhere, ultraconservative Tea Party activists energized the Republican Party.[15] Far-right politicians, ascendant in the Republican Party, elected numerous state-level offices and reclaimed control of Congress.[16]

Republicans won majorities in both bodies of the Maine Legislature and the governorship, controlling all three for the first time in nearly 40 years. LePage won with 38 percent of the vote. LePage and independent candidate

Eliot Cutler opposed organized labor. Maine's labor unions lined up behind third-place finisher Democrat Libby Mitchell, denouncing Cutler and LePage for their closeness with big business. Despite not winning a majority of votes in the general election, LePage believed that he and the Republican-controlled Legislature had secured a mandate to pass antiunion legislation, including right-to-work. Nationally and in Maine, conservatives and labor unions geared up for battle in the changing political landscape.[17]

The first significant public opposition to this national conservative agenda appeared on Valentine's Day, 2011. The Teaching Assistants Association at the University of Wisconsin-Madison organized a demonstration against Republican Governor Scott Walker's plan to sharply limit public-sector unions' ability to bargain collectively.[18] Closely linked to billionaire industrialists like the Koch brothers, newly elected conservatives viewed state budget shortfalls and economic precarity as an opportunity to reduce public-sector employment.[19] Efforts began to curtail the influence of public-sector unions and introduce right-to-work legislation in union strongholds.

On February 15, tens of thousands of protesters occupied the Wisconsin capitol building in protest against the proposed legislation. During the National Governors Association meeting in Washington, D.C., on February 26, Paul LePage announced that his administration would emulate Walker by "going after right to work."[20] Recognizing that passing the legislation was "going to be a battle" the governor predicted that there would be similar protests in the state. He suggested that labor activists were "going to leave Wisconsin and come to Maine" once they learned of plans for renegotiating labor relations in the state.[21] Emboldened by the fight in Wisconsin, LePage sought to curtail labor unions by passing right-to-work legislation. He also tried to erase the most visible symbols of Maine's labor history from public memory, replacing this history with a false neutrality narrative between workers and employers.

Controversy Erupts

Two months after Paul LePage was sworn in as Maine's 74th governor and four weeks after he announced his prioritization of right-to-work, the *New York Times* reported that he sought to remove the mural from the Department of Labor's reception area. On March 23, under the headline "Mural of Maine's Workers Becomes Political Target," the newspaper reported that this decision represented the latest in a wave of antilabor sentiment across the country. The *Times* cited LePage spokesperson Adrienne Bennett, who noted that it did not represent the interests of the Department of Labor, "a state agency that works very closely with both employees and employers, and we need to have a décor that represents neutrality."[22] The article discussed LePage's previous clashes with unions, his plans to rename conference rooms, and the possibility of moving the artwork to the state museum. Among the names removed was Maine's Frances Perkins, the Secretary of Labor from 1933 and the first woman appointed to the U.S. Cabinet. The director of the Frances Perkins Center called it "unthinkable to me that anyone would consider her an enemy of any part of American life, including business. I mean she was not anti-business."[23]

Coverage grew, with stories in the *Washington Post*, on National Public Radio, in Salon and Politico, and on MSNBC's "Rachel Maddow Show." Stories focused on the mural's removal for its pro-labor stance. A note from an unnamed Maine businessperson to the LePage administration called the piece's artistic style reminiscent of "communist North Korea, where they use these murals to brainwash the masses."[24] The director of the Labor Department secretly removed the art and put it into storage to be hung in a "suitable location" at a later date. The conflict escalated.[25] A few days later, the governor admitted that the removal was poorly timed, insisting that it "should have been done later on, not when we are trying to get a budget passed."[26] However, he refused to return the artwork to its former location. The U.S. Department of Labor, which provided a majority of the project's funding, requested that the LePage administration reimburse the federal government or display the painting in another state building. Democratic Congresswoman Chellie Pingree commented that "public art belongs to all of us, and I don't think the governor should have acted so hastily in taking it down. It wasn't a decision for one person."[27]

Created to tell Maine's labor story, the mural was thrust into a larger national conversation about public art. Its placement in storage prompted protests at the Capitol and a lawsuit to return it to the Department of Labor's reception area. Self-described "muralistas" sprang into action. Political commentator Edgar Allen Beem wrote that he was motivated by what he believed to be "government censorship" and "the cause of freedom of expression."[28]

The 2011 lawsuit argued that removing the mural "violated First Amendment rights protected in the U.S. Constitution, as well as the state's contract with the artist." LePage defended his administration's right to decide what could be on display in government offices. Thrown out by a federal judge, in 2012, the case got dismissed on appeal. In a second ruling, Judge John A. Woodcock Jr. determined that the governor had the right to decide what type of art was displayed. "To hold a jury trial and subject elected officials to cross-examination whenever a dissident group contends that a governmental action, which affects a governmental message, is politically motivated," he wrote, "would risk transforming the courts into stages for political theater."[29] While labor groups like the Maine AFL-CIO defended the work, Beem and many other 'muralistas' were seemingly motivated more by a commitment to good government than the cause of the working Mainer. The stage was set for a very public discussion on its content and what it meant to remove it from public view.

Unlikely Victory for Labor

Just weeks after the removal of the labor mural, Governor LePage submitted a budget met with fire by labor unions and their supporters. Among the proposals put forth were significant increases in the amount state workers contributed toward pensions, raising the age of retirement by two years, and freezing cost of living increases for retired state workers. This budget, which sought to balance the state expenses and close a pension shortfall by cutting benefits and increasing costs to public workers, was vehemently opposed by organized labor and liberal groups. Heading into the legislative session, many observers believed that these measures were likely to pass in Maine as they had already done in union strongholds like Wisconsin, Michigan, and elsewhere.[30]

However, commentators had not taken into account the fury aroused by the mural's removal and the role it would play in defeating the proposals. Newly elected Republicans faced pressure from their constituents after the AFL-CIO-affiliated canvassing organization, Working America, went door-to-door in Senate districts, including Waterville, Rockland, and Augusta.[31] The majority of voters in these cities, which had formerly employed large numbers of unionized wage-earners, voted Republican in the previous election.[32] Grassroots organizing, which mainly took place during the coldest days of winter, combined with growing anger at the poor reputation that the LePage administration had garnered across the country worked to ensure defeat for this priority legislation. Maine voters pressured their representatives to support the restoration of the mural, oppose right-to-work legislation, and generally oppose the LePage administration's push for austerity. By the end of the legislative session, a majority of Senators opposed right-to-work, and the Senate's Republican leadership decided to carry-over LD 788 to the next session. The shorter 2012 legislative session was no kinder to LePage. Right-to-work did not receive a vote in the 125th Legislature. Writing shortly after the end of the 2011 legislative session, the *Wall Street Journal* complained that LePage mishandled the controversy, which caused dissension in the legislative caucus, and ultimately, the defeat of almost all of the priority legislation related to labor. The mural controversy, combined with active grassroots campaigning, won an unlikely labor victory.[33]

Public Art and Right-to-Work: The Aftermath

In January 2013, two years after its removal from public view, the mural went back on display. Seeking to end the conflict, Bernard Fishman, curator of the Museum, had reached out to the LePage administration to have it loaned to the Maine State Museum and Archives. He hoped that the work's reappearance would "make people think about history, about the meaning of art, and about art in public places."[34] Commentator Edgar Allen Beem wrote that some in the pro-mural camp believed that the 2012 election, which saw majorities of Democrats elected to both bodies of the state legislature and "the appointment of Democratic [Attorney General] Janet Mills, who does not support LePage's mural ban, had something to do with [the labor mural] coming out of the closet."[35] Contrary to the wishes of some who sought to return it to the Labor Department reception area, the piece remains in the State Museum lobby and is on display six days a week to the general public. It is now on view for those passing through the complex, returning to the commemorative position it held before the 2011 controversy.[36]

Despite failing to pass right-to-work legislation in 2011 and 2012, LePage persistently reintroduced the bill several other times before being term-limited out of office following the 2018 gubernatorial election. In each instance, opponents were successful in stopping its passage. However, by 2017, the threat of a court ruling to force the end of service fees compelled changes in the ranks of organized labor. Bypassing the Legislature, the LePage administration successfully negotiated 'right-to-work' into contract negotiations with public-sector unions. In August 2017, the Maine State Employees Association (MSEA) and American Federation of State, County and Municipal Employees (AFSCME), concerned with a case before the U.S. Supreme Court that could end "fair share" or representation fees to public sector unions, approved a contract that eliminated the fair-share fee and in return won pay increases that were larger than expected. The *Bangor Daily News* wrote that this agreement, "can't be counted as anything other than a win for the governor."[37] Less than a year later, on June 27, 2018, the Supreme Court confirmed the union's fears and issued the long-expected ruling in the Janus case that requiring service fees from non-union members was unconstitutional. In a statement, AFL-CIO President Richard Trumka said that the decision demonstrated that the court had "conceded to the dark web of corporations and wealthy donors who wish to take away the freedoms of working people."[38]

Conclusion

Looking back on the mural saga, Kevin Raye, the president of the Republican-led Senate and Robert Shetterly, one of the artists who was a plaintiff in the lawsuit against the LePage administration, noted that the mural dust-up reflected a political moment during the early days of the LePage administration. Raye did not know about the mural and saw its removal as an "unnecessary and provocative action that created a divisive sideshow" from the work of governing. For Shetterly, the fight was indicative of the larger contentiousness of Maine politics. The mural was a "flashpoint" for the anger many felt about LePage's ascendency to the governorship. These perspectives illustrate how the Maine Labor Mural controversy served as both a symbol over the struggles of representation of labor history and the contentiousness of class conflict. Paul LePage won the governorship of Maine in 2010 with only 37.6 percent of the vote, with the other 62.4 percent split between the Democratic nominee and three independent candidates. The top independent, Eliot Cutler, received 36 percent of the vote and finished in second place ahead of the union-endorsed Democrat, Libby Mitchell. Less than a week before the election, Maine's largest labor unions had held a press conference criticizing Cutler and LePage.[39]

Public memorials in general, and art in particular, clearly have the power to animate public opinion. As cities and states debate the removal of Confederate monuments, arguments about the Civil War have re-entered the national discussion. Although working-class history has not received as much discussion, as pointed out in Erik Loomis's chapter eight on labor history and the National Park Service, the Maine Labor Mural controversy proves that the public memorialization of laborers can ignite passionate discourse. Occupy Wall Street, conversations about the "one percent", cuts to school budgets, teacher strikes, and a burgeoning socialist movement have made national headlines. While Maine was not Wisconsin, where thousands of people overwhelmed the Capitol building, Maine's activists and the labor community demanded that the mural be put back on public display. Ultimately, public pressure succeeded in having the piece placed in a much more visible location at the Maine State Museum. Animated by the controversy, the AFL-CIO's canvassing affiliate, Working America, channeled the public's frustration and successfully pressured Republican legislators to oppose right-

FIGURE 12.2. June 2011 prounion rally in Augusta, Maine, sponsored by the Maine State Employees Association. Photo credit: Maine Service Employees Association, SEIU Local 1989.

to-work legislation just as Republicans like Margaret Chase Smith had done generations earlier. Right-to-work legislation was rejected in Maine.[40]

The work reappeared in the public discourse in 2018. In a brief letter to the *Portland Press Herald* following the election of Democrat Janet Mills as Maine's next governor, Dan Turner of Parsonfield wrote: "a public request that she please, with all possible speed, restore Judy Taylor's labor-history mural to its rightful place in the Maine Department of Labor building." That this work of art, which had not been in the news since its relocation to the Maine State Museum in early 2013, would stir someone to write to the state's largest newspaper is indicative of the impact that the mural had on the general public's memory. Turner concluded that he "can't think of a more symbolic way that she [Governor-Elect Mills] could indicate her determination to restore the respect for the working folks of Maine that has been so sadly absent in the eight years of the LePage administration."[41]

Given the national controversy surrounding these panels, it is important to consider the role that public art might play in future labor struggles. Can memorialized labor history, such as statues of famous figures like Mother Jones or César Chávez or generalized depictions of famous labor battles like Ludlow or Homestead, galvanize the public to understand this too-hidden history of the United States? Threats to installations of public history and art ignite broad-based passion in ways that bread-and-butter issues like wages, collective bargaining agreements, and work stoppages sometimes do not.

Known for his series "Americans Who Tell the Truth," public artist and activist Robert Shetterly, once noted:

> Generally I think public art, by itself, plays a minor role in public perception. For many people, it becomes empty background after a while . . . My experience is that people will walk by public art and not ask themselves basic questions about its purpose unless reminded of its importance.[42]

For several years, Maine's labor mural controversy shone a bright light on the cause of working people, allowing activists like Shetterly to bring "attention to history many people were ignorant of." Largely ignored before the controversy, the threatened removal or destruction of public art became a focal point in the conversation between labor and capital during a period of rising class conflict, thus reminding us of how public renderings of historical moments can shape discussion even without initially intending to do so.[43]

Notes

1. Robert Shetterly. Email to authors. December 8, 2018. Robert Shetterly of Brooksville, Maine, is an award-winning artist and activist who was prominent in the movement to restore the labor mural for public viewing. He founded the *Americans Who Tell the Truth* project in 2002. AWTT produces "portraits and narratives [which] highlight citizens who courageously address issues of social, environmental, and economic fairness." www.americanswhotellthetruth.org/.

2. Despite Maine's overwhelmingly white population, people of color have played significant roles in the state from its founding. For example, Portland had a significant free black community before the Civil War, which provided most of the longshoremen for the city's transatlantic port. Black sailors played a significant role in nineteenth-century trade out of Portland. See W. Jeffrey Bolster, *Black Jacks: African American Seamen in the Age of Sail* (Cambridge, MA: Harvard University Press, 1997) and Michael C. Connolly, *Seated by the Sea: The Maritime History of Portland, Maine, and Its Irish Longshoremen* (Gainesville: University Press of Florida, 2010).

3. As Paul LePage's tenure as governor of Maine ended, the *Portland Press Herald*, the state's largest newspaper, compiled a retrospective of LePage's most audacious quotes that demonstrate this capacity for language: "Paul LePage's Greatest Hits," *Portland Press Herald*, December 30, 2018.

4. In March 2020, union electrician and state representative Scott Cuddy intro-duced a joint resolution honoring the strikers, which passed unanimously. Efforts are underway to place a memorial at the nearby Crescent Beach State Park, which overlooks the island: Joint Resolution Commemorating the First Strike Over Working Conditions in What Would Become the United States," State of Maine Legislature, http://www.mainelegislature.org/LawMakerWeb/summary.asp?ID=280076837. For more on the striking lobstermen see E. A. Churchill, "A Most Ordinary Lot of Men: The Fishermen at Richmond Island, Maine, in the Early Seventeenth Century," *New England Quarterly* 57, no. 2 (1984): 184–204.

5. "The Truth About Right to Work Laws," Bureau of Labor Education, University of Maine, April 2011. https://umaine.edu/ble/wp-content/uploads/sites/181/2011/04/RighttoWork_Laws.pdf. Senator Margaret Chase Smith is one of Maine's most famous politicians. She was the first woman to serve in both houses of the United States Congress and is most well known for her "Declaration of Conscience" speech in 1950, which made her one of the first senators to criticize McCarthyism openly.

6. The difference between official (governmental) and vernacular (from the ground up) is outlined in John E. Bodnar, *Remaking America: Public Memory, Commemora-tion, and Patriotism in the Twentieth Century* (Princeton, N.J.: Princeton University Press, 1991).

7. Interconnections between public art and labor have a long history. For example, in the 1930s, the federal government employed numerous artists in the Works Prog-ress Administration's Art, Music, Theatre, and Writers Projects. See Barbara Melosh, *Engendering Culture: Manhood and Womanhood in New Deal Public Art and Theater* (Washington: Smithsonian Institution Press, 1991). Federal funding for art projects flowed from the National Endowment for the Arts, starting in 1965 ("About the NEA," National Endowment for the Arts, https://www.arts.gov/about-nea.). Such funding also came from state and city budgets ("Grants," National Endowment for the Arts, https://www.arts.gov/grants-organizations/public-art-resources).

8. Judy Taylor, "The Maine Department of Labor Mural," *Judy Taylor Studio*, http://www.judytaylorstudio.com/mural1.html.

9. Craig Crosby, "Labor of Love," *Kennebec Journal*, August 23, 2008, *Judy Taylor Studio*, http://www.judytaylorstudio.com/1crosby.html. Many of the articles used for this analysis come from links that Taylor herself provided on her website.

10. Robert Levin, "Artist labors on epic work," *The Mount Desert Islander*, June 12, 2008, *Judy Taylor Studio*, http://www.judytaylorstudio.com/levin.html.

11. Robert Shetterly, email to authors, December 8, 2018.

12. Scontras is the preeminent Maine labor historian. He published 19 books on the topic between 1966 and 2017. His face is replicated onto a worker depicted in the panel.

13. Crosby, "Labor of Love," *Kennebec Journal*. For more on the strike itself and others like it, see Charles A. Scontras, *Organized Labor in Maine: War, Reaction, Depression and the Rise of the CIO 1914–1943*, Bureau of Labor Education, The Uni-versity of Maine, 2002.

14. John Buell, "Mural shows off Maine's social history," *Bangor Daily News*, July 8, 2008, *Judy Taylor Studio*, http://www.judytaylorstudio.com/buell.html.

15. Abby Goodnough, "Maine Governor: Energized Base Tilts Rightward," *New York Times*, October 28, 2010.

16. In one incident emblematic of conservative anger at organized labor, delegates to the Maine Republican Party convention tore down pro-labor posters. They left an anonymous note in an eighth-grade classroom at King Middle School in Portland. It read, "A Republican was here. What gives you the right to propagandize impressionable kids?" Kevin Miller, "Maine GOP apologizes for convention incident," *Bangor Daily News*, May 12, 2010.

17. Christopher Cousins, "Labor union members attack records of LePage, Cutler," *Bangor Daily News*, October 27, 2010.

18. Deborah Ziff, "On Campus: UW-Madison students to Walker: "Don't Break My ♥," *Wisconsin State Journal*, updated May 22, 2012.

19. Eric Lipton, "Billionaire Brothers' Money Plays Role in Wisconsin Dispute," *New York Times*, February 21, 2011.

20. Stephen Hohmann, "LePage: 'We're going after right-to-work,'" *Politico*, February 26, 2011.

21. Ibid.

22. Steven Greenhouse, "Mural of Maine's Workers Becomes Political Target," *New York Times*, March 23, 2011.

23. Besides Perkins, rooms were named for other well-known labor figures, including Cesar Chavez. The Department of Labor announced that it had launched a contest to rename the rooms. Susan Sharon, "Maine Takes Down Labor Mural," National Public Radio, March 24, 2011, https://www.npr.org/2011/03/24/134832723/ Maine-Takes-Down-Labor-Mural; Steven Greenhouse, "Mural of Maine's Workers Becomes Political Target," *New York Times*, March 23, 2011.

24. Jennifer Epstein, "Maine governor removes labor mural," *Politico*, March 28, 2011.

25. Ros Kransey, "Revisionist art history as Maine removes labor mural," *Reuters*, March 29, 2011.

26. Tom Bell, "Governor: Mural was removed at a bad time," *Portland Press Herald*, April 1, 2011.

27. Tom Bell, "U.S. Labor Department asks for return of Maine mural funding," *Portland Press Herald*, April 5, 2011.

28. Greenhouse, "Mural of Maine's Workers Becomes Political Target," *New York Times*, March 23, 2011. Edgar Allen Beem, "Maine Labor History Mural Restored," *New England Living*, January 16, 2013.

29. Staff Reports, "Judge rules removal of labor mural was justified," *Portland Press Herald*, March 23, 2012.

30. Kevin Miller, "LePage budget draws fire from union," *Bangor Daily News*, March 3, 2011.

31. Thomas MacMillan, a coauthor of this chapter, worked as a canvasser for Work-

ing America briefly during this campaign. An internal memorandum produced by the organization claimed that it signed up 7,000 new, nonunion members in Maine as a result of their organizing efforts. *Working America* (June 2011), *Pension Rap 1.0, Internal Report of Working America*, Unpublished.

32. In Augusta, a resident wrote a letter to the editor attacking Working America for going door-to-door in the low-income Sand Hill neighborhood. Using Tea Party rhetoric, he argued against the organization and its strategy, instead writing that "Responsible, taxpaying citizens need to stand up and take control of our neighborhoods and our government." State Senator Roger Katz, an Augusta Republican, was a top target of the AFL-CIO in their bid to defeat "right-to-work" and austerity in the state budget. Eddie Kutniewski, "Time to make 'Hope and Change' Happen," *Kennebec Journal*, April 13, 2011.

33. In an email to the authors, former Senate President Kevin Raye noted, "Very simply, I believe Governor LePage overplayed his hand. Many Republicans, including me, appreciate the fundamental value of unions, even though I believe some modern-day unions have likewise overplayed their hand with unreasonable demands that have had a negative impact on jobs and the economy," November 29, 2018; Allysia Finley, "How Bad Art Killed Good Labor Reforms; Maine's governor picks the wrong fight with unions," *Wall Street Journal*, July 9, 2011.

34. Clarke Canfield, "Labor mural removed by Maine gov. back on display," *Salon*, January 15, 2013.

35. Edgar Allen Beem, "Maine Labor History Mural Restored," *New England Living*, January 16, 2013, https://newengland.com/today/living/new-england-environment/maine-labor-history-mural-restored/.

36. "Maine Labor History Mural," *Maine State Museum*, January 14, 2013. https://mainestatemuseum.org/exhibit/maine-labor-history-mural/. There was also a play produced by Deering High School that dramatized the events depicted in the eleven panels but did not address its controversial removal. See "Deering High to present Maine labor mural play," *Central Maine*, February 18, 2013.

37. "Maine state union members vote to accept LePage's 'right to work' contract language," *Bangor Daily News*, August 31, 2017.

38. Kenneth Quinnell, "Working People Stand Resolute in the Face of Janus Ruling," AFL-CIO, June 27, 2018.

39. Kevin Raye, email to authors, November 29, 2018; Robert Shetterly, email to authors, December 8, 2018. See: Christopher Cousins, "Labor union members attack records of LePage, Cutler," *Bangor Daily News*, October 27, 2010.

40. Christopher Burns, "Decades in decline: The fall of unions in Maine," *Bangor Daily News*, May 6, 2016.

41. "Letter to the editor: Gov.-elect Mills, time to bring back the labor mural," *Portland Press Herald*, November 17, 2018.

42. Shetterly email to authors, December 8, 2018.

43. Ibid.

Contributors

Editors

ROBERT FORRANT, a University of Massachusetts Lowell Professor of History and Lawrence History Center board member, worked extensively on community-based programs dedicated to the centennial anniversary of the 1912 Bread & Roses Strike. Publications include *The Great Lawrence Textile Strike of 1912: New Scholarship on the Bread & Roses Strike* (2014), *The Big Move: Immigrant Voices from a Mill City* with Christoph Strobel (2011), and *Metal Fatigue: American Bosch and the Demise of Metalworking in the Connecticut River Valley* (2009). A participant in public history and digital history projects funded by Mass Humanities, the National Endowment for the Humanities, and the Lowell National Historical Park, he is working on a digital immigration history website and an immigration history monograph on Lowell, Massachusetts (forthcoming).

MARY ANNE TRASCIATTI directs the Labor Studies program and is Professor of Rhetoric and Public Advocacy at Hofstra University. She is also president of Remember the Triangle Fire Coalition. Since 2010, she has helped organize the annual official Triangle fire commemoration. She is leading the project to build the Triangle Fire Memorial, scheduled for dedication in 2023. She is coeditor of the forthcoming anthology *Talking to the Girls: Intimate and Political Essays on the Triangle Shirtwaist Factory Fire* (2022). She wrote the foreword for *My Life as a Political Prisoner: The Rebel Girl Becomes "No. 11710"* (2019), the prison memoir of radical labor activist Elizabeth Gurley Flynn, and is completing *The Rebel Girl, Democracy, and Revolution: Elizabeth Gurley Flynn's Civil Liberties Activism 1909–1964* (forthcoming).

Authors

JIM BEAUCHESNE has served as the Visitor Services Supervisor at Lawrence Heritage State Park since 1998. He has been a member of the Bread and Roses Heritage Committee for the same period, serving as Chairman for several years. Born and raised in Lawrence, Massachusetts, he holds an MA in Public History from Northeastern University.

REBEKAH BRYER is a doctoral candidate in the Interdisciplinary PhD in Theatre and Drama program at Northwestern University. Her research examines the intersection of performance and public memory in American history and culture. Her work is in the *Atlas of Boston History* (2019) and *Liminalities*, an online performance studies journal. She has helped curate exhibits for the Humanities Action Lab and John Fitzgerald Kennedy National Historic Site. Before Northwestern, she received an MA in Public History from Northeastern University and worked at multiple theaters in Maine and Massachusetts.

REBECCA BUSH is Curator of History/Exhibitions Manager at the Columbus Museum in Georgia. Ms. Bush earned a BA in History from Kansas State University and an MA in Public History from the University of South Carolina. Interests include community history, multiple-perspective interpretation, and interdisciplinary museum exhibitions, and her research is often on the social history of the American South in the late nineteenth and early twentieth centuries. On the editorial board of *The Public Historian* and the board of the Georgia Association of Museums, she is coeditor and contributing author to *Art and Public History: Approaches, Opportunities, and Challenges* (2017).

CONOR M. CASEY, Labor Archivist, and Director, Labor Archives of Washington at the University of Washington, has an MA in Library & Information Science from San Jose State University and an MA in History from San Francisco State University. Building and organizing the University of Washington's labor archives, he has published in the *Pacific Northwest Quarterly* and the *Public Historian* and served as editor to the *Labor Archives in the United States and Canada: A Directory*, prepared by the Labor Archives Roundtable of the Society of American Archivists.

RACHEL DONALDSON trained as a historian and a historic preservationist. She is a Public Historian in the History Department at the College of Charleston. There, her work focuses on the intersections of labor history and historic preservation. She worked as the chief historian revising the

Labor History Theme Study for the National Park Service (under review) and is a co-facilitator of the National Council on Public History's Public History of Labor working group. Her work has appeared in *the Journal of Popular Culture, History of Education Quarterly, The Public Historian, Left History,* and *Labor* (forthcoming). As a member of Charleston Alliance for Fair Employment, she participates in labor activism in the South Carolina Low Country.

KATHLEEN S. FLYNN has supported the Lawrence History Center since the 1980s as a volunteer and board member, serving in several capacities, including President. She is a graduate of Regis College and holds advanced degrees from Northeastern University and Fitchburg State College. She is currently head researcher at the LHC and has authored several Lawrence books that feature the history of the Catholic cemeteries and the Catherine McCarthy Memorial Trust.

ELIJAH GADDIS is an Assistant Professor of History at Auburn University. A public and digital historian, he has curated a variety of exhibits, built numerous online archives and projects, and run oral history initiatives. Much of his recent public history work has been through the Community Histories Workshop based at the University of North Carolina at Chapel Hill, which he cofounded. He studies the spatial, material, and cultural histories of the nineteenth and twentieth century South and is currently completing his first book, tentatively titled *Gruesome Looking Objects: A Material History of Lynching.*

SUSAN GRABSKI, MEd, has been executive director of the Lawrence History Center (LHC) since 2011. She serves as a member of the Massachusetts State Historical Records Advisory Board and is a Commissioner for the Essex National Heritage Area. In 2013, she coauthored *Lawrence, Massachusetts and the 1912 Bread & Roses Strike* with Robert Forrant. The LHC online exhibition, *Bread and Roses Strike of 1912: Two Months in Lawrence, Massachusetts, that Changed Labor History,* is included among other stories of national significance on the Digital Public Library of America.

AMANDA KAY GUSTIN holds degrees in history and museum work from both Tufts University and Middlebury College. The Public Program Manager of the Vermont Historical Society, where, since 2012, she coordinates programs and exhibitions, she has worked in archives, libraries, museums, and historical societies for nearly twenty years.

KAREN LANE served as director of the Aldrich Public Library in Barre, Vermont, from 1989 to 2015. Vice President of the Barre Historical Society, she has been instrumental in the preservation of Barre's Socialist Labor Party Hall, a National Historic Landmark.

ROB LINNÉ, a professor in the Ruth S. Ammon School of Education at Adelphi University, serves on the board of *The Remember the Triangle Fire Coalition*. With a PhD in Language and Literacy Studies/Composition Studies from The University of Texas at Austin, he has published widely on integrating labor education in the schools and coedited *Organizing the Curriculum: Perspectives on Teaching the U.S. Labor Movement* (2009).

ERIK LOOMIS is an Associate Professor of History and Director of History Graduate Studies at the University of Rhode Island. He is the author of *Empire of Timber: Labor Unions and the Pacific Northwest Forests* (2016) and *Out of Sight: The Long and Disturbing Story of Corporations Outsourcing Catastrophe* (2015). His newest book is *A History of America in Ten Strikes* (2018).

THOMAS MACMILLAN is a PhD student studying History at Concordia University in Montreal. Born and raised in Portland, Maine, he earned his BA from Clark University and an MA from the University of Maine. His MA thesis is on the alliance of the business interests and nativists in stemming class conflict with a particular emphasis on the Ku Klux Klan in the 1920s. His research is on the intersection of working-class history and left-wing politics in North America.

LOU MARTIN, a founding board member of the West Virginia Mine Wars Museum, and an honorary member of UMWA Local 1440, is an Associate Professor of History at Chatham University. Author of *Smokestacks in the Hills: Rural-Industrial Workers in West Virginia*, published in 2015 as part of the University of Illinois Press's series The Working Class in American History, his latest project explores different values and understandings of place in the coal industry—from investors to workers to policymakers—during its collapse in the 1950s and 1960s.

SCOTT A. McLAUGHLIN, PhD, is the executive director of the Vermont Granite Museum of Barre and a college lecturer. Since 1986, he has worked in Vermont as an archaeologist, educator, and museum professional.

KRISTIN O'BRASSILL-KULFAN is a public historian and scholar of early American social history in the History Department at Rutgers University, where she coordinates the Undergraduate Public History Program. She holds a PhD in History from the University of Leicester and an MA from Queens University Belfast, and researches poverty, labor, mobility, and crime and punishment in the early American northeast, as well as public historical and commemorative representations of these subjects. The author of *Vagrants and Vagabonds: Poverty and Mobility in the Early American Republic* (2019), she has previously worked as an archivist and research analyst for the Pennsylvania House of Representatives Archives, and with museums, archives, and libraries in the U.S. and the U.K. curating exhibits, managing archival collections, and creating inclusive public programming.

KAREN SIEBER is the Humanities Specialist for the McGillicuddy Humanities Center at the University of Maine and also serves as the Research and Outreach Coordinator for the Theodore Roosevelt Center and Digital Library. She is the creator of many digital humanities and public history projects, including Digital Loray, Visualizing the Red Summer, and H is for Hayti.

KATRINA WINDON is the Collections Management and Processing Unit Head for the University of Arkansas Special Collections. She holds an MSIS in Information Studies from the University of Texas at Austin and is a Certified Archivist. She curated an exhibit commemorating the one-hundredth anniversary of the 1919 Elaine Massacre, which resulted, over eight days, in what many researchers now believe to be more than two hundred African Americans killed.

Index

The Working Class in American History

The University of Illinois Press
is a founding member of the
Association of University Presses.

———————————————

University of Illinois Press
1325 South Oak Street
Champaign, IL 61820-6903
www.press.uillinois.edu